Additional praise for
Customer's New Voice: Extreme Relevancy and Experience through Volunteered Customer Information

"The always connected digital lifestyle means consumers are continuously sharing information about their specific wants and desires. Is your business positioned to take advantage of this shift? The *Customer's New Voice* points the way with actionable information as to how your organization can confidently move forward.

—Kathy Koontz, Associate Vice President, Customer Information Management, Nationwide Insurance

"In the *Customer's New Voice,* McKean's astute insights force us to take a hard look at chasing customer mediocrity by only building information proxies of what's inside the customer's head. He creditably demonstrates that the most effective path toward driving tomorrow's profitably is not only by businesses answering questions about customers, but increasingly how businesses inspire customers to volunteer their own answers to business's questions."

—Marc Teerlink, Chief Business Strategist, IBM Watson Group, IBM

"The *Customer's New Voice* brings us the blunt reality that the most advanced technology or analytics will only reach a fraction of its full potential without integrating the insights that exist inside the heads of our customers. In the context of the new connected and "sharing" consumer, McKean clearly illustrates the steps taken by today's business innovators to inspire new levels of volunteered customer knowledge for the win/win of unprecedented levels of product relevancy and customer experience."

—Dr. Mark Jeffery, Director of Technology Initiatives, Center for Research on Technology and Innovation at the Kellogg School of Management, Northwestern University

"The consumer view of big data analytics is a critical perspective that is essential to the ultimate realization of the value potential made possible by today's information revolution. John's refreshing viewpoint on the empowerment of the individual in taking ownership and control of data assets is an indispensable read for anyone who wants to understand the future of big data analytic."

—Stephen Brobst, Chief Technology Officer, Teradata Corporation

"Customer generated information is mind boggling and the amount of insight available is growing at a far faster pace than businesses can process. That's why I love John's new book. The history of how we got here is intriguing, but the practical guide to "what do I need to do today" in invaluable. Driving change through an organization is no small feat. Having a roadmap to start with is priceless."
—Joni Newkirk, CEO Integrated Insight; former Senior Vice President, Business Insight & Improvement—Walt Disney Parks and Resorts

"In The *Customer's New Voice* John McKean has comprehensively documented the "we" economy of customers who are connected 24/7, never more than a click or a swipe away from your business. But don't even think about trying to compete if you don't have your customer's trust."
—Don Peppers, Author, Thought Leader, Founding Partner, Peppers & Rogers Group

"John McKean is a twenty-first century pioneer exploring the emerging personal data economy. The *Customer's New Voice* is a foray into the future of consumer interactions and reveals how your business can capitalize."
—John Lovett, Senior Partner, Web Analytics Demystified, Former President, Digital Analytics Association and Sr. Analyst at Forrester Research

"McKean's the *Customer's New Voice* is a thorough handbook for the paradigm shift with the consumer now in control! This book's cases and tool sets will guide navigation in the new digital economy with benefits based on currency minted in trust and respect."
—Cathy Burrows, Director, Strategic Initiatives & Infrastructure at RBC (Royal Bank of Canada)

"John McKean's concise and thoroughly researched the *Customer's New Voice* provides a detailed account of the history and current technology to which consumer's behaviour has been reactive, and less than predictable. Defining terms and new behaviours of those consumers and the models to which modern and next generation businesses will be expected to interact, in a candid and deep assessment of the next generation of consumer behaviour and business/systems requirements. Practical history, statistics, and examples are widely used, this book will become the Information Purveyors' bible of who/what/how, and should be on the desk of anyone who designs, implements, and interacts with consumer systems of any kind."
—Michael McIntire, Distinguished Architect, TapJoy; former Chief Technology Officer—Analytics Sears Holdings, Chief Architect User Data at Yahoo!, Chief Architect Data Warehousing at eBay.

"In the *Customer's New Voice,* McKean makes clear our transition to a digital world doesn't change the fact that we seek and value advice from those we trust, and understand they must know us—and what matters to us—to provide it. This truth and McKean's roadmap for implementing it digitally will obsolete the naïve view that massive investments in collecting and analyzing the digital bits and pieces of our lives we inadvertently leave behind can ever substitute for chosen, trusted and engaged relationships."

—Dr. Blake Johnson, Management Science and
Engineering, Stanford University

"Supported by powerful facts and compelling statistics, the *Customer's New Voice* presents an insightful view of today's brave new world where consumers have sharing discretion over the most valuable dimensions of information that exists in the current business environment. McKean provides concrete examples of how businesses can transform their performance metrics by motivating this sharing while creating a safe and trusted sustainable sharing environment."

—Klaas Wierenga, Senior Engineer, CTO (Chief Technology Officer)
Office Enterprise Networking, Cisco Systems

"What happens when the big-data-driven organization meets the info-empowered consumer? The *Customer's New Voice* will prepare you for the next big shift in company-consumer communication where the data marketplace becomes a two-way street moderated by data aggregation services, infomediaries, and personal data agents."

—Jim Sterne, Founder, eMetrics Summit and Digital
Analytics Association

"I was inspired by reading McKean's new book–*Customer's New Voice* as it clearly shows us the immense impact that can occur when customers and their volunteered insights are placed at the epicenter of any business with all information, processes and systems in place to empower the customer."

—Darren Herman,VP of Content Services, Mozilla, Named in Top 25
Marketing Innovators and Thought Leaders by iMedia
and named "Media All Star" by Media Post.

"The *Customer's New Voice* brings much needed clarity to a topic that has long been regarded as mysterious: Understanding and acting on your customer's personal beliefs and preferences. McKean shows you how to engage your customers and act on their specific needs using straightforward analytics and communications."

—David Sonnen, President, Integrated Spatial Solutions, Inc.
Global Analyst—Geospatial Technologies—International
Data Corporation, Member: Editorial Board Member—GeoWorld

Customer's New Voice

Customer's New Voice

Extreme Relevancy
and Experience through
Volunteered Customer Information

JOHN McKEAN

WILEY

Published by John Wiley & Sons, Inc., Hoboken, New Jersey.
Published simultaneously in Canada.

For general information on our other products and services or for technical
support, please contact our Customer Care Department within the United States at
(800) 762-2974, outside the United States at (317) 572-3993 or fax (317) 572-4002.

Wiley publishes in a variety of print and electronic formats and by print-on-demand.
Some material included with standard print versions of this book may not be included
in e-books or in print-on-demand. If this book refers to media such as a CD or DVD
that is not included in the version you purchased, you may download this material
at http://booksupport.wiley.com. For more information about Wiley products, visit
www.wiley.com.

Library of Congress Cataloging-in-Publication Data:

ISBN 978-1-119-00232-1 (Hardcover)
ISBN 978-1-119-00420-2 (ePDF)
ISBN 978-1-119-00436-3 (ePub)

Printed in the United States of America

10 9 8 7 6 5 4 3 2 1

To my loving mother, Barbara McKean.

Contents

Foreword

In every apple you'll find five seeds. Plant those and the result will be five different trees, bearing five different fruits, as unlike each other as they are of their parent. This is because apple seeds are *heterozygous*, meaning they produce different individuals in a variety that trends toward the infinite. All the familiar varieties of apples—McIntosh, Delicious, Granny Smith, Fuji—come from trees grown from twigs of parents grafted onto saplings that are nothing more than rooted trunks.

The normalizing of apple varieties through grafting is one of civilization's oldest industrial practices, and serves as a model for the way industry today normalizes another heterozygous species: Homo sapiens. To any company doing mass marketing, you are not a distinct and different human being. You are a rootstock for a graft that produces cash. The graft is a template: a controlled and generic set of appetites the company wishes to fill. In some cases the company seeks customers like you, which they understand in terms of demographics, regions, sectors, income levels, tested preferences, and so on. In some cases the company creates appetites through advertising, promotion, and other marketing methods. But in all cases the need for *scale* outweighs the need to respect customers' differences as human beings.

For evidence of how one-sided this is, go to a bookstore or a library and visit the business section. See if you can find a book about what individual customers bring to the marketplace, other than cash, credit, and loyalty cards. You won't find much. While there are plenty of books that are respectful of customers, and talk about how companies can "relate" to customers, the default assumption is that companies are in charge. Even when you hear talk about "giving the customer a seat at the board table," it's still the company doing the giving. Such flattering jive is the exception to the rule of subordinating individual customers to the imperatives of scale. This is why you still hear sales and marketing people talking about "targeting," "capturing," "acquiring," "controlling," "managing," and "locking in" customers as if they were cattle or slaves. The mentality behind this talk not only dismisses customers' individual differences, but also their ability to contribute more to a business than cash and coerced loyalty.

This mentality took root after Industry won the Industrial Revolution. Before then, the power advantage was on the customers' side. The expression "supply and demand," for example, was coined as "demand and supply" by James Denham-Steuart in *An Inquiry into the Principles of Political Oeconomy*, written in 1767.[1] In his *Inquiry*, Denham-Steuart described seven natures of demand, the sixth of which was "to encourage industry." In *The Wealth of Nations*, published nine years later, Adam Smith wrote, "The real and effectual discipline which is exercised over a workman is that of his customers. It is the fear of losing their employment which restrains his frauds and corrects his negligence."[2]

Once the Industrial Age got rolling in the early 1800s, power piled up on the supply side. Mass manufacture and distribution eventually led to mass markets and marketing. Conversation between company and customer became a cost to be minimized, rather than a direct source of intelligence and discipline. While treating customers as templates was an efficiency required for scale, it also denied what is most human about us as individuals. Not only are we all different from each other, but each of us also differs in what we think, feel, know, and do, from one context and moment to the next.

When the Internet took its current form in 1995 (ISPs, browsers, e-mail, and websites galore), many expected the balance of power to shift from businesses to what Smith called their employers: the customers. That's because the Net, by design, regards everyone and everything connected to it as a peer, and places them all at a functional distance apart of zero. By this simple design, the Net also had no privacy, no control over the manners of people, businesses, governments, or anything. On the Internet, everybody could do what they pleased—for themselves, for each other, and *to* each other.

So, while business has become more connected than ever, it has not become more involved with customers—at least not directly. In fact, business may be *less* involved with customers, thanks to "big data" gathering, analytics, and programmatic marketing. These provide ways for companies to know more about customers without actually engaging

---

[1] James Denham-Steuart, *An Inquiry into the Principles of Political Economy* (London: Printed for A. Millar, and T. Cadell, in *The Strand*, 1767).
[2] Adam Smith, *An Inquiry into the Nature and Causes of the Wealth of Nations*, Book I, Chapter X, Part I, I.10.86. http://www.econlib.org/library/Smith/smWN4.html#I.10.86. (Accessed August 1, 2014.)

them directly. We see this rationalized in a 2012 promotional piece by IBM titled *Welcome to the Era of the Chief Executive Customer*. One excerpt:

> *CMOs used to try to shape customers' desires; now they're actually learning how to predict them. Sophisticated analytics help them take a holistic view of the customer experience and create new methods of engagement, using data to create not just a snapshot of a customer, but a lifetime view that can improve with every interaction. Predictive analytics brings science to the art of customer engagement, helping create a seamless experience that can give customers what they want, when they want it.*[3]

Note how the company is still totally in charge: it creates the methods of engagement, predicts what the customer will do, and controls the customer's experience. The customer in this fantasy is not a fully human being, but an ever-changing "snapshot."

Little of the data feeding this system is volunteered. Instead it is either coerced or obtained by surveillance. This is both unfriendly and inefficient. Improving guesswork is no substitute for direct knowledge, voluntarily given, by customers.

What would happen if customers had full control over their sides of relationships with companies—and if those relationships were genuine rather than coerced? How much more valuable would customer information be if it was offered directly and voluntarily, for the good of both sides? And how much more useful is it for customers to express their true intentions, rather than having those intentions guessed at constantly?

These are the kinds of questions that have driven my work in the world over the past two decades. I wrote up some answers in *The Cluetrain Manifesto* (Basic Books: 2000, 2010) and in *The Intention Economy: When Customers Take Charge* (Harvard Business Review Press: 2012), which begins with this prophesy:

> *Over the coming years, customers will be emancipated from systems built to control them. They will become free and independent actors in the marketplace, equipped to tell vendors what they want, how they want it, where, and when—even how much they'd like to pay—outside of any vendor's system of customer control.*

---

[3] *Welcome to the Era of the Chief Executive Customer*. International Business Machines Corporation 2012. http://ibm.co/1o7KUpp. (Accessed August 1, 2014.)

On the matter of personal data, I wrote this:

Each customer will come to market equipped with his or her own means for collecting and storing personal data, expressing demand, making choices, setting preferences, proffering terms of engagement, offering payments, and participating in relationships—whether those relationships are shallow or deep, and whether they last for moments or years.

The question this begs is *How?* John McKean answers that question—and many more—in *The Customer's New Voice.* For companies that want to know how to engage fully empowered customers, there is no better guide than this book.

There will always be a need for scale. Companies successfully explored the limits of that need throughout the Industrial Age. Now it's the customers' turn. We have the tools to start making scale work for us, and we will get more of them. Count on it.

The best time to invest is in the past. That's where we are now. Companies that place their bets with customers today are the ones that will see the biggest payoffs in the future. In this book, John McKean tells you exactly where companies should invest their money, time and attention today and in the coming years, as customer self-empowerment blooms in the wilds of the networked world.

Read on and prosper.

—Doc Searls, author of *The Intention Economy*
and co-author of *The Cluetrain Manifesto*

Preface: New Voice, New Competencies

For the first time in history, individuals are developing the ability and willingness to share any information at any scale with anyone.

Whether it is with their rapidly evolving smart phones, smart homes, smart vehicles, wearable technology, or anything connected via the Internet of Things . . .

This is their new voice . . . rapidly evolving and radically empowering.

It is transforming their lives, cultures, countries, and the very fabric of our society.

Individuals as customers and consumers are intentionally sharing this new voice with those businesses today that have created the new competencies required to inspire the sharing of this new voice while safeguarding their shared information.

The result: a new generation of win-win.

Customers/consumers get what they want . . . extreme levels of product relevancy, exceptional experiences, and ultra-personalized interactions.

Business shareholders get what they want . . . significantly higher and expanded revenue generation opportunities, ultra-product relevancy (higher campaign conversion rates), operational cost reductions and efficiencies, and incomparable customer experiences.

A new generation of business innovators has begun leveraging the customer's new voice with initial results reaching as high as 20 percent to 50 percent for purchase relevancy with extreme levels of customer experience and personalization.

Customers/consumers are *not* sharing this new voice with businesses that are still caught in the legacy approaches of "chasing" them using arm's-length, second-hand "inferences" as to what they actually really want and need. Nor are they willing to share their most valuable information with businesses without sufficient motivators and safeguards.

The traditional inference-based business model only achieves an average success rate of 2 percent to 5 percent and has remained at this level for decades. That is, only 2 percent to 5 percent of a business's inference-based marketing offers are deemed sufficiently relevant for purchase. Equally important is that 70 percent of a business's cost infrastructure exists to compensate for these low success rates; that is, compensating for not knowing what your customers and consumers already know.

The blunt reality is that the most advanced technology or analytics will only achieve a fraction of its full potential without integrating the insights that exist inside the heads of consumers and your customers.

So better hurry. . . . They're waiting for you to inspire their new voice . . .

Acknowledgments

I want to express great appreciation for the intellect, creativity, and courage of my colleagues, friends, and family who have inspired my thinking around the *Customer's New Voice*.

Adam Dawes
Adam Goldberg
Alan Karp
Alex McKean
Amy McKean
Amy K Johnson
Andy Dale
Anne Robinson
Anthony Rodio
Ben Gillis
Bill Franks
Bill Mills
Blake Johnson
Bob Page
Bryant Cutler
Chad Meley
Chris Twogood
Chuck Mortimore, VP
Craig Gard
Craig Hackett
Daniel Gerber, VP
Darren Herman
David Howell
David Pinter
David Rocci
David Schrader
Dean Furness
DeAnna Blair
Deanna Decker

Digant Kasundra
Doc Searls
Dr. Catriona Wallacerant
Dr. Hugh J. Watson
Dr. Jeffrey Gersbach
Drummond Reed
Eric Sachs
Erik Brynjolfsson
George Fletcher
Geraldine McBride
Gregory Leproux
Griffin McKean
Guy Kawasaki
Hani S. Mahmassani
Helen Cho
Iain Henderson
Jack Greenberg
James Donovan
James Semenak
James Sheire
Jaron Lanier
Jeffrey Hayzlett
Jeffrey Jones
Jessica McKean
Jim Sterne
Joe Andrieu
John Lovett
Jonathan Zittrain
Kaliya Hamlin

Kazue Sako
Kimberly Little
Klaas Wierenga
Lee Rainie
Leland Modesitt
Linda McKean
Loie Levine
Marc Stiegler
Marius Scurtescu
Mark Jeffery
Mark Swenson
Mary Ruddy
Matthew Berry
Matthew Sutton
Michael Engan
Michael McIntire
Mike Jones
Morteza Ansari
Nathan Dors
Naveen Agarwal
Neil Harris
Pat Patterson
Pattie Maes
Phil Hunt
Phil Windley
Philip Filleul
Porter Gale

Prateek Mishra
Rob Tuttle
Ron Monzillo
Roshni Chandrashekhar
Sarah Davies
Scott Gnau
Sean Bohan
Sean Brooks
Seth Godin
Shadron Ruffin
Sheck Cho
Shon Shah
Srisupa Ruangsuk
Stefan Magdalinski
Stefanos Giampanis
Stephen Brobst
Steve Greenberg
Taylor Davidson
Tom Davenport
Tom Malone
Tony Ohlsson
Verna Allee
Vikas Jain, Mr
Vint Cerf
William Griffith
William Heath
Yue Lu

PART I

Dawn of the New Customer

Consumers are born and subsequently brought up in a world increasingly dominated by increasingly sophisticated and friendly personal information technology (e.g., smartphones, tablets, laptops) interconnected by an increasingly pervasive Internet and mobile infrastructure. Each succeeding year, consumers are exposed earlier in their lives and are more deeply immersed in the competencies of how to leverage the information components of these technologies. Their motivation is the opportunity to leverage the information to better fulfill their needs and wants (e.g., connect with family and friends, make their lives easier, save money, do their jobs, find information). The key transformational piece is the direct connection to information, people, and organizations. This is analogous to the original vision for the Internet— to "directly connect to anything without an intermediary."

This directness to information, people, and organizations has radically changed our lives forever and will continue to do so.

CHAPTER 1

New Information Masters

The new Information Masters of this era are not the expected technology-rich business contingent but in relative terms are the new direct consumers. Armed with mobile devices and the infinite network of the world's Internet infrastructure, the new direct consumer can directly view unbiased, unmediated, and unadulterated information about a business's products or services relative to any of its competitors in almost any market or geography. The consumer's view into a business's world is far more transparent than the business's view into the customer's world (i.e., asynchronous transparency). While businesses grapple with leveraging with the exponential increase in the amount of data that consumers unintentionally generate on a day-to-day basis, their lack of relative consumer knowledge is reflected by marketing accuracy of less than one in 10 offers.

In one minute, the new Information Masters produce 694,980 status updates and 522,080 tweets. The new Information Masters collect, share, and manage 300 petabytes of personal data in Facebook alone.[1]

Previously people would have an average of 150 friends (past, present, and future) in real life, whereas the new Information Masters can now communicate and engage with an average 245 friends (e.g., Facebook). The ability to have a wider pool and definition of friends is enabled by the new information environment. The new Information Masters have a broader span of intimacy where 82 percent of their online friends are known in real life and 60 percent are known through mutual friends. Because the new information environment is visual, they can choose new "friends" just by their appearance (29 percent of online friends are based on appearance).

The intent of the new Information Masters is not just about personal information mastery but is increasingly about mastering their personal information in the context of a business network. Some 11 percent of online friendships are related to business interactions and relationships.

Informed

Today's new Information Master is more informed and capable of sharing on a massive scale than at any other time in history. The proliferation of the Internet spans not only geography but also the demographics of gender, ethnicity, age, education level, income, and community type. An amazing 88 percent of individuals who were born 50 to 64 years ago access the Internet. On average, 87 percent of all U.S. adults use the Internet, including e-mail or accessing the Internet via a mobile device, as shown in Table 1.1.

Sharing

The new Information Masters can share almost anything, anytime, anywhere given that there is a motivating factor and that they feel safe in that particular sharing context.

Every 60 seconds, there are:

- 98,000+ tweets
- 695,000 status updates
- 11 million or so messages
- 698,144 Google searches
- 98,000,000+ e-mails sent
- 1,820 TB of data created
- 217 new mobile web users[2]

Philosopher Helen Newson notes that sharing (and privacy) is rooted in context. This reality started roughly 10 years ago when social media entered the everyday lives of our communities. Prior to social media, terrestrial (offline) sharing was more private by default, and great effort was required to share personal information broadly in public. In contrast, social media is "public by default" and "private with effort."[3] As a result, individuals share prolifically intentionally and incidentally. As Figure 1.1 shows, 73 percent of adults who are online use some type of social networking site (42 percent of adults who are online use multiple social networking sites).

Mobile

The new Information Masters are more informed, more capable of sharing, and more capable of doing both of these activities any place, at any time, because of new mobile device platforms. Mobile platforms are not confined

TABLE 1.1 Internet Users in 2014

Among adults, the % who use the Internet, e-mail, or access the Internet via a mobile device

All adults	Use Internet 87%
Sex	
a Men	87
b Women	86
Race/ethnicity*	
a White	85
b African American	81
c Hispanic	83
Age group	
a 18–29	97[cd]
b 30–49	93[d]
c 50–64	88[d]
d 65+	57
Education level	
a High school grad or less	76
b Some college	91[a]
c College+	97[ab]
Household income	
a Less than $30,000/yr	77
b $30,000–$49,999	85
c $50,000–$74,999	93[ab]
d $75,000+	99[ab]
Community type	
a Urban	88
b Suburban	87
c Rural	83

* The results for race/ethnicity are based off a combined sample from two weekly omnibus surveys, January 9–12 and January 23–26, 2014. The combined total n for these surveys was 2,008; n = 1,421 for whites, n = 197 for African Americans, and n = 236 for Hispanics.

Note: Percentages marked with a superscript letter (e.g.,[a]) indicate a statistically significant difference between that row and the row designated by that superscript letter, among categories of each demographic characteristic (e.g., age).

Source: Pew Research Center Internet Project Survey, January 9–12, 2014. N = 1,006 adults.

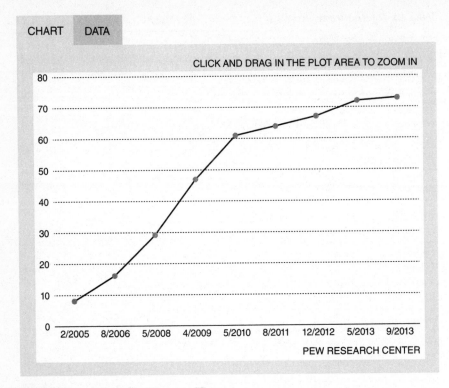

FIGURE 1.1 Social Media Use over Time

Source: Pew Research Center, www.pewinternet.org/2013/12/30/social-media-update-2013/.

to smartphones or tablets but extend into a proliferation of wearable technology and drivable technology (i.e., vehicle automation).

In just the category of smartphones, starting roughly in 2006 their use has been steadily climbing. Beginning in about 2010, the popularity of tablet computers has experienced a significant increase in usage. Of U.S. adults,

- Ninety percent have a cell phone.
- Fifty-eight percent have a smartphone.
- Thirty-two percent own an e-reader.
- Forty-two percent own a tablet computer.[4]

Mobile statistician Tomi Ahonen recently published his *Tomi Ahonen Almanac 2013*, which features a wealth of information about mobile usage.

Tomi claims that there are now 7.1 billion individuals in the world, of which there are:

- 6.7 billion mobile accounts
- 5.2 billion mobile phones in use
- 4.3 billion unique users

Individuals check their phones an average of 150 times a day. They check their mobile phones for:

- Messages 23 times per day
- Voice calls 22 times per day
- Time of day 18 times per day
- Their music player 13 times per day
- Gaming 12 times per day
- Social media 9 times per day
- Camera 8 times per day
- News and alerts 6 times per day
- Calendar 5 times per day
- Search 3 times per day
- Other random web browsing 3 times per day
- Voice mail 1 time per day
- Other miscellaneous uses 10 times per day[5]

Most important, information mobility elicits deep-seated emotions from connected individuals. When smartphone owners were asked how social and communication capabilities of smartphones made them feel, they responded as follows on a scale of zero (weakest) to 10 (strongest):

Connected	7
Excited	4
Curious/interested	2
Productive	1
Hip/trendy/cool	1
Loved	1
Popular	0.8
Special	0.7
Overwhelmed	0.3
Stressed out	0.2
Burdened/anxious	0.2
Lonely	0.1

Note: Relative Sentiment Index[6]

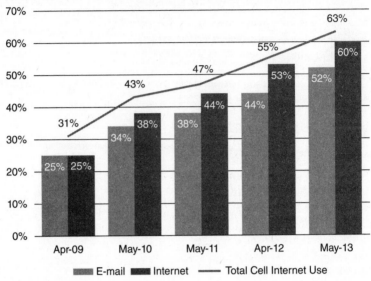

FIGURE 1.2 Cell Phone Owners Use Phones to Go Online
Note: N = 2,076 cell phone owners ages 18+. Interviews were conducted in English and Spanish and on landline and cell phones. The margin of error for results based on cell phone owners is +/− 2.4 percentage points.
Source: Pew Internet & American Life Project Spring Tracking Survey, April 17, 2013-May 19, 2013.

Sixty-three percent of cell phone owners go online with their phones, according to the Pew Research Center's Internet & American Life Project, as illustrated in Figure 1.2. This is not surprising since 91 percent of Americans own a cell phone. The percentage of cell owners who go online with their cell phones has doubled since 2009.[7] This percentage will likely increase significantly over the next couple of years.

Future Masters

The new Information Masters have raised the bar on businesses' need to be relevant and transparent. The harbingers of future Information Masters are digital natives, that is, individuals born or brought up with digital technology and therefore familiar with computers, mobile devices, and

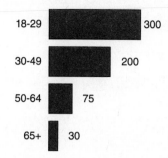

FIGURE 1.3 Facebook Friend Counts
Source: Pew Research Center's Internet Project Survey, August 7,
2013-September 16, 2013.

the Internet from an early age. These technologies are not segmented
in their minds as pieces of technology but rather are an integral part of
their lives.

Every aspect of digital natives shows the increasing expense of leveraging the information-sharing aspects of the web and social media.
Looking at the number of Facebook friends relative to age groups shows
that the digital natives far outpace older generations in terms of their
social networking preferences and abilities. In the 18 to 29 age group,
the median number of friends on Facebook totaled 300, more than three
times the number of friends that their parents have on Facebook (see
Figure 1.3).

As shown in Figure 1.4, the future Information Masters will prefer to
interact digitally rather than face-to-face. Today the most effective channel
for engaging consumers in financial services is face-to-face, but within two
years it will be social media. Figure 1.4 shows the evolution of channel effectiveness for financial services consumers.

Pragmatic but Digitally Aware

The digital natives are digitally pragmatic about being on the grid yet have
a sense that sharing information for no explicit utility or reward does not
justify the sharing. This is particularly evident in the space of mobile apps,
as many teens uninstall or avoid overlaps that ask for too much personal
information without providing an explicit motivator for them; they'll share
almost anything but they need a reason and some control. Teenage girls

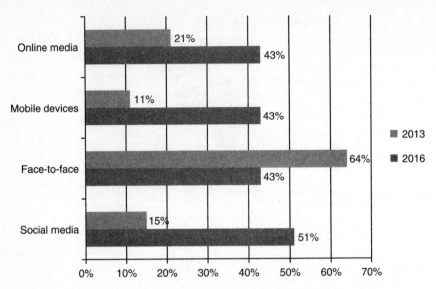

FIGURE 1.4 Evolution of Channel Effectiveness for Financial Services Consumers

are particularly sensitive to location-tracking features on their cell phones or in apps.

A study by Coleman Parkes Research for Accenture found that 80 percent of 20- to 40-year-old consumers believe total privacy in the digital space no longer exists. Forty-nine percent of respondents said they would not object to having their behavior tracked if in return they received relevant promotional offers. Eighty-seven percent of the respondents believe that adequate safety measures are not in place to protect personal information, and 64 percent are concerned about websites tracking their buying behavior. Fifty-six percent say that they do not allow their credit card information to be saved on e-commerce sites, citing theft concerns.

U.S. and UK consumers believe that digital privacy is a thing of the past, according to a study by Maidstone, England–based custom research firm Coleman Parkes Research for Chicago-based management consulting firm Accenture.[8]

On the surface, this new digital pragmatism appears as if the digital natives' prolific sharing is with complete abandon and disregard for a sense of privacy. In actuality, most have some sense of administering some control over their personal information with either controlling the access to their posts or controlling access to the meaning of their posts.[9]

% within each age group who go online

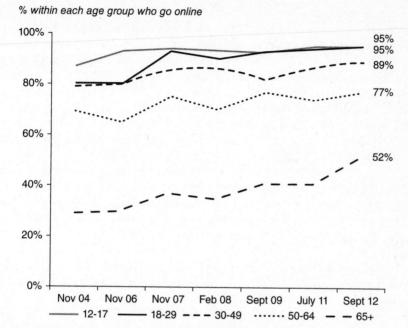

FIGURE 1.5 Internet Use over Time by Teens and Adults
Source: Pew Internet Research Project, Teens Fact Sheet.

Survey findings from September 2012 illustrated in Figure 1.5 indicate the behavioral differences between 12- and 17-year-olds and adults. Of U.S. teenagers:

- Fifty-eight percent downloaded apps to their cell phone or tablet computer.
- Fifty-one percent avoided particular apps due to privacy concerns.
- Twenty-six percent have uninstalled apps because they preferred not to share personal information.
- Forty-six percent turned off location tracking features because of privacy concerns.[10]
- Ninety-five percent of teenagers (ages 12 to 17) are now online.

Digital Natives

The most recent generations have entered the world in a relatively mature web/mobile infrastructure. Generational factors coalesce to produce a new behavioral norm for the motivation and competency to share personal information. This new sharing norm is based on an emerging acceptance and pragmatism about being on the grid (online) while still being sensitive to potential negative impacts from personal information sharing. Coupled with this new pragmatism is still a portion of digital naïveté regarding the full life cycle and/or monetization of their personal information. The digital natives (Millennials or Gen Y), now roughly 10 to 30 years old, will have a $200 billion annual spend by 2017 and will spend $10 trillion in their lifetimes.[11] The information and technology competency of Generation Z (the generation following the Millennials) raises the bar even further.

Consumers will make strides in the explicit monetization of the personal data toward the second half of this stage. Consumers begin this stage with essentially zero monetization of the personal data, whereas businesses have achieved a company capitalization of personal data of over $500 billion (e.g., Google, Facebook, Yahoo!, LinkedIn, Experian, Twitter, Trans Union, and Equifax).

The birth of the new Information Masters as an informed, sharing, and mobile force garners a new level of transparency and ultimately absolute power.

Notes

1. Craig Smith, DMR editor/owner, "By the Numbers: 925 Amazing Facebook User Statistics," Digital Marketing Ramblings, Expanded Ramblings.com, March 13, 2014. http://expandedramblings.com/index.php/by-the-numbers-17-amazing-facebook-stats/#.U868MfldUoM.
2. Kerry Matre, Hewlett-Packard, "How Using Big Data in Security Helps (and Hurts) Us." https://privacyassociation.org/conference/global-privacy-summit-2014/breakout-sessions-s14/.
3. Danah Boyd, *It's Complicated: The Social Lives of Networked Teens* (London: Yale University Press, 2014).
4. Pew Research Center, "Device Ownership over Time"; "Three Technology Revolutions." www.pewinternet.org/three-technology-revolutions/.
5. Mobile Marketing Association, "How Does the Rest of the World Use Mobile Marketing," MMA Forum Singapore, August 22–23, 2013, *Tomi Ahonen Almanac 2013*. www.mmaglobal.com/events/sites/default/files/8_tomiahonen.pdf.
6. Mary Meeker and Liang Wu, KPCB, "Internet Trends," D11 Conference, May 29, 2013, IDC 3/13 Facebook-sponsored research.
7. Maeve Duggan and Arron Smith, "Cell Internet Use 2013," Pew Research Center.

8. Molly Soat, "Digital Privacy Study, Consumers Harbor Mixed Feelings about Digital Privacy, Survey Says," Marketing News Exclusives, www.ama.org. https://www.ama.org/publications/eNewsletters/MNE/Pages/digital-privacy-study.aspx.

9. Danah Boyd, *It's Complicated: The Social Lives of Networked Teens*.

10. Mary Madden, Amanda Lenhart, Sandra Cortesi, and Urs Gasser, "Teens and Mobile Apps Privacy," Pew Internet Research Project. http://www.pewinternet.org/2013/08/22/teens-and-mobile-apps-privacy/.

11. Erin Mulligan Nelson, "Millennials Want to Party with Your Brand but on Their Own Terms." http://adage.com/article/digitalnext/millennials-party-brand-terms/236444/.

of the power transformation is the evolution of mountains, seen

CHAPTER 2

Power and Transparency

Complete open access to information creates new transparency. This new transparency creates absolute power. It is this access to information that has given birth to a new customer and the relative evolution of absolute customer power.

The commercial world has witnessed an inversion of the consumer/ business power structure. Since the early 1900s when Henry Ford pronounced that "any customer can have a car painted any color that he wants so long as it is black," customers have been subordinate to business. Today, the polar opposite is true: Consumers choose not only the color but every dimension of the who, what, where, when, and how of a product or service. If the consumer/business power structure is deconstructed, the core of the power transformation is the evolution of information. Technology has fundamentally changed the information equation. Technology enables information. Information enables power. The enabling technological chain that underpins the rapidly evolving direct consumer consists of four parts:

1. Technology—Internet/mobile infrastructure
2. Information—resulting by-product and the raison d'être of technology
3. Competency—and consumer's ability and willingness to use it
4. Culture—emerging new consumer behavioral norms

Absolute Power

The absolute power of today's consumer is unquestioned. The attributes of consumer power have radically evolved from a subservient, simple, mute, naive, defenseless entity to an assertive, vocal, influential, sophisticated, complex, and armed commercial force. The information-enabled power chain has involved the following set of direct consumer attributes:

- Independence
  - Looking and listening on business's time and terms have migrated to consumer's time and terms.
- Informed
  - Reliance on business's information has evolved to direct independent information sources.
- Complexity
  - Ten commercial interactions or transactions are now thousands.
- Disconnectability
  - Irrepressible advertising is increasingly consumer controllable (e.g., "Do not track," "Do not call," "Right to be forgotten," and inevitable future interactions of "Do not's").
- Manageability
  - Customer has evolved from managed consumer (customer relationship management) to manager.
- Speed
  - Speed standard of offline world (days) is now immediacy of online world (seconds).
- Sharing
  - Limited breadth and depth of shared personal information and audience have evolved to pervasive sharing of personal information (doubled each year).
- Learning
  - Confided concerted efforts are now limitless, immediate, and detailed.
- Identity
  - Real person identity moves to device (multiple) oriented identity.
- Expectations
  - Low expectations regarding product or service competitiveness have evolved to high expectations from completely transparent view of product, price, delivery, and experience.
- Digital information competency
  - Techie-oriented competency has evolved to essential and unconscious digital information competency in everyday life.

New Transparency

The new transparency is a two-sided coin. The customers' transparency is the degree to which they reveal or disclose their purchase intentions in the context of their lives to businesses and others. The businesses' transparency is the degree to which the characteristics of their reputation, quality, and brand are exposed or disclosed to their customers. Coupled with the consumer's new voice are new eyes and ears that have virtually unlimited access to the relative truths about almost any aspect of the business and its product offerings.

Customers choose not to be transparent to businesses unless there is a motivating factor and they feel safe being less transparent. In the new environment, businesses have no choice regarding their level of transparency. Businesses are fundamentally naked to the array of candid and direct customer feedback about their value propositions and their performance in delivering a good or bad value proposition and customer experience.

The future evolution of transparency will focus on building new business competencies to create an environment where this asynchronous transparency will evolve into a synchronous transparency.

Asynchronous Transparency

Asynchronous transparency is the world that the Internet and mobile devices have created. It is a one-way looking glass for consumers to research a business's products and services in great detail as well as its competitors' offerings. The consumer can research not only the attributes of products and services but also the direct experiences of others like themselves who have actually experienced the company's products and services as well as its service levels. While consumers have this new one-way lens, businesses have far less ability to view a consumer's purchasing intent and context with equal translucence.

Synchronous Transparency

Synchronous transparency is the world that we are evolving to where consumers not only can see businesses in great detail but also are motivated and feel safe enough to increasingly reveal themselves to businesses to achieve greater relevancy on both sides. Synchronous transparency enables extreme relevancy.

Simple truth: Relevancy is desired and desirable both by businesses and by consumers.

Death of B2C/C2B; Birth of C2W/W2C

This new transparency is not confined by limited discovery processes (e.g., single phone calls referenced from the Yellow Pages, a stroll through a shopping mall, a car ride downtown), but is now an unbounded discovery process starting with one click to the world. This has antiquated the premise of business to consumer (B2C) or consumer to business (C2B) models as if consumers were still bound to a myopic view of local markets.

The new model is consumer to world (C2W) and world to consumer (W2C). It is not only how the new consumers view their world but also the new process by which they create the perception of potential value from businesses. The competitive edict for a business is to provide products and services to consumers that have greater value than the consumer would expect from purchases from competitive businesses in similar markets. The consumer then weighs a business's offer relative to the perceived worth of competitive offers (i.e., "What do I get for what I paid?"). The consumer's new reference point is any business on the planet that is selling a similar product or service in a similar market. This includes unmitigated direct reviews of the product features relative to price as well as the waterfall of the experience, which could extend anywhere in the world and even across decades of product use. The consumer researches a business to determine how "somebody like me" felt about the product and the experience, ranging from product liability to responsiveness.

In the life of a consumer, the following waterfall of experiences in five areas represents typical points of determining how consumers develop their perception of relative value of a product or service. In the old B2C or C2B world, most of this learning happens after the purchase or product experience. In the new C2W world, these attributes can be discovered from virtually any location on the planet in seconds with a simple mobile device:

1. Product Research
   - Reliability—"I want it to be reliable."
   - Feature/function—"I want certain product features."
   - Ease of use—"It has to be easy to use."
   - Performance—"It has to work well."
2. Buying Process
   - Accessibility—"I want information easily accessible or, if not, a person to talk to."
   - Responsiveness—"I want my questions answered fast."
   - Knowledgeability/professionalism/automation—"I want all my questions answered completely."
   - Follow-up—"I want quick follow-up with any unanswered questions or delivery issues."
3. Delivery/Installation
   - Interval—"I want it delivered fast or faster."
   - Delivery/installation when promised—"I want the stated delivery time met or exceeded."

- Progress report—"Let me know the status before the actual delivery."
- Follow-up—"Follow up with me if things are different than promised."
- No initial failure—"When I get it, I want it to work."

4. Return/Exchange/Repair
   - Fast—"I want it to be fast and easy."
   - When promised—"I want it when promised"
   - Progress report—"Let me know what's going on during the process."
   - Follow-up—"Check to make sure I'm satisfied."
   - No repeat troubles—"Don't let it happen again."

5. Receipt/Invoice/Bill
   - No surprises—"Make sure there is nothing unexpected after the fact."
   - Easy to understand—"Make it really easy to understand."
   - Timely—"Make it fast."
   - Easy to resolve problems—"Make it easy to resolve any issues I have."[1]

Whether the product or service is a travel destination or some esoteric collectible, the business will thrive or struggle based on what its customer's feedback is online for the world to see.

The other important dimension of moving from a B2C or C2B world model to a C2W/W2C world is that the added view increases the consumer's choices. As a result, the number of competitors a business has increases. The more competitive choices a consumer has to choose from, the higher the expectations become. The higher the consumer expectations are, the less tolerant consumers are of any performance other than excellent along any one of the waterfall elements. Statistically, businesses must score in the 90th percentile or above in terms of executing in a combined excellence rating to prompt a strong "likelihood to recommend" score. Once the overall total customer experience score drops below the 80th percentile, the "likelihood to recommend" score drops off precipitously. This is referred to as the slippery slope where, after the initial purchase, execution excellence is the only performance level that creates a follow-on purchase as well as a recommendation to others to purchase.

Note

1. Raymond Kordupleski, former AT&T customer satisfaction director.

CHAPTER 3

Age of Sharing

It is our nature to share. It is as much a part of our survival as a species as it is a central part of our self-actualization as human beings. We share because we have the enabling tools and motivation to share. When we don't share, either we don't have the tools or we lack sufficient motivation or safety to share. The following points are the essence of why and how we share:

- Given the right motivation (e.g., make my life easier, save me money, make me feel good as a person)
- Sense of safety (if I share information with you, nothing negative/no harm will come from it)
- Sharing enablers (with mobile phones, tablets, the Internet, wearable technology, and sensors, we have the propensity to share virtually any information with anyone)

Historical Sharing Tools

Sharing personal information is what people do as human beings. It has been the nature of human beings since the beginning of time. Until recent history, sharing was confined to physical one-to-one communication and its content was determined by the level of trust and intimacy. Communication tools evolved because human beings wanted to share more information beyond just words. Human beings' need to share has driven prolific inventions and has historically shaped our behavior:

- 1814: First photograph
- 1829: Braille (system of reading for the blind)
- 1831: Electric telegraph
- 1835: Morse code
- 1843: First long-distance telegraph line

- 1843: First fax machine
- 1861: Pony Express established
- 1867: Typewriter invented
- 1876: Mimeograph patented
- 1876: Telephone invented
- 1876: Dewey Decimal System invented (system for classifying books in the library)
- 1876: Phonograph invented
- 1884: Fountain pen invented
- 1888: Roll film camera invented
- 1895: First radio promoted
- 1915: Mechanical pencil invented
- 1925: First television invented
- 1935: Ballpoint pen invented
- 1938: Xerography invented (process of copying paper without ink)
- 1956: Liquid Paper invented
- 1960: First cell phone invented
- 1963: Zip codes created
- 1969: First form of Internet created[1]

The age of sharing is driven by the ease of sharing. When contrasting the effort and competency required to use some of the predecessors of today's communication devices (smartphones, tablets, netbooks, and laptops), we see that the ease of sharing is driving much of this new sharing age. Consider just a few years ago, when fax machines where still fairly prevalent, the time and effort required to fax a 30-page document to 200 people. Hours of time to complete this task are now measured in seconds. Other communication tools such as speech recognition are also enabling sharing to be much more natural while still being very efficient. It is not only the ease of sharing a simple item but the ability to share massive amounts of information to a broad number of entities that is transforming our world. Sharing is truly the new behavioral norm. This comes with all of the pluses and minuses of the new etiquette of sharing.

Sharing Statistics

One of the most telling sharing statistics is how often individuals are searching for words related to sharing. Over the past 10 years, the word *privacy* as a search word has slowly declined, and it is predicted to decline even further. This is indicative of the new digital pragmatism of today's consumer. On the surface, this may indicate that individuals are caring less about privacy issues. Individuals continue to be aware of privacy issues but are more pragmatic about their privacy awareness.

The amount of global digital information that was created and shared (e.g., documents, pictures, tweets) grew nine times in five years in 2011.[2]

Demographically, global averages indicated that individuals under the age of 35 (81 percent) are most likely to share any type of content on social media sites compared with individuals aged 35 to 49 (69 percent) and 50 to 64 (55 percent). Women (74 percent) edge out men (69 percent) in having shared content in the past month. Those with a high level of education (74 percent) are more likely than those with low and medium levels of education and income to share content.[3]

In the beginning of 2014, there was no sign that how much individuals were sharing was going to slow down. This is not to say that they do not value privacy—they do. Events such as Edward Snowden's global surveillance disclosures and other notable organizational data breaches will help keep their new digital pragmatism in check. Here are some of the latest sharing statistics, primarily on Facebook:

- Instagram alone has 200 million users as of the beginning of 2014, with 200 billion photos shared total and 60 million photos shared daily.
- The number of Facebook users grew to 1.28 billion, with monthly active users registering at 1.23 billion. This is not a youth phenomenon.
- Forty-five percent of Internet users who are 65 years or older use Facebook.
- Sixty-two percent of Facebook users post about what they are doing, where they are, and who they are with.
- The total number of location-tagged Facebook posts is 17 billion.
- The total number of uploaded Facebook photos is 250 billion.
- The average number of photos uploaded per Facebook user is 217 photos.
- The average number of items shared by Facebook users daily is 4.75 billion items.
- The average time spent on Facebook totaled per day is 20 billion minutes.
- The average number of minutes users spent on Facebook mobile is 914 minutes compared to Facebook.com, which is 351 minutes.
- Thirty percent of Americans get their news on Facebook.[4]

On the surface, the declining frequency of searches on the word *privacy* seems to indicate a declining interest or concern with privacy. Taking this trend in the context of other privacy research, though, the exponential increase in shared personal information does not necessarily indicate

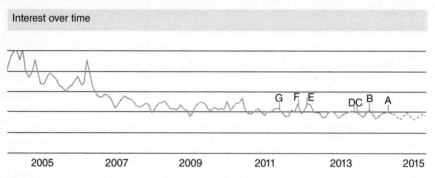

FIGURE 3.1 Trend of Google Searches on the Word *Privacy*
Source: Google Trends.

that the concern for privacy is lessening. The concern for privacy is being melded into a new digital pragmatism coupled with some level of digital naïveté (see Figure 3.1).

According to Intel's "Mobile Etiquette" survey, 85 percent of U.S. adults share information online with 25 percent of U.S. adults sharing information at least once a day; 23 percent of U.S. adults experience fear of missing out (FoMo) if they are unable to share their consumer information online.

Twenty-seven percent of the respondents stated they are an "open book" both online and offline, with very little in their lives they would not share; 51 percent of U.S. adults said they would be comfortable if all of their online activity were made public tomorrow. This reflects the new digital pragmatism as well as a level of digital naïveté; that is, they do not fully understand the full life cycle of personal information.

The fact that only about half of U.S. adults would feel comfortable if all of their online activity were made public might be because 27 percent of U.S. adults admit to having a different personality online than in person, and one in five U.S. adults (19 percent) report that they have shared false information online.

Most U.S. adults (81 percent) believe that mobile manners are becoming worse (compared to 75 percent of U.S. adults surveyed a year ago), and 92 percent of U.S. adults wish people practiced better mobile etiquette in public. As a follow-up to Intel's "Mobile Etiquette" surveys in 2009 and 2011, U.S. adults continue to report that the top three pet peeves are texting or typing while driving a car (77 percent), talking on a device loudly in a public place (64 percent), and having the volume too loud in a public place (55 percent).[5]

The age of sharing is across the globe, with compelling statistics on most generations' transformation into a sharing norm. The following are sharing statistics from around the world.

Brazil

■ Twenty-three percent of teens constantly share throughout the day.
■ Forty-three percent of adults share sports-related information via mobile Internet-enabled devices.
■ Sixty-five percent of adults say the top reason to share is to express opinions or make statements.
■ Fifty-four percent share online to make new friends.
■ Eighty percent of teens constantly check to see what friends are sharing.

China

■ Seventy-seven percent of adults regard themselves as an "open book" online; there is little they would not share online.
■ Fifty-one percent admit they share too much personal information online (i.e., sharing compulsion versus rational decision).
■ Eighty-two percent of adults post or share online once a week or more.
■ Thirty-one percent share throughout the day.
■ Sixty-five percent of adults feel more comfortable sharing online than in person.
■ Sixty-two percent of adults report that the top reason for sharing is to express opinions or make statements.
■ Sixty-two percent of adults feel they are missing out if they are unable to share or consume information online (i.e., fear of missing out [FoMo]).

France

■ Eighty percent of teens share online at least once a week.
■ Forty-seven percent of adults share as frequently as teens.
■ Forty-one percent of teens are more comfortable sharing online than in public settings.

India

■ Eighty-one percent of adults share information online once a week or more.
■ Forty-eight percent of adults share once a day or more.
■ Sixty-four percent of adults are more comfortable sharing online than in person.
■ Sixty-nine percent of teens feel they're missing out if they are unable to share their consumer information online.
■ Forty-three percent of teens try to make sure that every moment of life is captured online.
■ Fifty-six percent of teens communicate with their family more online than in person.

- Sixty-seven percent of teens communicate with their friends more online than in person.

Indonesia
- Ninety-one percent of adults always feel connected with family and friends because they share online.
- Seventy-nine percent of teens always feel connected with family and friends because they share online.
- Forty-six percent of adults share online because they cannot share openly in other offline settings.
- Fifty-two percent of adults feel they are missing out if they are not able to share or consume information online.
- Sixty-eight percent of adults share information online about the moment they are currently in.
- Forty-nine percent of teens admit they share too much personal information online.

Japan
- Thirty-seven percent of adults say they feel connected to family and friends anywhere because they can connect online.
- Fifty-five percent of adults who share report they have different personalities online and in person.
- Thirty-eight percent of adults share product and service reviews and recommendations online via mobile Internet-enabled devices.

United States
- Ninety percent of adults believe they share too much personal information online (i.e., sharing compulsion versus rational decision).
- Eighty-five percent of adults share information online.
- Twenty-six percent of adults share once or more a day.
- Nineteen percent of adults admit to sharing false information online.
- Forty-two percent of teens feel they are missing out if they are unable to share or consume information online.
- Forty-two percent of teens are more comfortable sharing personal information online than in offline public environments.[6]

Intentional versus Incidental

Intentionally shared information is becoming increasingly more common and holds the richest and most valuable dimensions of shared information—for example, "I (consumer) feel motivated and secure about directly communicating to you (business) highly relevant information about me relative to your product or service." Intentionally shared information is still less than 10 percent of what businesses operate on. An example would be a consumer agreeing to install an insurance company's monitoring device into the vehicle for a potentially better insurance rate. Intentionally shared information is typically a more overt and explicit win-win proposition for both the business and the consumer. Another example would be the proliferation of mobile apps where information is exchanged for utility or reward (e.g., "I'll reveal my location if you help me navigate to my favorite restaurant and give me a coupon"). In a perfect world, if businesses could sufficiently motivate consumers to share 100 percent of their personal knowledge, business operational effectiveness and marketing conversion rates would approach 90 percent, with cost infrastructures being reduced by as much as 70 percent.[7] As enablers of sharing continue to proliferate (smarter phones, Internet of Things, smarter homes and vehicles, wearable technology, and mobile health), it will become easier to intentionally share information with businesses.

Incidentally shared information is over 95 percent of our "big data" universe and is the most available and lowest-value form of shared information—for example, "We (business) see that a 'device' purchased X item and also searched on three Y items on Thursday, so we think you (consumer) may also purchase Z item related to Y item sometime in the future." Currently, 90 percent of information businesses use to predict what consumers will buy is this type of incidentally shared information.

The reality is that businesses will need both intentionally and incidentally shared information to predict accurately what and why consumers will purchase in the future. The race to the highest level of consumer relevancy will be determined by the businesses that (more quickly than their competitors) create the competencies required to motivate consumers to increase their level of intentionally volunteered information from the business's existing mix of 90 percent incidental/10 percent intentional.

This age of sharing will accelerate this migration to balance between intentionally and incidentally shared information. Tapping into intentionally shared information is tapping into our very nature as human beings to share. The rapid proliferation of communication tools (e.g., Internet, mobile devices) will proliferate sharing further. This digital environment enables us to share almost any information with almost any audience for almost any purpose. This same digital world creates exponentially more incidentally shared information from our intentional sharing or just everyday activities that capture our lives. A major distinction between intentionally and incidentally shared information is that intentionally shared information has an intended audience and purpose whereas incidentally shared information is typically not the result of a premeditated act of intentional sharing.

Understanding the difference between intentional and incidental sharing requires understanding the chain of sharing.

The chain of sharing has three dimensions:

1. The "what"—what information I shared
2. The "who"—the intended audience
3. The "why"—the purpose for sharing

The chain of intention can be broken in any one of the three dimensions. An individual could intentionally share specific personal information with one audience and have it migrate to an unintended audience. An individual can also intentionally share specific personal information with an intended audience and the intended audience could use information for an unintended purpose. The following are example iterations of the chain of intentional sharing:

- Intentional information → Intentional audience → Intended purpose
  - Example: Facebook post meant for Facebook friends who read post.
- Intentional information → Intentional audience → Unintended purpose
  - Example: Facebook post meant for Facebook friends is sold to business.
  - Example: Vehicle registration for local government is sold to business.
- Intentional information → Unintended audience → Unintended purpose
  - Example: TripAdvisor hotel review meant for fellow travelers is leveraged by competitive hotels for cross-selling.
- Unintentional information → Unintended audience → Unintended purpose
  - Example: Google product search is purchased/accessed by a business or other public organization for product marketing or organizational intelligence.

The key will be for businesses to offer an explicit and overt motivating value proposition in an environment where the consumer feels safe regarding the exchange for volunteering more revealing information. Businesses will need to engage the consumer early and directly in the sharing intention chain with an explicit and overt motivating value proposition in exchange for more direct and relevant information. The motivating value proposition will need to be offered in an environment where the consumer feels safe about sharing increasingly revealing dimensions of buying intention and context.

Value of Intent and Context

The value of intent for a business is knowing what is inside the consumer's head in terms of what, where, when, and how he or she will buy something in the next minute, hour, day, week, month, and year.

The value of context for a business is knowing every variable that is influencing the purchase intent both emotionally and rationally, down to subtle human nuances of decision making.

If a business had perfect knowledge of both a consumer's intent and context, that knowledge would radically change the business's revenue generation effectiveness (i.e., each consumer offer would generate a sale) and the business's cost infrastructure (i.e., there would be up to 70 percent cost reduction or reallocation ranging from required associates to inventory).

Ninety percent of the data generated today by consumers is not meant to be used to predict their purchase intent or to give context to that intent. When collected and analyzed by a business, it does a relatively poor job at actually predicting intent or explaining the full context of the decision.

The higher the intent component across the shared information, audience, and purpose, the higher the value of the information both to the individual and to the business or organization leveraging or seeking to leverage the information. If a consumer is motivated and feels secure about sharing high-quality personal information with an intended audience for an intended purpose, the likelihood that the information will be highly relevant will be much greater; for example, "If you give me another 5 percent off and two-day home delivery on your high-end mountain bike with the following accessories, I will share my identity, my mountain bike purchase history, and my exact purchase criteria and will promote your product with my large mountain biking club." If the consumer is unmotivated to share and feels insecure about sharing high-quality personal information with an unintended audience for an unintended purpose, the likelihood that the information will be relevant is much lower. For example, a consumer searches online for two weeks for a mountain bike for his wife, until his wife tells him that she doesn't want a mountain bike anymore; the business's analytics engage to continually serve up online ads for women's mountain bikes for seven to 10 days after he has found out that his wife no longer wants a mountain bike.

Today, there are five realities of consumer sharing:

1. More than 90 percent of the massive amounts of data created by consumers is unintentionally shared.
2. Some 90 percent of information businesses use to predict consumers' actions is unintentionally shared data.
3. Accuracy from unintentionally shared data is less than 10 percent and has remained at that level for decades.

4. Ninety percent of the time, consumers know their buying intent, and are now ready to share if motivated.
5. Consumers' true buying intentions reside in intentionally and discretionarily shared information.

The race to consumer relevancy will be defined by businesses that unlock the secrets of intentional and discretionary sharing of the consumer's direct knowledge.

Science of Consumer Sharing

Facebook CEO Mark Zuckerberg's law states that the average amount of information that an individual shares doubles every year or so.

Zuckerberg's Law of Sharing

$$Y = C * 2 \wedge X$$

where:

Y is what is shared
C is a constant
X is time

When individuals have far more control over what they share, they share far more.

When individuals have control over what they share, their sharing explodes. Snapchat is an excellent example. Snapchat is a photo messaging application where one can take photos, record videos, add text and drawings, and send them to a controlled list of recipients with a set time limit for how long recipients can view their Snaps (one to 10 seconds). After this time, shared content is hidden from the recipients and deleted from Snapchat's servers. At the end of 2012, there were 20 million photos shared per day on Snapchat. At the end of 2013, there were 400 million photos shared per day on Snapchat—a 20-fold increase in one year.[8] In the exponentially larger platform of Facebook (in 2013 Facebook had 780 million users versus Snapchat's 26 million users) where individuals have far less control of their photo sharing, only 350 million photos were uploaded daily.[9]

Why Consumers Share/Don't Share

Studies at Harvard University's department of psychology found that individuals devote 30 to 40 percent of their speech to informing others about their experiences. They found that individuals take advantage of opportunities

Sharing Motivators	Sharing Inhibitors
Self-Interest	**Self-Protection**
Make my life easier (utility)	Protect me/my information
Improve my experience	Give me control
Personalize our interactions	Give me choice
Reward me financially	Be transparent
Be relevant	Give me data portability

FIGURE 3.2 Consumer Information Sharing Equation
Copyright JohnMcKean@InformationMasters.com.

to communicate their thoughts and feelings to others because the act of sharing engages neural and cognitive mechanisms associated with psychological rewards for the individual. The very act of self-disclosure is directly linked to increased activity in the brain's reward pathways of the mesolimbic dopamine system. The research findings indicate that even simple sharing or communicating information to others induces psychological rewards for individuals. The researchers' conclusion was that disclosing information ranging from a complex personal experience to simple information about oneself is intrinsically rewarding.[10]

The behavioral mechanics of sharing personal information are simple. There are two primary dimensions: One is a motivator (positive) and the other is an inhibitor (negative). In this model, there is a balancing dynamic of perceived relativity. If the motivators' side of the equation is perceived to be extremely high, the inhibitors' side of the equation is perceived to be less important to the consumer. Conversely, if the inhibitors are extremely high, the motivators are perceived to be less important (see Figure 3.2).

(+) Sharing Motivators (I want to share because I can now do or get something)
- Self-interest
  - Utility (When I share this information, I can now do this...)
    - Find a restaurant, find a professional, find my size pants, help me share achievements/life with friends/family, improve my experience
  - Reward (When I share this information, I can now get this...)
    - Low-order
      - Product, service, discount, coupon
    - High-order
      - Likes on Facebook, many comments from friends on my post, many followers on Twitter, many hits on YouTube

(–) Sharing Inhibitors (I don't want to share because I can't control the bad things that may happen to me)
- Fear/anxiety
  - Control and/or choice mitigates fear.[11]

An increasing amount of information that individuals share is volunteered on social networking sites.

Intel's "Mobile Etiquette" survey found that a majority of U.S. adults (85 percent) share online, one-quarter of U.S. adults share at least once a day, and 23 percent of U.S. adults feel they are missing out when they haven't shared or consumed information online.

Why Is Sharing (Self-Disclosure) Important?

Divulging personal information about ourselves stimulates regions in the brain associated with a sense of satisfaction regarding food, money, and/or sex. Eighty percent of social media posts are about the individual who is posting. Of the 250 million photos that are updated daily, 35 percent of posters tag themselves in the photos. In fact, nine out of 10 Americans believe that most people share too much personal information online. Based on this clinical sharing need, Facebook has tested whether users would pay to have their sharing highlighted. There is also a sharing gradient where individuals with higher levels of narcissism or potentially low self-esteem spend far more time on social media sites (e.g., Facebook) than those with higher self-esteem. Amazingly, 40 percent of everyday dialogue is about how we think or feel. Harvard University has conducted brain imaging and behavioral experiments that point to the neurological underpinnings of the rewards to share personal information. Bottom line: When we share, we positively stimulate brain cells and synapses. These positive stimuli are in the same category as the stimulus we get from consuming food or acquiring money. People will even sacrifice money in order to share more about themselves. The Harvard researchers found that individuals were willing to give up 17 percent to 25 percent of potential earnings (in the study) so they could reveal more personal information.[12]

Fear of Missing Out

Fear of missing out (FoMo) is another important human driver of sharing. Millennials and earlier generations are particularly driven by social online FoMo. It is their norm to use texting and status updates to stay in touch with friends and family far more easily than with phone calls. FoMo not only drives individuals to share and interact on social sites but also manifests behaviorally as a compulsion:

- Twenty-seven percent of individuals check social networks when they wake up, and 51 percent log in periodically throughout the day.
- Fifty-six percent believe that not regularly checking sites means they're potentially missing out on important updates, content, or events.[13]

Social Validation

Social validation is different for every individual. In face-to-face interactions, social validation will come in the form of a smile or a kind word. In online interactions, it can come in the form of a Facebook like. It is a social affirmation as well as a confirmation of our existence. Skills are then developed to maximize the affirmations online.[14] Some of the psychological underpinnings of FoMo emanate from our instinct to survive within our groups.

As Dr. Stephanie Rutledge explains, "We have a brain wired for collaboration, compromise, restraint, comprehending, and managing one's place in shifting alliances." When individuals witness other activities that are going on without them, it can trigger primal instincts of survival. These reactions can be heightened with younger generations who are still in the process of establishing their survival skills such as personal and professional identities that support an economically viable existence (i.e., surviving in the world).[15] Individuals can rate their own FoMo score at www.ratemyfomo.com/.

Ego

A person' s emotional motivation to share personal information on social networks is more tied to the audience than the generic need to connect socially with other individuals. Individuals' focus on themselves drives them to update their status or tag themselves in photos. They are essentially trying to create a personal or professional brand when they share information on social networks such as Facebook, LinkedIn, or Twitter.[16]

One of the measurements of whether other people actually care about what an individual shares (i.e., social influence) is a Klout Score. Klout is a website and mobile app that ranks people according to their online social influence via the Klout Score. The Klout Score is a numerical value between 1 and 100 that measures the size of a person's social media network and correlates the content created to measure how other people interact with their content.

Klout and American Airlines partnered to offer a promotion with two dimensions:

1. Boost people's Klout Score and redeem a prize via increased interaction with Klout.
2. Earn a bonus when sharing the promotion with friends.

The prize was access to an American Airlines' VIP lounge for those who received a Klout Score of 55 or higher.[17]

This is a subtle way to capitalize on driving egos to share more while promoting a particular business. Klout is leveraging this further by partnering with other major brands such as Sony, Nike, Microsoft, Disney, Audi, and Gilt to encourage individuals to boost their personal brand while simultaneously promoting commercial brands.

Social Comparison

It is natural for individuals to compare themselves to others, particularly in their peer group. It is part of our instinct to survive relative to others; that is, the most fit will survive. Individuals compare a wide range of dimensions, including physical and emotional traits (e.g., physical appearance, feelings, strengths, weaknesses, abilities, attitudes, and beliefs). In most cases, individuals compare themselves to peers or those in a similar situation. Individuals compare themselves to others who are perceived as better than they are (upward social comparison) and those who are worse off (downward social comparison). This is tied to the development and maintenance of self-esteem.[18]

Social Space Underpinning New Sharing Norm

The social and search organizations (e.g., Facebook and Google) have been leading the incidentally shared information evolution, with Facebook setting the pace and testing the boundaries of how much information individuals are willing to share and how much monetization they can extract. When privacy backlashes occur from individuals, governments, or advocacy groups, Facebook typically acquiesces.

The largest opportunity is in the intentionally volunteered information area. This holds the most promise for businesses that want to achieve extremely high levels of relevancy. Whereas the incidentally shared information will still need to be analyzed to create inferred buying intentions, intentionally volunteered information can be managed to generate actual buying intentions.

Social sites give individuals an opportunity for easier self-disclosure. Self-disclosure is a central component of creating and developing intimacy (e.g., friendship, love). Social sites give individuals who have a harder time with face-to-face sharing an easier road to socializing. Individuals with lower self-esteem oftentimes are hesitant to disclose personal information on an ongoing basis in intimate relationships.[19]

What Consumers Share

Individuals continue to make dramatic increases in their propensity and competency to share personal information via social media such as Facebook, LinkedIn, and Twitter. With over one billion Facebook users, 650 million of them are active daily posting some of the most intimate details of their lives, and 750 million of them are sharing their personal information via their mobile phones. These numbers grow exponentially when the numbers of friend connections multiply. Currently, there are 150 billion friend connections on Facebook. Individuals reveal their personal feelings (likes) about everything from people to products. Facebook's likes total 1.13 trillion since its launch—4.5 billion per day. Perhaps some of the most revealing aspects of Facebook are the photos that individuals post, which many times convey far more than words. Individuals post 350 million photos a day on average to Facebook. An important trend that is occurring with Facebook is that while younger generations (Y and Z) are still sharing their personal information, they are tightening their privacy settings and regularly deleting and editing previous posts.[20]

Despite this propensity to share personal information, only 75 percent of Facebook users would consider clicking on a Facebook advertisement, and a full 35 percent state they would never click on a Facebook ad. The object lesson here is that using the best incidentally volunteered personal information and advanced algorithms, individuals are highly unlikely to respond to even highly targeted "push" marketing.[21] From a business perspective, Generation Y's purchasing power alone approaches $200 billion, with influence over half of all economic spending in the United States.[22]

This behavior indicates that they still have the propensity to share personal information but want more control over who sees it and how it is used. This indicates a discernible shared information maturation process when Generations Y and Z (Y = born 1980–2000; Z = born 2000–present) migrate from an almost complete apathy toward privacy issues to being far more attuned to the privacy controls they manage regarding their personal sharing. In a survey, 70 percent of Millennials agreed with the statement "No one should ever be allowed to have access to my personal data or web behavior," and 77 percent of individuals over 35 agreed. Gen Yers also indicated that they are more likely to share their location in order to receive discounts than Generation Xers (Gen Yers 56 percent versus Gen Xers 42 percent). Twenty-five percent of Gen Yers indicated that they would share personal information to get more relevant advertising, versus 19 percent of Gen Xers. More broadly, over half of Millennials said they would share information with a company if they got something in return, versus 40 percent of those 35 and over.[23]

In another recent survey, 28,500 individuals indicated that they are willing to share personal information with their preferred retailers regarding their media usage (75 percent), demographics (73 percent), identification such as name and address (61 percent), lifestyle (59 percent), and location (56 percent) in return for sufficient utility or reward.[24] Beyond just Millennials, 85 percent of cross-generational online consumers know that websites track their online shopping behavior, and they have a basic awareness that this tracking will help companies present more relevant offers and content. Seventy-five percent of online consumers are comfortable with retailers using a certain level of personal information to improve their shopping experience, and 64 percent of online consumers believe that revealing personal information will be sufficiently rewarded by the companies' increase in offer relevancy. Conversely, 36 percent of online consumers believe that the trade-off in relinquishing their privacy is not worth the reward in added offer relevancy.[25]

Pew Research Center's Internet Project revealed the three main dimensions of how and why individuals share their locations. Many individuals use their smartphones to navigate the world; 74 percent of adult smartphone owners ages 18 and older use their smartphones for directions or information about their current locations; 30 percent (up from 14 percent in 2012) of these smartphone owners also include their location in their social media posts. There is a slight decline (18 percent down to 12 percent of adult smartphone owners) in the number of smartphone owners who check in while using location services. This is likely due to the fact that the utility or reward for doing so is insufficient to compensate them for the additional location information or effort to do so. Of these geo-social service users, 30 percent check in to places on Facebook, 18 percent to Foursquare, and 14 percent to Google Plus. Overall, statistics show a steady increase in divulging location.[26]

Despite the growth, divulging one's location is still cause for concern and prompts mobile users from all age groups to turn off location tracking features at some point due to privacy concerns. Forty-six percent of teen app users indicated they turned off their location tracking feature because of concerns that people or businesses would access this information.

There still is a growing trend for individuals in most generations to reveal their physical locations in order to receive some type of text alert for discounts or location-specific offers. A recent survey found that 31 percent of individuals are at least somewhat interested in receiving such texts, which was a 5 percent increase from the previous survey. In addition, 10 percent were very interested in receiving text alerts, which was an increase of 5 percent from a previous survey. Fifty-three percent of individuals view texts as a more compelling communication medium, as texts are typically more succinct, simpler, and easier to act upon than traditional ads, coupons, e-mails, and direct mail. Seventy-three percent of individuals say they are likely to visit a store after receiving a geo-targeted text message, while 71 percent actually made a retail store visit, with 61 percent making a purchase after receiving the alert.

Another interesting dynamic when individuals agree to share their locations is that their expectations increase; that is, they anticipate the special offer when in the proximity of certain stores. Combining the individual's location data with other dynamic data such as weather, traffic, events, loyalty information, past purchases, user data, and demographics dramatically increases the offer's relevance to the individual and thus the business's conversion rates. Geo-fencing is also applicable not just to store-based locations but also to places that the targeted individuals are likely to frequent (e.g., sports arenas, concerts, ski resorts, airports, gyms, and parks). Also, adding an incentive to signing up for the location-based text alerts will increase the participation up to twofold.[27]

In a broader context, an individual's willingness to reveal location supports the advancements in the broader geo-spatial analytics. Dr. Waldo Tobler (American-Swiss geographer and cartographer, and professor emeritus at the University of California, Santa Barbara, department of geography) theorized that "Everything is related to everything else, but near things are more related to each other." This conclusion is referred to as the first law of geography. To extend Dr. Tobler's theory to an individual's value of things, something that an individual intends to purchase has a certain perceived value, but near things have a higher perceived value; that is, proximity of an item defines its perceived value to an individual.

Just as the concepts of Isaac Newton's law of universal gravitation are synonymous with the concept of spatial dependence, perceived value is spatially dependent. Individuals' perception of value typically centers on the perception of time expenditure relative to other related activities (i.e., convenience and any associated travel costs). This is supported by the gravity model of trip distribution and the law of demand in that the probability of traveling to a location to purchase an item is inversely proportional to the cost of the travel, and therefore changes the perception of value at that location and at that point in time. To have a complete behavioral picture of the relationship between an individual and the items he or she has bought or will buy in the future, the location of each individual and each item is critical as "everything and everyone has to be somewhere." Not only are these dimensions critical in creating a more accurate current picture, but they also help in anticipating the next event. When a business can combine operational and event-driven analytics against an individual's location, it can create a higher value proposition for the individual and more efficiency for its operations.

Businesses can extend this value proposition to an individual by using augmented reality, where a business marries its product or service to a physical, real-world environment with relevant information based on the customer's geographical location. As individuals are hiking with their iPhones, they point the iPhones at the mountain peak they are about to climb and get a readout on the relevant information about the ensuing hike based on their location information. The central value of augmented reality is that it is a relevant information feed in real time and in a semantic context with the individuals and their physical environment. To extend this concept, a business can also use virtual reality to simulate an individual using its product and service based on the information that the individual volunteers to the business (e.g., the mountain in front of the hiker is 12,000 feet high with dense fog, a Park Service hiking restriction is currently in place, and it will take seven hours to reach the summit based on the individual's physical condition and history).

Another characteristic is that the individual can interact with the augmented reality intelligence and digitally manipulate the assessment. The individual points the iPhone to another peak and suggests climbing this new mountain on a clear day. The mobile app responds with the new time frame and a suggested day based on the weather forecast. So the value of the information is based not only on the location of the individual and the physical mountain but also on the individual's process of interacting with the mountain. With the individual volunteering his or her location information and streaming intelligence, the individual evolves from a passive user of the information to a participant and co-creator of the experience.[28]

	Past	Now	Emerging
Design paradigm	Expert driven	Human centered	Facilitated
Audience role	Customer	User	Participant
Activity	Consume	Experience	Co-create
	• Shop	• Use	• Adapt/modify/extend
	• Buy	• Interact	• Design
	• Own	• Communicate	• Make

This observation is embedded in the gravity model of trip distribution. It is also related to the law of demand, in that interactions between places are inversely proportional to the cost of travel, which is much like the probability of purchasing products that is inversely proportional to the cost.

Another interesting trend is that the nature of personal information sharing is changing for Generations Y and Z. These generations are migrating from Facebook to microblogs like Twitter and Pheed. Twitter's demographics saw a doubling of teenagers' use in 2012. Teenagers share their tweets more publicly on Twitter than they do their Facebook posts (i.e., public tweeting versus Facebook posts to friends only). It's interesting to note that while social networking websites like Facebook, MySpace, and LinkedIn also have a microblog sharing feature, called "status update," Twitter is the most popular, with 500 million users sharing 400 million tweets per day.

Texting is another information sharing practice that is more prevalent in generations Y and Z with staggering frequency. Generations Y and Z send 10 times the number of texts than older generations do. U.S. individuals with smartphones between the ages of 18 and 24 send 2,022 texts per month on average (67 texts per day), and receive an additional 1,831 texts.[29] That is double the number of texts that smartphone users ages 25 to 34 send.

It is important to look at Generations Y and Z, as they are the harbingers for personal information sharing. Generationally, these individuals have also shown a tremendous growth in information sharing competency and sophistication that was unheard of a decade ago. Particularly with these generations who are information natives (i.e., born into an "informated world"), the generational effect of individuals being born into a world of computers, tablets, smartphones, and apps is raising not only innate personal information competencies but also the propensity and capability to share information. Generationally, individuals are showing more and have less sensitivity to privacy issues, particularly the later generations Y and Z. This refers to incidentally volunteered personal information. There is a high likelihood that this will also be the case for intentionally volunteered personal information given the right motivations and control.

Individuals are showing a strong willingness to share their physical locations via their smartphones' Global Positioning System (GPS) capability. Many comprehensive location-based offerings from Foursquare, Facebook, Yelp, and increasingly Groupon have provided a steady stream of location-based opportunities for individuals. As with any mobile app, individuals must perceive the utility to relinquish their personal location. These geographically referenced social networks ask individuals to check in to various locations such as coffee shops, bars, or homes, and share their location information with other friends on the network. These location-based services provide information not only on current locations but also on future locations—that is, the individual's next destination. This functionality operates from the GPS locator on the individual's mobile device, allowing the social network to know where the person is. Yelp's utility to individuals is that it is a "consumer review aggregator" that aggregates individuals' reviews of product and service offerings. There is a growing comfort for individuals to opt in, in order to reveal their location to benefit from location-based offers by businesses.

Geo-fencing is an important dimension of how individuals receive the utility in return for revealing their location (e.g., an individual caught in a rainstorm receiving a special on umbrellas that is within a five-mile radius). The geo-fence is a dynamically generated radius, reference point, or boundary of the individual as the individual changes locations—for example, radius around one's home, radius around a store, radius around the seat of an automobile (a specific point), a school zone (notification the child is exiting the zone). When an individual enables the GPS function on his or her smartphone and has a location-based marketing (LBM) app such as ShopAlerts (Placecast), a merchant or manufacturer can communicate timely and relevant products and special promotions when the individual enters or exits the geo-fence. The use of geo-fencing is represented by a cross section of industries (e.g., retailers, manufacturers, hospitality, transportation). Top brands, including North Face, Starbucks, L'Oréal, Subway, Kohl's, Kmart, Hewlett-Packard, JetBlue, and SC Johnson have/are using ShopAlerts programs. Ten million individuals perceive that the value they gain from Placecast's ShopAlerts warrants revealing their location information. ShopAlerts is licensed by Telefonica O2 in Europe and AT&T and DDR in the United States and is used by millions of individuals.

Google has begun integrating an individual's location usage of Google Maps with the individual's Google Plus social community of friends. As the individual travels and indicates favorite locations and businesses, both the individual and the circle of friends benefit. The individual's behavior also captures the decision process. For example, the individual travels to Los Angeles and queries Google Maps about Thai restaurants. The individual reviews the menus of three Thai restaurants on Google Maps, then briefly stops at one of the locations, and continues on to spend one hour at the final restaurant; the individual considered these three options, the second runner-up was X restaurant, and the person chose Y restaurant. Another aspect of Google is the intelligence gained at the nexus between location and search (i.e., intent).

This willingness to share personal buying information occurs when businesses have provided a clear utility and/or reward to individuals for sharing their personal information directly with the business. Some examples include My Lowe's (planning future home improvement projects), Meredith's My Recipes (recipes for future meals), Aviva (monitor your driving to lower your insurance premiums), and Amazon (Wish List of what the individual explicitly indicates he or she would like to buy in the future).

These examples of information sharing on social sites and microblogs are considered *active* sharing of personal information. This decade has seen a tremendous growth in another category of personal shared information—*passive* information sharing. This passive information sharing is primarily enabled by direct personal information feeds from smart objects and wearable devices (e.g., Nike smart watches, Volt electric cars, Colorado Springs Utilities self-monitoring). In passive information sharing, the individual's personal activities stream in information flow of data to the individual and/or other external entities (e.g., running with their Nike FuelBand or Apple iWatch, driving their Volt electric car, monitoring their home's electricity consumption). In context, a Boeing 737 engine generates 10 terabytes of data every 30 minutes, and a six-hour flight from New York to Los Angeles on a twin-engine aircraft creates 240 terabytes of data on the engines' performance and health.[30]

The best examples of burgeoning subindustries that have emerged in this decade for volunteered consumer intelligence are "quantified self" (QS) (data acquisition on a person's daily life activities), the Internet of Things (everyday smart devices that are fully integrated via the web), and mHealth (individuals monitoring their own health supported by mobile devices). Much of the activity has been centered on the explosion of mobile apps technology, which extracts volunteered buying context and future buying intent or plans directly from the individual. More detailed examples of "quantifying yourself" and the Internet of Things will be illustrated later in the book (Chapter 7). In the subcategory of mHealth, it's estimated that 30 percent of smartphone users have installed wellness apps. There are 500-plus mobile health projects worldwide and 40,000 medical apps available for smartphones and tablets. Twenty-nine percent of 18- to 29-year-olds research health information on their smartphones; 18 percent of 30- to 49-year-olds and 8 percent of 65+-year-olds do so.[31] At the current rate, mobile health downloads are doubling each year; they are used to manage sleep, eat healthier, manage moods, track pregnancies, manage prescriptions, monitor blood pressure, check nearby pollen levels, and so on. Some 2.8 million individuals use a home monitoring service with integrated connectivity. This figure does not include individuals who use monitoring devices connected to a PC or mobile phone.[32]

Another subindustry of volunteered customer intelligence is professional intelligence. LinkedIn, Viadeo, and XING are some of the leading players where individuals share their personal occupational details on social networking websites to serve their professional occupation and aspirations. LinkedIn is clearly the leader in this information sharing space. LinkedIn is an important object lesson for the dynamics of an individual's personal information sharing and what businesses need to create to compel individuals to share their personal information directly with the business. LinkedIn is a social platform for professionals. The information that the individual shares about his or her professional history and details is personal professional information regarding the individual. Some 230 million individuals of LinkedIn's user base perceive great value in sharing their personal professional information, because there is explicit reward and/or utility. The individual has the ability to control the distribution and use of the information.

In fact, there is a fledgling industry supporting intentionally volunteered customer information, with some roots extending back to the last decade, such as project vendor relationship management (VRM). This new industry represents a new set of start-ups and emerging industry standards organizations, consortiums, work groups, and protocols that will evolve over the coming decades.

In summary, the first half of this decade has demonstrated that individuals are significantly increasing their propensity to share personal information when there is personal utility and/or reward for doing so. Individuals have also shown a clear ability to manage a more complex personal data environment as well as leverage the information capabilities of mobile and web infrastructures like no other previous decade has seen. In fact, individuals are currently a decade ahead of businesses informationally and are primed to engage directly with businesses once the business enables innovation on the individual's behalf (demand side). Demand-side innovation will once again unlock supply-side innovation as in previous decades (e.g., data warehouses, business intelligence, and web analytics).

Notes

1. Kirk Nichols, "30 Communication Inventions from the 1800s to 2010." www.timetoast.com/timelines/67104.
2. John Gantz and David Reinsel, "Extracting Value from Chaos," IDC Reports, sponsored by EMC Corporation, June 2011.
3. Ipsos Open Thinking Exchange study. https://www.ipsos-na.com/research/media-content-technology/.
4. Craig Smith, editor/owner Digital Marketing Ramblings. Expanded Ramblings.com.
5. Intel "Mobile Etiquette" survey, conducted by Ipsos Observer, Santa Clara, CA, September 5, 2012.
6. Ibid.
7. 2014 Center of Information-Based Competition research study.
8. Billy Gallagher, "You Know What's Cool? A Billion Snapchats: App Sees over 20 Million Photos Shared per Day, Releases on Android," *TechCrunch*, October 29, 2012.

9. Craig Smith, editor/owner Digital Marketing Ramblings, Expanded Ramblings.com.

10. Diana I. Tamir and Jason P. Mitchell, "Disclosing Information about the Self Is Intrinsically Rewarding," Department of Psychology, Cambridge, MA: Harvard University, May 22, 2012.

11. 2014 Center for Information-Based Competition research study.

12. Robert Lee Hotz, "Science Reveals Why We Brag so Much," Health & Wellness, *Wall Street Journal*, May 7, 2012. sciencejournal@wsj.com. Diana Tamir and Jason Mitchell of Harvard University conducted the experiments.

13. MyLife.com survey, "Social Media Survey Says: We're Overwhelmed!" July 9, 2013.

14. Tom Lowery, "Psychology of Social Media—Why Marketers should Care," Thinking Out Loud (blog), September 2013. http://tomlthinking outloud.blogspot.com/2013/09/psychology-of-social-media-why.html. E-mail interview with Dr. Stephanie Rutledge.

15. Tom Lowery, "Why Social Media Is so Addictive (And Why Marketers Should Care)," Business 2 Community, September 2, 2013. https://smallbusiness.yahoo.com/advisor/why-social-media-addictive-why-marketers-care-192533900.html.

16. Ibid. Tom Lowery, "Psychology of Social Media—Why Marketers should Care," Thinking Out Loud (blog), September 2013. http://tomlthinkingoutloud.blogspot.com/2013/09/psychology-of-social-media-why.html. E-mail interview with Dr. Stephanie Rutledge.

17. Don Hoang, "American Airlines' Admirals Club Welcomes Klout Users in Nearly 40 Locations," May 7th, 2013. http://blog.klout.com/2013/05/american-airlines-klout/.

18. Kendra Cherry, "What Is the Social Comparison Process?" http://psychology.about.com/od/sindex/g/Socialcomp.htm.

19. Amanda L. Forest and Joanne V. Wood, "Facebook Is Not Such a Good Thing for Those with Low Self-Esteem." www.psychologicalscience.org/index.php/news/releases/facebook-is-not-such-a-good-thing-for-those-with-low-self-esteem.html.

20. Pew Internet and American Life Project, "Facebook's Total 'Likes' Is 1.13 Trillion." www.infographicscreator.com/2014/04/03/infographic-every-business-use-facebook/.

21. Retail-digital.com, "Whisbi Launches Tech for Monetizing Facebook—Retail Digital," www.retail-digital.com/retail_technology/whisbi-launches-tech-for-monetizing-face.

22. Ashley Archer, "Direct Marketing to Generation Y," Hanover research. www.hanoverresearch.com/insights/direct-marketing-to-generation-y/?i=automotive.

23. University of Southern California's Center for the Digital Future survey, "Is Online Privacy Over? Findings from the USC Annenberg Center for the Digital Future Show Millennials Embrace a New Online Reality," April 22, 2013, digitalcenter.org. http://annenberg.usc.edu/News%20 and%20Events/News/130422CDF_Millennials.aspx.

24. "IBM's State of Marketing Survey 2012: Marketers' Biggest Challenges and Opportunities Reveal the Rise of the Empowered Customer," March 16, 2013. www.club-cmmc.it/lettura/ibm_marketing.pdf.

25. Janice Y. Tsai, Serge Egelman, Lorrie Cranor, and Alessandro Acquisti, "The Effect of Online Privacy Information on Purchasing Behavior: An Experimental Study." www.heinz.cmu.edu/~acquisti/papers/acquisti-onlinepurchasing-privacy.pdf.

26. Kathryn Zickuhr, "Location-Based Services," Princeton Survey Research Associates International, September 12, 2013. www.pewinternet .org/2013/09/12/location-based-services/.

27. Placecast, "Consumer Interest in Mobile Offers Increases 19 Points since 2009, Providing Promise to Brands and Publishers." http://techcrunch .com/2010/02/25/placecast-debuts-location-based-mobile-marketing-technology-shopalerts/; www.placecast.net/press/releases/PR_harris_ local_offers.pdf.

28. Tobler's first law of geography wiki; augmented reality wiki; David Sonnen (IDC). http://geospatial.referata.com/wiki/First_Law_of_Geography.

29. Experian/Pew study. www.businessinsider.com/chart-of-the-day-number-of-texts-sent-2013-3

30. Paul Mathai, applied research lead, Manufacturing and Hightech, "Big Data-Catalyzing Performance and Manufacturing," Wipro Technologies. www.wipro.com/documents/big%20data.pdf.

31. Maggie Wirtanen, "Smartphone = Smarter Healthcare?" AlliedHealth-World.com, September 21, 2012. www.alliedhealthworld.com/ visuals/smartphone-healthcare.html; Sam Laird, "How Smartphones Are Changing Health Care," September 26, 2012. http://mashable .com/2012/09/26/smartphones-health-care-infographic/.

32. Johan Fagerberg and Lars Kurkinen, "mHealth and Home Monitoring," Berg Insight, M2M research series. www.berginsight.com/ReportPDF/ ProductSheet/bi-mhealth5-ps.pdf.

PART II

New Voice Innovators' Win-Win

Most businesses are a decade behind their customers. Personal technology has enabled customers to evolve far more rapidly than the corresponding business competencies that are required to leverage the customer's rapid technological ascent. There has been a group of business innovators that have adapted more quickly than their contemporaries. This group of business innovators includes some of the most powerful brands in the world, ranging from Amazon to Apple. Their initiatives to leverage the new era of volunteered customer information range from the most strategic (e.g., Ford's OpenXC smart vehicle initiatives) to the most tactical (e.g., North Face's mobile app).

The race to catch these new customers will be defined by the companies that can break free from yesterday's model and create today's new model by forging sustainable information partnerships that drive relevancy and value on both sides of the equation.

CHAPTER 4

Yesterday's Indirect Information Model

Yesterday's voice of the customer was present but without propulsion or power. Customers had the willingness but not the capability or competency that has rapidly evolved over the past decade to enable a radical transformation of their power as a consuming entity. As a result, 90 percent of how businesses predicted what customers wanted or needed was only a proxy of a direct voice without most of the real direct knowledge required to make an accurate prediction. Yesterday's voice was also missing the critical contextual variables of the purchase that could be sourced directly only with the discretionary sharing of the customer.

Yesterday's Model

Business has always been about collecting consumer information and then guessing what consumers would likely want or need. In prior centuries, businesses were direct with customers. The nature of economies was to be more localized, and businesses oftentimes had the luxury of being able to ask their customers face-to-face what they wanted or would need in the near future. Most of this information that businesses leveraged to determine what to order was directly and intentionally volunteered knowledge from their customers. The customers volunteered this information because they trusted the local business owner with their information and clearly understood the utility of providing information to the business: "I tell them what I want and they will provide it for me."

This was the business model of the proverbial corner store. Business's information gathering and analysis was the shop owner asking customers about their buying intentions and oftentimes knowing the context surrounding the intentions: "I know Mrs. Green will be buying a red dress next week because her daughter just got engaged, and Mrs. Green's favorite color is red." They knew the real identity of the consumer as well as the who, what, where, when, how, and why (context) attributes that now take the most advanced predictive analytics that businesses can muster. The challenges of "next best offer" (What is the next best thing we can offer this consumer?) or "attribution" (What did we do that actually caused the consumer to buy?) were just the natural flow of information in a small community.

As populations expanded and businesses became larger and more complex, this type of intimate relationship with consumers disappeared as the relationship became more distant. Person-to-person consumer information collection was ultimately replaced by businesses collecting a relatively small amount of information directly from consumers with primarily (90 percent) a myriad of other indirect data collection from secondary sources (e.g., data aggregators, public records, other businesses).

As consumers' lives became more digitized and mobile, businesses' data collection and analytics added in all the incidentally and indirectly shared consumer data from their new digital world—Google search, smartphone use, paying by credit card, posts on Facebook, and purchases from Amazon. Despite all the advances in technology and predictive analytics, businesses' guesses or extrapolations still produce a success rate of less than 10 percent, which has gone relatively unchanged for decades. It has been accepted because the sizable investments have been financially justifiable, and, more important, having consumers directly volunteer what they want and why has been infeasible.

Figure 4.1 shows the relative trajectories of the evolution of four corporate computing elements and the world's data growth rate.

These investments are justifiable with a positive return in investment (ROI) but are not incremental, not transformational.

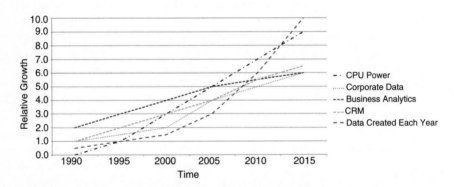

FIGURE 4.1 **Evolution of Business Computing Capabilities**
Data Source: Gartner, IDC, Radicati Group, Facebook, TR Research, Pew Internet, EMC, *Popular Science*, SINTEF (www.sintef.no), Center for Information Based Competition.

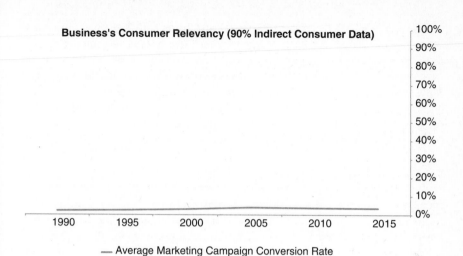

FIGURE 4.2 Business's Consumer Relevancy
Sources: c JohnMcKean@InformationMasters.com.

Figure 4.2 shows the evolution of a business's consumer relevancy: how often a business offered a consumer a product and how often the consumer found this product sufficiently relevant to purchase it (average marketing conversion rate). To achieve maximum relevancy, 90 percent of a business's data is from the consumer's indirect voice—that is, incidentally/unintentionally volunteered by the consumer. The indirect data is missing much of the consumer intention and broader context to create strong relevancy. The result is that 95 percent of the time, the consumer deems the business irrelevant.

These investments have not been just about buying the newest or biggest database computer or adding more consumer marketing applications—for example, customer relationship management (CRM), business intelligence (BI), campaign management, predictive analytics—but run deep into fundamental customer and consumer strategies and infrastructure that a business develops to operate in a complex environment.

As Amazon, eBay, Google, LinkedIn, Facebook, and YouTube became further embedded into the fabric of everyday behavior for consumers, new technology and marketing applications were added to the consumer information arsenal. With relatively little digital regulation compared with today, businesses have made significant strides in leveraging most of the incidentally volunteered information by consumers. This growing volume of multistructured data required businesses to address a larger volume of data as well as a more analytically intensive approach to both online and offline initiatives (e.g., enterprise data warehouse [EDW], BI, data warehouse, web analytics, CRM). Many business innovations resulted through most of this stage primarily based on inferred behavioral models. These innovations would ultimately slow down toward the end of this stage with only relatively small incremental performance improvements and innovations. Businesses finished this phase lagging behind the rapid digitization of the mobile consumer.

Legacy of Indirect Information

Businesses operate on information. When it comes to understanding and predicting what consumers will buy, businesses have collected and analyzed information from sources other than directly from the consumer. Businesses have been relegated to indirect sources for several decades because consumers have been unable and unwilling to communicate directly with businesses as to what they intend to buy and why they intent to buy it.

Most of these indirect sources involved collecting information that the consumer did not intend to be used to help businesses market to them. In businesses' pursuit of better indirect information, they have had to push the boundaries of privacy in an attempt to achieve more effective marketing results as well as greater efficiencies.

Businesses have built the information competencies for this indirect model over decades and as a result are deeply entrenched in everything that makes up a business's information competency.

The indirect information business model required a substantial information infrastructure with many different separate and supportive competencies to create an overall business information competency. The seven factors for driving competencies of an indirect information business model run parallel to the factors that drive tomorrow's direct information business model:

1. **People.** Associates' predisposition and skill set are invested in the indirect approach for collecting and analyzing consumer information. As associates, their employability and professional worth are their ability to execute indirect approaches.
2. **Process.** The processes are designed to optimize the collection and analysis of indirect information from a variety of indirect sources. Processes are also tied to delivering core value propositions based on indirect information. Without direct knowledge of the consumer's intent or identity, many additional processes must be put in place to compensate.

3. **Organizational structure.** The structure of organization that supports a business using primarily indirect information is geared toward collection, analysis, and executing a business model of indirect information.

4. **Culture.** The seemingly intangible aspects of a business's values, attitudes, standards, and beliefs that can define a business's focus on driving customer insights from indirect and secondary customer information sources rather than innovating to direct information sources.

5. **Leadership.** Leaders have obtained their executive positions because they have been successful at the indirect business model. The skills and strategies are what have defined their careers. It is where they are most comfortable executing and leading.

6. **Information.** The indirect information model is about building a proxy of the real world with 95 percent of big data being indirect, incidentally generated information. The information proxy is the vehicle that creates the entrance of future behavior. The multistructured nature of indirect data coupled with the multitude of indirect data sources (e.g., marketing data providers, credit bureaus, search services, public domain records, banks, local governments, cross-industry data, and utilities) add to the complexity of the indirect model.

7. **Technology.** Technology of the indirect approach has mostly been focused on businesses' internal technology as well as the enabling technology of the environment and third-party data providers (e.g., corporate databases, intranets, Internet, e-mail, social networks).

Figure 4.3 depicts the major flows of the indirect approach, which all seven information competencies must support.[1]

Once the data buckets have been defined, now the data flows can be addressed. Indirect data flows 1 through 4 are the primary vehicles of the secondary flows.

Data flow 1 represents the flow between My Data and Your Data. From a data sovereignty perspective, businesses extract data from the individuals' personal data resulting from their personal and commercial activities (e.g., interactions, transactions, questionnaires).

Data flow 2 represents the data flow inside the Our Data group of organizations. For example, the organization that an individual obtains a driver's license from sells the person's car ownership information to other organizations in countries where this type of information is required. Another example would be a telecommunication firm selling aspects of that data to marketing companies, or Google AdWords selling the individual's behavior online to other organizations. Mail-order businesses also monetize their customer lists in a similar fashion.

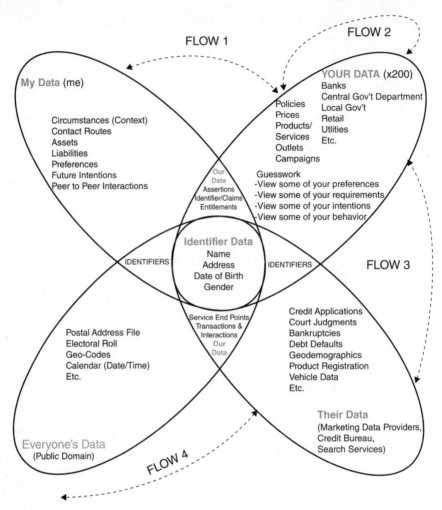

FIGURE 4.3 Data Sovereignty and Flow
Source: Iain Henderson, Information Answers, www.informationanswers.com.

Data flow 3 illustrates the data flow between Your Data and Their Data, which again is organizations sharing and monetizing personal data between organizations. This data flow also incorporates data flows from Our Data into Their Data as well. The best example of this type of data flow is the oftentimes not explicit question: "May we share your personal data with other companies?" with a tick box that may or may not be auto-selected. This also includes whatever personal data results from the data industry monetizing the individual's activity (e.g., warranty cards, product registrations).

Data flow 4 demonstrates the flow between Everybody's Data and Their Data, which essentially is the data industry using public data (e.g., electoral rolls, court records). Data aggregators such as Axiom, Equifax, Experian, and LexisNexis extract information from public records and then package that information and offer it for resale. These data aggregators use the existing public domain information sources and apply analytics and categorization to initiate new commercial data value from the original data.

Privacy Not

For most of the past several decades when the Internet and mobile technology were starting to become part of consumers' everyday life, legislation and advocacy group efforts significantly lagged behind curtailing businesses' collection and use of personal consumer information. Consequently, businesses had a free hand to leverage personal consumer data in the most profitable manner.

Government legislation and advocacy groups spent this stage attempting to catch up to the rapidly emerging digital nature of life and consumerism with a clear trajectory toward increasing the consumer's personal data protection and control. Although government is still behind in legislative initiatives, it was much further behind in the early digital Wild West days.

The following list represents the Wild West days for businesses' relatively unrestrained exploitation and monetization of personal data:

- 1994 Yahoo!
- 1994 World of Warcraft (WoW) multiplayer online role-playing game.
- 1994 Netscape launches first browser.
- 1994 Beginning of banner ads.
- 1995 MSN.
- 1995 Amazon opens for business.
- 1995 Internet Explorer adds support for cookies.
- 1995 eBay.
- 1995 Craigslist: classified ads for jobs, housing, personals, for sale, items wanted.
- 1995 First wiki—mainstream in 2000s.
- 1996 Ask Jeeves.
- 1997 Mobile commerce hits $800 million.
- 1997 Netflix.
- 1998 Google.
- 1999 Napster.

- 1999 *E-commerce* becomes the new buzzword as Internet shopping rapidly spreads.
- 1999 MySpace.com is launched.

In these early Wild West days, relatively little legislation was created:

- 1995 European Union passes Data Protection Directive.
- 1996 U.S. Federal Trade Commission (FTC) holds first cookie hearings.
- 1996 Telecommunications Act—privacy protection on telecom information.
- 2000 Children's Online Privacy Protection Act—restricts collection of data from children under 13.
- 2001 Gramm-Leach-Bliley Act—restricts disclosure of personally identifiable information by financial institutions.

Businesses could creatively leverage most of the information that consumers created digitally (intentionally or unintentionally).

As the consumer's digital life continued to expand, the business's indirect information model expanded in depth and reach. Google, for example, started with several thousand searches and is now part of the fabric of many individuals' daily activities ("I'll just Google it"). The purpose of the section is not to detail these important Internet entrances into the world but to serve as a quick review of the timing and sequence of this digital lineage of volunteered personal information. The following is a time line of some of the more significant online ventures during the first decade of the new millennium, many of which are still running strong today. A key point is that during the beginning phases of these significant online initiatives, little regulation would control the personal information that was generated until much later in the decade.

The following list contains significant online start-ups with interspersed governmental regulation, privacy initiatives, and data breaches. It's important to note that the regulations are fairly sparse throughout the time line relative to the number of significant online initiatives. The other trend to note is that regulation tends to increase toward the latter part of this decade. This increase in legislation and advocacy work presents increasing challenges for businesses.

- 2000 TripAdvisor.com, travel website that assists customers, posting reviews.
- 2000 America Online buys Time Warner for $16 billion.
- 2000 Dot-com bust.
- 2000 U.S. retail sales are $800 billion, and online shopping is $25 billion to $30 billion.

- 2000 Google AdWords.
- 2001 StumbleUpon.
- 2001 Napster peaks with 26.4 million users.
- 2001 Wikipedia; wiki is website type while Wikipedia is a website that uses wiki format.
- 2002 AOL Time Warner reports biggest quarterly loss in U.S. history.
- 2002 Plaxo.
- 2003 Taobao Marketplace: China website for online shopping, similar to eBay and Amazon.
- 2003 Amazon posts first yearly profit.
- 2003 eBay acquires PayPal.
- 2003 Google AdSense.
- 2003 Apple launches iTunes, digital rights management to prevent file sharing.
- 2003 Spam, unsolicited e-mail, accounts for about half of all e-mails.
- 2003 LinkedIn.
- 2003 California Security Breach Information Act (SB-1386)—requiring organizations to inform individuals if the security of their information is compromised.
- 2003 Fair and Accurate Credit Transactions Act (U.S.)—allows consumers to request and obtain a free credit report once every 12 months from each consumer credit reporting company.
- 2004 Facebook.
- 2004 National Do Not Call Registry.
- 2004 Flickr; acquired by Yahoo! in 2005.
- 2004 Gmail is launched.
- 2004 Identity Theft Penalty Enhancement Act—enacted by U.S. Congress; increased criminal penalties for identity theft (i.e., aggravated identity theft). Read more: www.ehow.com/facts_6371292_aggravated-id-theft_.html#ixzz2aX1ATBvd.
- 2005 YouTube; purchased by Google in 2006.
- 2005 LexisNexis has personal records stolen from more than 310,000 individuals.
- 2005 Online pharmacies increase in popularity due to convenience and price.
- 2005 Retailers begin "Cyber Monday" kickoff of holiday online shopping.
- 2005 Yahoo! pays $35 million for Flickr.
- 2005 Placecast location-based ShopAlerts.
- 2005 ChoicePoint (information broker) sells 145,000 individuals' information to inadequately vetted bogus businesses.
- 2005 Bank of America loses computer tapes (or they are stolen) with account information on 1.2 million federal employee credit cards (among them those of U.S. senators and Pentagon employees).

- 2006 WikiLeaks.
- 2006 Project VRM, Doc Searls, Berkman Center for Internet & Society at Harvard University.
- 2006 Twitter.
- 2006 SlideShare.
- 2006 U.S. Veterans Affairs Department loses (stolen from employee) 26.5 million veterans'/active duty troops' personal information.
- 2006 Mint.com; Intuit, Quicken, and TurboTax bought it in 2009.
- 2006 Tripit, www.tripit.com.
- 2006 Nike+ allows customers to track performance.
- 2007 Tumblr, microblogging platform and social networking website, post multimedia in short-form blog.
- 2007 Netflix announces its billionth delivery.
- 2007 World of Warcraft's online game hits a milestone when it surpasses nine million subscribers.
- 2007 Microsoft HealthVault; store and maintain health and fitness information.
- 2007 TJX Companies ($17.4 billion retailer that owns T.J. Maxx, Home Goods, and A.J. Wright) has 45.7 million credit/debit card numbers (perhaps 200 million) stolen from wireless network.
- 2007 Zynga, provider of social game services, 12 percent of Facebook revenue in 2012.
- 2007 Apple delivers first iPhone.
- 2008 Google Health, volunteer health records; canceled in 2011, and Google abandons project.
- 2008 Groupon.
- 2008 Amazon launches the Kindle, a device for reading electronic books.
- 2008 Best Buy buys Napster for $121 million.
- 2008 Number of devices connected to the Internet exceeds number of people on Earth.
- 2008 Apple launches mobile app store.
- 2009 Foursquare, location-based social networking website for mobile devices.
- 2009 Bing.
- 2009 Health Information Technology for Economic and Clinical Health Act (U.S. HITECH Act) incentivizes health care organizations to adopt more secure electronic medical records.
- 2009 Facebook turns cash flow positive for the first time.
- 2009 Yahoo! makes source code Hadoop available to the public.
- 2009 T-Mobile employee steals and sells millions of personal account details to rival firms.

- 2009 Klout uses Twitter, Facebook, Google Plus, LinkedIn, Foursquare, Wikipedia, and Instagram to create Klout Score to measure breadth and strength of one's online influence.[2]

As consumers began to create more intentionally and incidentally volunteered data online (e.g., LinkedIn, YouTube, eBay, Wikipedia, Red Beacon, Mint.com, SlideShare, TripAdvisor, Flickr, Personal.com, and Microsoft HealthVault), government and adequacy groups ramped up an increasingly restrictive environment for businesses' personal consumer data utilization.

Notes

1. Data Sovereignty and Flow graphic, Iain Henderson, Information Answers, www.informationanswers.com.
2. Respective wikis.

CHAPTER 5

Emerging Customer's New Voice Business Information Model

The emerging customer's new voice business model is fundamentally about the new flow of information. It is the first time in history that customers can communicate at scale to businesses directly. The key here is *directly*. Historically, businesses have "pushed" information to customers and consumers in an effort to sell the products and services based on their predictions or guesses as to what customers need or want. Now businesses are learning how to work the information flows first so that a direct stream of information can emanate from customers to radically enhance the information and ultimately the knowledge the businesses have about their current and potential customers.

Customer-Direct Information Model

The opportunity for businesses is to begin the journey to leverage individuals' growing willingness, competency, and/or capability to directly share far more personal information than they have ever shared previously throughout the history of commerce. The vision of a 360-degree view of the customer or one version of the truth has proved to be only that: a lofty vision that has played out to be implausible without directly engaging the information source itself—the customer. Many businesses have come to the conclusion that the only 360-degree view or one version of the truth has and will always lie in only one place—inside the minds and hearts of the customer.

Many leading businesses have made positive strides toward engaging the source of this truth—the new customers with their new voice. As their new voice evolves, they will balance out the monetization and control of their personal data to engage in an equal and fair direct partnership with business. In this partnership, they will exchange their truth and knowledge for added value from the business.

The new customer's voice has created a new edict for businesses to migrate from a predominately indirect information model to a consumer-direct information model. Each of the following industry leaders has begun its journey to this new consumer-direct information model:

- Amazon
- Apple
- AT&T
- Aviva
- Bancorp
- Colorado Springs Utilities
- eBay
- FIS
- Ford
- General Motors/Chevrolet
- Google
- Home Depot
- Intuit
- Jaguar
- Kellogg
- Kraft
- Lowe's
- MasterCard
- Meijer
- Mercedes-Benz
- Microsoft
- Nike
- North Face
- Oklahoma Gas & Electric
- Procter & Gamble
- Sony
- Southern California Edison
- State Farm
- Tesco
- Verizon Communications
- Virgin Atlantic
- Zappos

Each organization has initiatives ranging from technical to major strategic transformations. The fundamentals for these initiatives are to reward consumers for intentionally (versus incidentally) sharing personal information directly with the business in exchange for some form of personal utility or reward. Businesses are realizing that they are no longer relegated to using the historical customer data model approaches of inferring future buying behavior from indirect data sources through behavioral information proxies versus sourcing data directly from individuals. The historical approach has continued to this point because it was previously the best option for understanding an individual's future buying behavior. In this current decade with the megatrends of the web, mobile, and personal information sharing, this historical approach will increasingly become less effective and efficient and will ultimately become antiquated. It is the unnerving realization that the most advanced corporate in-house data and analytic capability will never match the efficiencies and effectiveness of a world where customer behavioral models are primarily sourced directly from individuals sharing their information themselves.

This presents innovators with the potential for game-changing relevancy for both revenue growth and cost reduction. Initial results with direct-from-consumer knowledge approaches are producing success rates up to 20 to 50 percent. As effectiveness for revenue generation increases, business costs decrease. Up to 70 percent of a business's cost infrastructure exists to compensate for the inaccuracies of extrapolations relative to the accuracies of consumers directly communicating their actual knowledge of buying intentions and context. Despite this potential, businesses' far slower evolution relative to today's consumers has cause businesses to find themselves anchored to decades of building competencies around indirect consumer information approaches. The evolution from indirect to direct approaches involves changes not only to information and technology but also to people, processes, culture, leadership, and organizational structures. Success drives change, and today's innovators are experiencing successes in catching today's consumer with their new direct-to-consumer information approaches: *"We'll make your life easier and/or reward you financially relative to our products in exchange for direct knowledge of your buying intentions and context."* The information vehicles for these direct information initiatives range from mobile apps to smart object sensors.

This opens up great opportunities for businesses to evolve from an inference-based model to a direct customer knowledge model.

The inference-based models were the best approach until customers can now communicate directly with businesses. With the past decades of megatrends, personal technology is not only reshaping the individual's lives but also the fundamental strategies of how businesses must operate in the future.

Forces Driving New Voice Engagement

Every business on the planet is driven by customer wants and needs. If businesses aren't, they die. The new voice takes customer expectation levels to previously unthought-of heights for customer relevancy and experience while at the same time helping businesses navigate the potential future gauntlets of privacy.

Customers want relevancy, and businesses need customer relevancy to prosper. It is the first time that a true win-win between customers and businesses is possible given the potential of the customer's new voice.

Customers Want Relevancy

Consumers don't want to be sold anymore. They want relevancy. In most cases, consumers want immediate relevancy. Businesses' track record for consumer relevancy is less than 10 percent with an indirect information approach. It is the unnerving realization that the most advanced corporate in-house data and analytic capability will not match the potential relevancy created from engaging consumers directly rather than guessing about what they want or need. When relevancy is low, revenue effectiveness is low and costs are higher.

The plausibility of a consumer-direct information model as an information end state where businesses could feasibly operate their customer information models based on information directly provided by the consumer was not technologically or behaviorally possible previously. It is difficult for businesses to fathom how different their information environment would be today if the information architecture were designed to fully leverage the next decade's information environment where individuals could opt in to provide select businesses with relevant dimensions of their Google Glass information feed as the individuals experienced every part of the personal and professional world. Compare this future information architecture with the current information architecture where marketing and operational decisions are primarily based on behavioral inference and secondhand information proxies of future behavioral intent.

The end state of this new information model will be the final catharsis of a data-driven business whose myriad of unobtainable information directives such as a 360-dgree view or single version of the truth can finally be realistically achieved through this emerging information model. This will require businesses to build a new culture and competency to make the long-term migration from an in-house customer data model approach to an externally focused "information direct from customer" information model. Many leading businesses have already made positive initial strides in beginning the journey from operating under the historical approach of applying customer information models built from in-house structured, transactional data, or from unstructured data integrated from the web and by third-party data suppliers such as Axiom, Experian, and Rapleaf. Their trajectory is to operate on a new customer behavioral model that sources customer information directly from the individuals themselves—that is, "bring your own information" (BYOI).

Businesses Want Relevancy

Businesses know that relevancy is the key to almost any business performance metric. If a business is less relevant than its competitor in the short term, the competitor wins. In the long term, the business ultimately dies.

A business's revenue-generating ability and the cost efficiencies associated with that have a direct correlation to how good the information is upon which the business operates. Businesses are continually driven to boost their conversion rates and their selling efficiencies. The historical indirect approach is relatively inaccurate, with a success rate of less than 10 percent that has been relatively unchanged for decades despite continual technological advancements in data and analytics. It has been accepted because the investments have been financially justifiable, and, more important, having consumers directly volunteer what they want and why has been infeasible. In the rapid evolution of technology and cultural information sharing norms, consumers now have the ability and willingness to directly share personal information. The amount of personal information consumers share has been doubling every year.

The opportunities for revenue performance and cost efficiencies are unprecedented with the change in business accuracy levels moving from less than 5 percent to 20 to 50 percent accuracy levels. These efficiencies come from a legacy cost infrastructure that was largely put in place because of the fundamental inaccuracies of inferring a future rather than having a customer actually communicate their future intentions in the context of their complete lives.

Direct New Voice Navigates Privacy

Governments and advocacy groups have demonstrated a noticeable acceleration in this decade to give consumers further personal data protection, powers, and control, from "Do Not Track" (U.S.) to "Right to Be Forgotten" (EU) initiatives. These groups are still not synchronized but are directionally consistent.

This significant legislative activity that indicates the balance of power and control over an individual's personal information will continue to shift from businesses to the individual. While governments are clearly attempting to strike a balance between individuals' increasing need for their personal data to be protected and businesses' need to monetize their personal data, the nature of information of the web and its potential risks and abuses have driven legislators to provide increasing protection and control to individuals more than the businesses that serve them (e.g., United States' Do Not Track and Consumer Privacy Bill of Rights, and the European Parliament's personal data protection, midata, Right to Be Forgotten, and ban on profiling).

Governments in different regions around the world have been quite active in attempting to address the increasing challenge of managing privacy and balancing corporate interests. The following time line lists some of the major personal information legislation that is in progress for this decade to date. As the time line indicates, advances are being made in giving the individual more control and rights over both incidentally and intentionally volunteered personal information.

The last point will be the evolution of governments to mature their legislation to protect citizens and their personal data sovereignty, which will likely result in nearly complete control and ownership over individuals' personally generated information as well as their identity management. Just the first three years of the current decade have yielded legislation that functions as a harbinger for the next iteration of personal data protection and ownership.

Government/Advocacy Event Time Line

- **2010**: U.S. Federal Trade Commission (FTC) issues a privacy report that calls for a "do not track" system.
- **2010**: National Institute of Standards and Technology publishes 800-122—"Guide to Protecting the Confidentiality of Personally Identifiable Information (PII)."
- **2010**: Do Not Track (DNT) begins with several browsers.
- **2010**: Federal Trade Commission issues preliminary FTC staff report—protecting consumer privacy in an era of rapid change, the proposed framework for businesses and policy makers.
- **2011**: National Strategy for Trusted Identities in Cyberspace (NSTIC) Guideline: secure online identity.
- **2011**: Kerry/McCain Commercial Privacy Bill of Rights Act strikes a compromise between business and consumer interests, with the bill having the support of Microsoft, Intel, and eBay.
- **2011**: HR2577—Secure and Fortify Electronic Data Act or SAFE Data Act: to protect consumers by requiring reasonable security policies and procedures to protect data containing personal information, and to provide for nationwide notice in the event of a security breach.

- **2011**: UK government announces its midata initiative and legislation to enforce midata—consumers' right to request an electronic copy of data held by company (still moving ahead as of April 2013).
- **2011**: Britain's spy agency GCHQ begins "Tempora" digital surveillance (i.e., analyzing world's phone calls/Internet traffic), which it is sharing with U.S. National Security Agency (NSA).
- **2011**: India adopts new privacy regulations: Information Technology Rules—Reasonable Security Practices and Procedures and Sensitive Personal Data or Information. India's large outsourcing industry is exempt from these rules.
- **2011**: Groupe Speciale Mobile Association (GSMA) represents mobile operators in 220 countries and has published Mobile Privacy Principles regarding how individuals' personal information generated from their mobile devices should be respected and protected.
- **2011**: EU passes cookie directive.
- **2012**: Federal Trade Commission (FTC) final report—protecting consumer privacy in an era of rapid change, the proposed framework for businesses and policy makers.
- **2012**: Consumer Privacy Bill of Rights is proposed by Obama administration.
- **2012**: European Parliament: personal data protection—processing and free movement of data (General Data Protection Regulation).
- **2012**: European Commission proposes comprehensive reform of EU's 1995: data protection rules.
- **2012**: European commission publishes "Cloud Computing" Report for Europe.
- **2012**: California Department of Justice forges agreement with leading operators of mobile application platforms to improve privacy protections for individuals around the world who access the Internet through mobile apps.
- **2012**: Customer Commons, a nonprofit, is established to educate, research, and advocate for individuals.
- **2013**: Cyber Intelligence Sharing and Protection Act (CISPA) is proposed: sharing of Internet traffic information between U.S. government and technology and manufacturing companies. CISPA would "waive every single privacy law ever enacted in the name of cybersecurity." CISPA is controversial because it overrules all existing federal and state laws by saying companies may share certain information "with any other entity, including the federal government." To date 208 organizations have registered to lobby on this bill (e.g., Google, AT&T).
- **2013**: United States' interagency National Science and Technology Council releases "Smart Disclosure and Consumer Decision Making: Report of the Task Force on Smart Disclosure"—the first comprehensive description of

the federal government's efforts to promote the smart disclosure of information that can help consumers make wise decisions in the marketplace. Power shift addresses a number of transparency and privacy concerns many have about how our personal data are collected and used.

- **2013**: U.S. Department of Health and Human Services (HHS) releases final Health Insurance Portability and Accountability Act (HIPAA)'s privacy, security, enforcement, and breach notification (e.g., imposes direct liability on business associates).
- **2013**: Midata rights are included in the UK Enterprise and Regulatory Reform Bill, which is currently in the committee stage in the House of Lords.
- **2013**: European Parliament's Legal Affairs Committee (JURI)—Right to Be Forgotten, explicit consent, ban on profiling.
- **2013**: Firefox to begin blocking third-party cookies by default.
- **2013**: Network Advertising Initiative (NAI—self-regulatory body governing third parties in the online advertising space) releases draft revised code of conduct for public comment (last updated its code of conduct in late 2008).
- **2013**: California Department of Justice publishes "Privacy on the Go"— recommendations for the mobile ecosystem.
- **2013**: EU's Article 29 Data Protection Working Party publishes a new set of privacy recommendations and opinions on mobile apps.
- **2013**: European Interactive Digital Advertising Alliance (EDAA) launches pan-European consumer awareness campaign for individuals relative to online behavioral advertising (OBA) and their privacy choices.
- **2013**: UK's Internet Advertising Bureau (IAB) launches ad campaign giving individuals greater control over targeted online ads.
- **2013**: Smart Disclosure—Providing consumers access to data in user-friendly electronic formats, in order to fuel the creation of products and tools that benefit consumers. Pushes control of personal data from business toward the individual.
- **2013**: U.S. Federal Communications Commission (FCC) issues declaratory ruling on customer proprietary network information (CPNI); for example, when mobile carriers collect information about customers' use of the network, including using preinstalled apps, carriers are required to protect that information in the same way they are required to protect CPNI on the network.

Direct Competencies Required

The new consumer has driven the need for businesses to create extensions to some competencies and evolve other competencies. When all of these competencies have been built over decades, the reality of evolving from

90 percent indirect to an increasing percentage of direct data will be an iterative process with all the complexities of corporations. Consumers have been able to evolve much more quickly than businesses relative to their use of technology and the competencies surrounding personal information. Organizations are likely a decade behind consumers in terms of their relative abilities and willingness to have direct personal information exchange. The relative speed of the consumer's evolution will likely outpace business if personal technologies keep evolving at their current pace (e.g., more devices, more personal quantification, more sensor technology). The more realistic aspirations of businesses will not be how to catch up to the consumer but how to minimize the gap between business and consumer.

Many other businesses have begun strategic and/or tactical initiatives to leverage the new digital consumer by enabling "direct from consumer" information sourcing with either a "personal data for personal utility" exchange or a "personal data for monetary reward" exchange.

As these initiatives and the consumer's personal data ecosystem mature, most businesses are still based on inference behavioral models, and as a result many are overrun and outrun by the digital consumer's production of big data volumes with the added enigma of the data's unstructured nature.

Big data and its analytics hold promise in this area and have managed to hold their ground in terms of marketing performance metrics so far this decade.

Information/Value Exchange Competency

In order to unlock discretionary sharing, the first competency that requires extension into this new commercial world is one that involves extending the delivery of other core value propositions to include an informational exchange component. It is no longer sufficient to deliver a business's core value proposition in its product or service without adding an additional layer of utility or reward in exchange for direct consumer knowledge. This direct consumer knowledge then gets fed back directly to the business for significantly improved relevancy and with that provides benefits to both revenue generation and cost efficiencies. This is the key to unlocking discretionary information sharing from the consumer. This model is akin to the mobile app value proposition.

The five primary steps are:

1. Determine what direct consumer knowledge is most valuable to the business.
2. Determine what synergistic utility/reward can be delivered in exchange for this knowledge.

3. Proactively minimize consumer information sharing inhibitors.
4. Deliver utility/reward in sync with current core value proposition delivery.
5. Communicate and reinforce utility/reward delivery and information well-being.

The business must deliver explicit sharing motivators to the consumer while creating a safe information environment for the consumer to engage.

When the consumer feels safe, his or her sharing greatly increases. Snapchat is an excellent example. Snapchat is a photo messaging application where one can take photos, record videos, add text and drawings, and send them to a controlled list of recipients with a set time limit for how long recipients can view their Snaps (1 to 10 seconds). After this time, shared content is hidden from the recipients and deleted from Snapchat's servers. At the end of 2012, there were 20 million photos shared per day on Snapchat; at the end of 2013, there were 400 million photos shared per day—a 20-fold increase in one year.[1] In the exponentially larger platform of Facebook (in 2013 780 million users versus Snapchat's 26 million users), where individuals have far less control of their photo sharing, only 350 million photos were uploaded daily.[2]

The following are examples of the types of intentionally volunteered customer knowledge that offer businesses the opportunity to provide significantly greater consumer relevancy and in turn far greater revenue effectiveness and cost efficiencies:

- "I intend to buy X in the future; help me buy the best X, at the best price."
- "Here's my smart object's activity data; advise me on product relevancy, pricing, and consumption."
- "Here's my location data; advise me of and/or coordinate my location-based products/services."
- "I have spent money in these things; show me where my future savings opportunities are."
- "I want to buy X, Y, and Z on A, B, and C dates; manage my savings and spending to enable my purchases."
- "I am buying X, Y, and Z now; adjust my price to reflect competitive pricing."
- "I intend to achieve this personal goal; help me achieve it with product and/or service suggestions."
- "I intend to do X activity; tell me how to do it, and then help me buy the supporting products wisely."
- "Here are my personal tastes for this service; adjust my experience and environment accordingly."

- "I need to better manage my disparate service providers; help me better manage my service information and better leverage future service providers."
- "Here are my physical activity data and goals; help me achieve my goals compared to others."
- "Here are my medical vital statistics and location; advise me on alerts and new services."
- "As I experience my personal and professional life, passively and proactively stream me relevant information and suggestions."[3]

Direct Information Competency

The second set of competencies that need to evolve from an indirect-based information competency to a direct-based information competency comprise the people, process, culture, organization, culture, leadership, information, and technology that all add up to a business's broad information competency.

The complexities of this indirect information business model require a massive information infrastructure with many different separate and supportive competencies to create an overall business information competency. For a business to build broad and deep overall information competency, as with indirect information competencies, it needs to invest in these seven broad competencies that parallel its existing competencies of indirect information:

1. People
2. Process
3. Organizational structure
4. Culture
5. Leadership
6. Information
7. Technology

As businesses evolve from an indirect information competency model to a direct information competency model, each of the separate competencies must evolve to achieve the new direct-from-consumer information competency.

PEOPLE A broad range of associated skills is related to collecting and analyzing consumer information that is not being volunteered directly but is primarily incidentally shared without the consumers being conscious of the data they are producing. Just the thinking and strategy around a business world driven by consumers and their information is not only an incremental skill set shift but also an evolving mind-set shift.

PROCESS   The processes of collecting and analyzing indirect data in the context of a commercial world are becoming far more complex and unstructured with the continuing increase in privacy regulation and advocacy groups for tracking consumers' behavior. With direct consumer information, the consumer will increasingly be the initiator of interactions and transactions, so business processes will need to evolve toward reversing processes.

ORGANIZATIONAL STRUCTURE   The structure of an organization that supports a business using primarily indirect information has far more complexity to it than one that is based on direct information, because of the added complexity and uncertainty of the indirect environment. The restructuring of an organization over time to support a go-to-market strategy where the consumers are increasingly the initiators of interactions and transactions will be incremental. Despite this, the changes will likely be disconcerting to the long-standing indirect structures of the organization.

LEADERSHIP   Leaders' career paths have been based on their acumen of building a business based on indirect marketing campaigns. There is always greater uncertainty for the leader who is the innovator and is stepping outside an excepted business model that has been historically justifiable despite being relatively inaccurate. This also means developing new skill sets other than the ones that initially brought the leader personal success.

INFORMATION   The specific challenge of indirect information that is the extrapolation or proxy of the real knowledge of the consumer has exponentially higher challenges (e.g., relevancy, recency, accuracy, reliability). Another aspect is the flow of information emanating from the consumer and then back in to the organization. This will be an incremental process to allow consumers to begin editing, changing, or adding their own data to an internal corporate database. The world of bring your own information (BYOI) will be a gradual change for organizations. Future incarnations of direct consumer information will also include a world where consumers manage and monetize their own data externally from the organization.

TECHNOLOGY   In most technological infrastructure diagrams, technology is built to flow information internally or flow from inside the business's infrastructure to outside in the form of marketing offers or campaigns to consumers. The information that is internal to the organization is mostly collected from external secondary sources other than the consumer. Within direct consumer information flow, the technology will need to be rewired for reverse flows where consumers not only can bring their own information but also can bring their own device or technology (e.g., smartphone, tablet, laptop).

Unlocking Consumers' Intent

Unlocking the secrets of future purchase intent is the key to any business operation. It drives revenue performance, operational performance, and cost efficiencies. It is the organization that best understands a consumer/ customer's intention that can provide the highest relevancy, greatest customer experience, and detailed personalization.

Intent Continuum

The secrets of consumer buying intent and context are a single dimension of the information continuum. If businesses had the direct "I intend to buy and why" feed from individuals in real time (i.e., intent and context), they could cut up to 70 percent of their workforce and reduce other corporate infrastructure by the same percentage. But they don't ... yet.

First, it's important to acknowledge that individuals don't always know what they intend to buy. Steve Jobs has said, "It's really hard to design products by focus groups. A lot of times, people don't know what they want until you show it to them." His philosophy was: "Don't ask what your customers want; tell them what they want." Henry Ford is also famous for saying, "If I had asked people what they wanted, they would have said faster horses." While their point is valid, most would agree that this is the exception rather than the rule.

The underlying key is not to focus on what the product is but rather on the problem, challenge, or need of the individual—what *and* why individuals buy (intent and context).

Understanding intent and context is not a new construct. This is ultimately what all businesses are attempting to solve, starting with product development and market research and continuing to management of the bottom of their marketing and sales funnel.

Intent answers the future "buy" questions of:

- What (I intend to buy a Canon EOS 5D Mark III camera ...)
- When (this weekend ...)

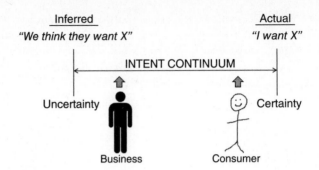

FIGURE 5.1 Intent Continuum

- Where (from Best Buy ...)
- How (online with my birthday gift card and the balance on my Visa credit card)

Intent is not an absolute; it is a continuum of uncertainty and certainty (see Figure 5.1). Of this continuum, the highest degree of certainty lives with its data source—the individual consumer. Individuals are the data source that has the most complete and up-to-date knowledge of who they are, what they're going to do, and why they are going to do it. It is the holy grail of business and consumer intelligence.

As shown in Figure 5.2, context is the "why" of the future and historical buy intentions.

- Why did I buy "what I bought"?
- Why did I buy it "when I bought it"?
- Why did I buy it "at that place"?
- Why did I buy it "in that way"?

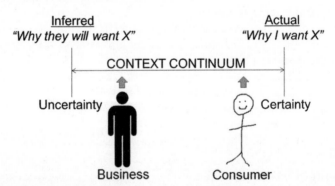

FIGURE 5.2 Context Continuum

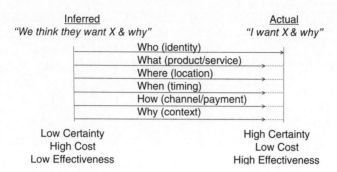

FIGURE 5.3 Inferred versus Actual

From the simple beginnings of baby or wedding registries, businesses have attempted to elicit direct buying intent and context from individuals. Businesses realize that input from the individual that communicates actual buying intent and context almost always trumps inferred intent and context. There are many factors for this. Businesses are typically information-myopic. They have a relatively narrow view of all the dimensions that go into a person's motivational factors to purchase. The business's 360-degree view is actually a 360-degree view of a 5 percent view relative to an individual's actual buying dimensions.

If we combine the continua of intent and context for each of their respective dimensions, we have a more holistic view of the dynamics of marketing effectiveness and efficiency (see Figure 5.3).

Businesses are compelled to migrate from inferred to actual (left to right) in order to achieve the highest level of marketing effectiveness and cost infrastructure efficiency. An important dimension that is not reflected in this chart is the individual's perception of the business's value relative to competitor offers. The dotted lines to the right acknowledge that individuals don't always know what they want to purchase but will typically know what their basic needs are.

What has changed is the willingness and ability for individuals to communicate far more actual buying intent and context to businesses than businesses are currently leveraging.

Life of Intent and Context

First and foremost, intent and context emanate from the hearts and minds of individuals. A small fraction is communicated to the world through words, tone, body language, and related behaviors. Albert Mehrabian, professor

FIGURE 5.4 Business Can Only See the Past Whereas the Customer Knows the Future
Source: http://commons.wikimedia.org/wiki/File:Fjordn_surface_wave_boat.jpg.

emeritus of psychology at the University of California at Los Angeles (UCLA), is best known by his publications on the relative importance of verbal and nonverbal messages (i.e., words account for 7 percent, tone of voice accounts for 38 percent, and body language accounts for 55 percent of the "liking.")[4]

Living in the world, individuals leave clues as to what were the intent and context of their actions. As individuals become more digitized, this is predominantly a "digital wake," as it has a ripple effect to other digital activities and concerns (see Figure 5.4).

Historically, intention and context clues are represented from not only businesses, customers, and their interactions and transactions but also from other traditional sources:

- Federal and local governments
- Utilities
- Credit applications
- Court judgments
- Bankruptcies
- Geo-demographics
- Postal addresses
- Electoral rolls
- Credit bureaus

Indirect Voice of Purchase Intent/Context

The indirect voice of purchase intent and context is the digital exhaust from the consumers' everyday lives. This indirect voice is incidental and unintentional relative to what they shared, the audience that it ultimately is shared with, and the actual use independent of context in which they originally shared the information. It's what businesses primarily monetize in order to market their products.

The indirect voice's marketing landscape can be thought of as the digital wake of an individual's online behavior. The landscape includes not only the behavior exhibited on different digital landscapes (e.g., search on Google, purchase on Amazon, or their own business's website), but also the ecosystem that harvests, enables, and analyzes this digital wake to support businesses.

- Sources
- Harvesters
- Buying engines
- Analytics

Sources of intent are the digital real estate upon which the individual behaves—for example, searches Google, posts a picture on Facebook, buys a camera on Amazon, queries Google Maps for a restaurant, or posts a video on Vine. These digital behaviors infer buying intent. Harvesters are the companies that extract and data mine the individual's behavior with those sources (e.g., Chango, Bluekai, Go Chime, MasterCard, and Nielsen). Buying engines are advertising platforms that enable advertisers and agencies to target individuals based on how they behave on the various digital real estate (e.g., Yieldbot, Optimal, Criteo, tapad, eBay, and Videology). Analytics are businesses that provide analytic platforms to enable marketers and agencies to analyze behaviors and trends of individuals for future web and campaign optimization.

Each of the indirect categories—sources, harvesters, buying engines, and analytics—has subcategories, each of which occupies a specific space relative to extracting and understanding buying intent in their specific digital space, as shown in Figure 5.5.

Sources

Sources of intent can be thought of as six subcategories:

1. **Search**—Google, Bing, Yahoo!
2. **Social**—Facebook, LinkedIn, Pinterest, Twitter
3. **Display**—Google, Yahoo!, AOL, Microsoft, IGN Entertainment, Weather Channel, Ask.com, CBS Interactive, Glam Media, Turner Digital, CNET, Meredith
4. **Location**—AT&T, Samsung, Waze, Foursquare, Apple
5. **Transaction**—Amazon, eBay, Walmart
6. **Video**—YouTube, Vimeo, Daily Motion, Hulu, VHX

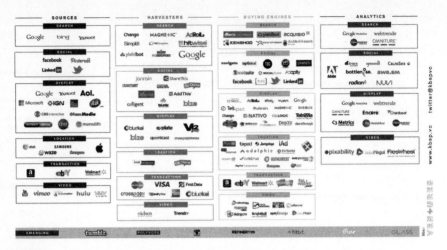

FIGURE 5.5 The Intent Marketing Landscape
Source: kbs+ Ventures.

SEARCH INTENT AND CONTEXT SOURCES One of the most natural and organic origins of inferred intent is search. Individuals search on a regular basis for basic knowledge about almost anything. Google, Bing, and Yahoo! are now the primary organic search engines. Google is clearly the dominant leader, with roughly 67 percent of the search market share. When an individual does a search for "best pet food for mature dogs," the search has enough specificity to it to narrow down the intent to the area of food for older dogs. Although there are many other variables that go into the purchase decision, it's a reasonable place for advertisers to place their ads relative to inferred intent. Bing has roughly 18 percent with Yahoo!'s share being 12 percent. Ask and AOL search are also calculated but the numbers are quite small.

Google	67%
Microsoft (Bing)	18%
Yahoo!	11%
Ask Network	3%
AOL, Inc.	1%

When an individual searches for information on Google that may represent travel intent (e.g., information on Hawaii), the search results appear in the middle of the page—and those links are never paid for (called "organic" search results). Advertisers pay money to appear on the right-hand side and sometimes at the top of the Google page to serve that intent (e.g., special tour packages to Hawaii). These ads are clearly marked as advertisements.[5] Bing and Yahoo! have similar mechanics. Google makes it a point that it never accepts money to improve rankings in organic searches. Google's massive "inferred intent" engine runs on one million servers, and processes over one billion search requests and roughly 24 petabytes of user-generated data each day.[6]

SOCIAL INTENT AND CONTEXT SOURCES   Another important category for intent sources are social networks, such as Facebook and Twitter. The amount of highly personal information that is posted on Facebook is unparalleled in other social networks as well as relative to historically shared personal information. Social media is a rich intent source because of the amount of personal information being shared.

Facebook's Intent Sourcing   In the case of Facebook, not only do individuals provide their profile information, but they also openly socialize with their friends and family. An individual provides important context around a predicted buying intent. On Facebook profiles, individuals share information about their sex, age, current city, relationship status, job, and school. They also indicate their interests in the postings on their time line, their friends' time lines, as well as their groups. They also give added context by the apps they use. Most of these intent indicators are done by keywords of posts and status updates (e.g., "My brother and I went fishing today in Lake X"). Facebook actually doesn't share an individual's information directly with advertisers, nor can advertisers see information about the individuals who view or click on their ads, because the individual's real identity is obscured.

Over the past several years, this type of shared personal information has almost doubled each year. Most of that information is then sold to advertisers to create intent indicators depending on the individual's privacy settings (e.g., 35-year-old female living in Ohio who likes gardening). This type of information increases the effectiveness for predicting intent (e.g., a 35-year-old female gardener may be interested in buying gardening tools). Based on this information, the advertiser would serve up gardening tool advertisements. If the individual directly volunteered actual intent, the advertiser would know that this 35-year-old female gardener just bought all her gardening tools last weekend and is now looking for flowers, plants, and fertilizers for this weekend's project. At her option, this 35-year-old gardener may also share her real identity, which adds to the quality of both intent and context (i.e., personalization, more specific demographics). This information is not linked to an individual's real identity, or it is aggregated to obscure the individual's real identity.[7]

The inferences of intent can be quite detailed. For instance, an advertiser can understand not only what music genre a Facebook user enjoys but also the actual artist or particular song. Dimensions of inferred intent also extend to other areas such as products, brands, religion, health status, and even political views. While these inferred intent dimensions are helpful, it is almost always desirable to extract actual intent. In regard to the music tastes, inferred intent dimensions may suggest that the advertiser will place ads for a particular artist's song without knowing whether the music lover actually has already purchased the song. The individual who is communicating actual intent would indicate that he or she already owns this particular artist's song and no longer is interested in purchasing.

Businesses integrate the intent information used from Facebook with their own offline customer data, which allows them to find past or existing customers on Facebook. Businesses can also model Facebook users who have similar characteristics to existing customers using Facebook's "Lookalike Audiences" to find new customers. Facebook also offers "partner categories" data to businesses that are its data aggregator partners.

Facebook's inferred intent pricing is based on cost per action (CPA), which moved away from the old model of per click or impression basis pricing to a model where businesses can pay for a specific number of likes, link clicks (clicks on a specific link, not the entire ad), or "offer claims."

Similar to businesses integrating Facebook intent data with their own offline customer data, Facebook's Exchange (FBX) integrates Facebook users' on-Facebook behavior with their off-Facebook online shopping behavior—for example, serving a real-time ad to a Facebook user who loves to travel and has just been visiting other travel sites to explore travel packages to Hawaii.[8]

Once advertisers have acquired the inferred intent and context dimensions from Facebook, they have their choice of displaying their advertisements on brand pages, display ads, sponsored stories, promoted posts, page post ads, mobile app install ads, and log-out screen ads.[9]

Pinterest   Pinterest uses an online scrapbook approach that allows individuals to create online bulletin boards of images and photos based on their interests in activities such as travel, decorating, or sports, with roughly 30 million unique visitors.[10] Pinterest's intent engine is not as advanced as Facebook's. Pinterest has taken the first step by offering new analytics to show businesses visitor metrics of their websites (e.g., Pinterest Web Analytics). Some of these metrics include giving site owners insights into how individuals are interacting with their "pins" that originate from the business's website.

In the early days of Pinterest, it had yet to display revenue-generating advertising on its website. Major brands such Gap, Patagonia, and Dell increasingly leverage the site to directly promote their products.[11]

Twitter Twitter's success in revealing intent and context is enabled by several acquisitions that specialize in global real-time bidding (e.g., MoPub). Twitter now has created a mobile ad network that uses Twitter's profile and location information from its users as a targeting device. Most other intent sources have a much higher degree of uncertainty about the location and identity of their users. Tracking cookies that enable targeting that exist on the desktop computers are missing in the mobile environment. The key for Twitter is that its users stay logged in on both the desktop and the mobile device. The MoPub technology allows Twitter to fairly accurately target both medias. Because individuals stay logged in, Twitter can infer intent by knowing their actual digital identities, what they have tweeted, and what webpages they have browsed. There is also a ubiquity about Twitter as the Internet is saturated with tweet buttons. This also allows for a larger intent window, as intent is discovered sooner over a longer time; for example, "I like Adele's new song and will probably like her new album that is coming out next year." Twitter accomplishes this by joining the individual's desktop browser Twitter login and mobile device login to follow the individual's "data exhaust" based on a consistent digital identity. The stream of inferred intent and context is far more persistent and consistent with digital IDs across devices.[12]

Armed with this inferred intent data, Twitter enables businesses to tweet into an individual's Twitter feeds (i.e., "promoted tweets"). Twitter also uses "promoted trends" by inserting a corporate-crafted hashtag into the Trending Topics list shows Tweets over time. Twitter allows individuals to edit their own photos on the site and post short videos with Vine. Other Twitter apps like #music keep individuals on the Twitter ecosystem instead of using services like Spotify or Rdio for new music. Twitter also reads intent and context through an individual's posts as well as profile. This way, advertisers can direct their promoted tweets and promoted trends with a real-time bidding to the right individuals, at the right time, in the right demographic, and at the right location. As mentioned, this is enabled by several acquisitions that specialize in real-time bidding in the mobile environment, such as MoPub. This is similar to Google's DoubleClick Ad Exchange. The $10 billion mobile advertising market is rife with opportunities if this type of intent and context data can be optimized.[13]

LinkedIn LinkedIn's market is an excellent example for comparing inferred intent and actual intent. LinkedIn is a social networking website for people in professional occupations who are seeking to both socialize as well as seek future career opportunities. It behooves professionals to explicitly communicate that they are looking for a particular role. In doing so,

LinkedIn can sell their recruiting solutions where recruiters and corporations pay for enhanced brand, search, or talent acquisition offerings. As a result, recruiters and corporations can advertise highly targeted campaigns to LinkedIn users because there is an explicit quid pro quo to professionals for placing their professional details on LinkedIn's website; that is, they want free professional exposure for their qualifications (context) and future aspirations (intent), and LinkedIn is happy to provide a platform for that professional intent and employment context exposure. In addition to the professional's profile, LinkedIn also monetizes the user's clicks to extract inferred intent and context (i.e., browser history). In return, LinkedIn is able to monetize each of its members' volunteered professional information to as much as $10,000 per year.[14]

Display (Digital) Advertising Intent and Context Sources

Display advertising providers are premium publishers like Yahoo!, AOL, CBS, and Meredith.

These providers form the next group of intent and context sources. Here is a representative list of the top digital display advertisers:

- Google
- Yahoo!
- AOL
- Microsoft
- IGN
- Weather Channel
- Ask.com
- CBS interactive
- Glam Media
- Turner Digital
- CNET
- Meredith

Each of these digital display advertisers is a core value and then displays it in parallel; that is, an individual searches for a particular car on Google, and a Google advertiser displays a car advertisement. In fact, Google monetizes an individual's inferred intent and context from searches beyond the gross national product (GNP) of the country of Panama and the 31 poorest countries in the world combined.[15] Google searches can run the gamut from highly uncertain inference-based intent to explicitly articulated actual intent (without a real identity attached). Most Google searches are biased more toward inference than actual intent indications.

Price of Inferred Intent and Context

The price a business is going to pay for a keyword represents the word's value to the business relative to giving it some indication of intent to purchase for a particular category. It starts when an individual searches for a particular word or phrase on Google. Google then reviews AdWord's advertising pool and determines whether it will initiate an auction. If one or more advertisers are bidding on keywords that Google deems relevant to the search query, an auction is initiated. Keywords are not search queries. Specific words (such as "pet medicine") may be entered into auctions for a wide range of search queries (such as "medicine for dogs" or "pet supplies"), depending on the word match. Advertisers identify specific keywords they are interested in bidding on, say how much they are willing to spend, and create groups of these keywords that are paired with their ads. Google then enters the keyword from the business's account that it determines has the most relevance in the auction, along with the business's maximum bid. The business can have only one entry in the query action for its account. Once the business enters into the auction, Google looks at two key factors to determine where the business ranks:

1. Maximum bid
2. Quality score

The quality score is a measurement to determine how relevant and useful the business's ad is to the Google searcher (components are click-through rate, relevance, and landing page). The business pays the minimum amount it can pay for the position it wins if its ad is clicked. The advertiser can pay less for a higher position due to its high quality score. These auctions are run billions of times each month with two ultimate goals:

1. Individuals perceive the ads as relevant to their online searches.
2. Advertisers economically connect with potential customers relative to their purchase intent.

As shown in Table 5.1, the attributes of intention are captured in the popularity of word searches.

The price and ultimate ranking is calculated by the following:

Calculating the price of intent
Advertiser's price = Ad rank of advertiser/
Advertiser's quality score + $0.01

As shown in Table 5.2, the calculation of the cost per click relative to the ability of a key search word to predict the customer's purchase intention

TABLE 5.1   KEYWORD RANKING FOR COST PER CLICK (CPC)

Rank	Keyword	Cost per Click	% of Total
1	Insurance	$54.91	24.0%
2	Loans	$44.28	12.8%
3	Mortgage	$47.12	9.0%
4	Attorney	$47.07	3.6%
5	Credit	$36.06	3.2%
6	Lawyer	$42.51	3.0%
7	Donate	$42.02	2.5%
8	Degree	$40.61	2.2%
9	Hosting	$31.91	2.2%
10	Claim	$45.51	1.4%
11	Conference call	$42.05	0.9%
12	Trading	$33.19	0.8%
13	Software	$35.29	0.8%
14	Recovery	$42.03	0.7%
15	Transfer	$29.86	0.6%
16	Gas/electricity	$52.62	0.6%
17	Classes	$35.04	0.5%
18	Rehab	$33.59	0.5%
19	Treatment	$37.18	0.3%
20	Cord blood	$27.80	0.2%

is a combination of the attributes of a maximum bid amount, a quality score, and an ad ranking.

The question for incidentally volunteered personal information is that if businesses are going to pay $54.91 for a click on "insurance" with a high degree of uncertainty, what would they be willing to pay directly to the consumer for intentionally volunteered personal information, which provides a far higher degree of certainty relative to the consumer's insurance needs? This inversion of the search industry will likely evolve over the next stage.

TABLE 5.2   COST PER CLICK CALCULATION FOR COMPETITIVE BIDDING

	Maximum Bid	Quality Score	Ad Rank	Cost per Click (CPC)
Advertiser A	2	10	20	16/10 + 0.01 = $1.61
Advertiser B	4	4	16	12/4 + 0.01 = $3.01
Advertiser C	6	2	12	8/2 + 0.01 = $4.01
Advertiser D	8	1	8	Highest CPC

Source: Wordstream.com.

Interesting note: "Cord blood" (20th top keyword) refers to more affluent parents who have a desire to preserve their children's umbilical cords with the notion that the umbilical cords' stem cells will have the potential to cure their diseases in the future. The storage of cord blood has a large up-front cost and substantial ongoing payments.

A good example of the value of even inferred intent is an online search on the word "insurance." It is the highest-priced keyword for searches and generates 24 percent of the top 20 keywords search income for Google. For example, an individual who is looking for auto insurance may search for "auto insurance price quotes." Relatively speaking, this research creates more questions than answers (What state? What driving record? Multiple cars? What is your age?). Despite this, it's the beginning of the insurance company qualifying this individual is a potential customer. A more detailed search string may fill in a broader context of this individual as a potential insurance customer and as a result reduce the uncertainty that remains from the initial search.

- Are you married?
- Do you have any roommates?
- How many miles a year do you drive?
- Have you had any at-fault accidents or moving violations in the past five years?
- Have you made other damage claims other than an accident?
- How much coverage do you want?
- Do you own a radar detector?[16]

These are other examples of top search queries that are helpful but in and of themselves are still quite ambiguous:

- Auto insurance price quotes
- California automobile insurance
- Building contents insurance
- Buy car insurance online
- Life insurance comparison quotes

Here's an example of the second most valuable paid search keyword: loans:

- Consolidate graduate student loans
- Fixed home equity loan rates
- Cheapest homeowner loans
- Fixed-rate secured loans[17]

Segmentation Uncertainty

The very nature of today's segmentation ranges from a segment of one individual to grouping millions of individuals into behavioral categories. In a world of indirect communications with individuals, most secondary sourced behavioral segmentation is helpful to businesses to improve their relevancy and marketing efficiency, as shown in Figure 5.6, which depicts Nielsen's technology adoption segmentation system at the household-level, Nielsen ConneXions®. As with Nielsen's segmentation system, most syndicated segmentation services are conducted at the household level, not the individual level. Although this type of segmentation is useful in today's business world, it is generally not done to the individual level, nor does it reference an individual's true identity. This type of individual information will likely be added into this behavioral segmentation as businesses become more directly connected to their customers. These behavioral assumptions include such things as predicted habits of shopping, financial, and technology preferences, as well as media habits (online and offline). The segments for these behavioral inferences are major inputs into a business's market planning, media strategy, customer acquisition activities, and cross-selling and retention initiatives. This level of segmentation is functional relative to historical metrics but still yields relevancy levels at only 10 percent or less. Offline segmentation to the household level has similar lack of specificity, as there is diversity within each household. Similarly, businesses must also make strategic decisions based on the high degree of uncertainty of indirect and secondary sources of individuals' information (e.g., best location for a business and trends in the market).[18]

For example, ConneXions® segment 16, named "Kids & Keyboards," refers to the segment of "Upper Mid Middle Age w/Kids." This type of behavioral segmentation is useful for targeting various groups with parts and services. As the following descriptions depict, these behavioral generalizations can be fairly accurate relative to predicting the group's behavior.

Upper Mid Middle Age w/Kids

In Kids & Keyboards, parents spend big on technology to entertain and educate their children. These upper-middle-class, middle-aged families fill their suburban and town homes with a wide assortment of electronic devices: multiple PCs and TVs, and video game systems. They favor cable TV packages that allow them to watch lots of kid-oriented programming on channels like Nickelodeon, Disney, and the Cartoon Network. And this segment ranks at the top for owning computer software for kids, with many of the computer-literate youngsters going online for gaming and watching streaming videos. To keep everyone connected, these households own both landlines and multiple cell phones. To keep their varied media accounts straight, they sign up for bundled plans covering cable, long-distance, and Internet access—the cheaper the deal, the better.[19]

01 Technovators	02 Plugged-In Families	03 Tech Nests
Wealthy Middle Age w/ Kids	Upscale Younger w/ Kids	Upper Mid Younger w/ Kids

04 Connected Country	05 You & I Tunes	06 High-Tech Society
Upscale Middle Age w/ Kids	Upper Mid Younger w/o Kids	Wealthy Older w/ Kids

07 Generation WiFi	08 Calling Circles	09 Dish Country
Upper Mid Younger w/o Kids	Midscale Younger w/ Kids	Midscale Younger w/ Kids

10 Smart Gamers	11 WiFi Warriors	12 Satellites & Silos
Wealthy Older w/ Kids	Wealthy Middle Age w/o Kids	Upper Mid Middle Age w/o Kids

13 Cyber Sophisticates	14 The Pragmatics	15 Bundled Burbs
Wealthy Middle Age w/o Kids	Upscale Younger w/o Kids	Upscale Middle Age w/ Kids

16 Kids & Keyboards	17 Time Shifters	18 New Technorati
Upper Mid Middle Age w/ Kids	Upper Mid Younger w/o Kids	Upper Mid Middle Age w/o Kids

19 Gadgets Galore	20 Cinemaniacs	21 Multimedia Families
Upscale Older w/ Kids	Upscale Older w/o Kids	Upper Mid Older w/ Kids

22 Analoggers	23 Cyber Strivers	24 Internet Hinterlands
Wealthy Older w/o Kids	Lower Mid Younger w/ Kids	Upscale Older Mostly w/o Kids

25 Low-Speed Boomers	26 Rural Transmissions	27 Video Vistas
Wealthy Older w/o Kids	Upper Mid Older Mostly w/o Kids	Lower Mid Middle Age w/ Kids

28 Big City, Small Tech	29 IM Nation	30 Techs and the City
Low Income Younger w/ Kids	Lower Mid Younger w/ Kids	Lower Mid Younger w/o Kids

31 Plug & Play	32 Family Dishes	33 Digital Dreamers
Upper Mid Middle Age w/o Kids	Lower Mid Middle Age Family Mix	Lower Mid Middle Age w/o Kids

34 Gearing Up	35 Broadband Boulevards	36 Opting Out
Low Income Younger w/o Kids	Upper Mid Older w/o Kids	Upper Mid Older w/o Kids

37 Techtown Lites	38 New Kids on the Grid	39 Video Homebodies
Lower Mid Older Family Mix	Downscale Middle Age Mostly w/o Kids	Downscale Older Family Mix

40 Low-Tech Country	41 Antenna Land	42 Tech Skeptics
Lower Mid Older Mostly w/o Kids	Midscale Older Mostly w/o Kids	Upper Mid Older w/o Kids

43 Bucolic Basics	44 Leisurely Adopters	45 Landline Living
Midscale Older w/o Kids	Low Income Older Mostly w/o Kids	Lower Mid Older Mostly w/o Kids

46 Old-Time Media	47 Discounts & Deals	48 Dial-Up Duos
Upper Mid Mature w/o Kids	Lower Mid Older Mostly w/o Kids	Midscale Mature w/o Kids

49 Satellite Seniors	50 Early-Bird TV	51 Tech-Free Frontier
Lower Mid Older w/o Kids	Lower Mid Mature w/o Kids	Downscale Mature w/o Kids

52 The Unconnected	53 Last to Adopt	
Downscale Mature w/o Kids	Low Income Mature w/o Kids	

FIGURE 5.6 Nielsen Segment Explorer
Source: Nielsen, ConneXions®
Segmentation and MyBestSegments (www.MyBestSegments.com) 2014.
Copyrighted information ©2014, of The Nielsen Company, licensed for use herein.

This Kids & Keyboards segment is one of five segments within the "Life-stage Group" of "Suburban Spenders."

The members of the Suburban Spenders group rank second in adopting new technology. Consisting of mid-scale to upscale families in the suburban sprawl, these five segments spend heavily to keep their families online, connected, and entertained. The households here typically own multiple cell phones, TV sets, MP3 players, and video gaming systems. They turn their computers into the focus of their family rooms, programming them with kid-oriented software for gaming, education, and e-mail. And most families have connected their TV sets to cable—with a fair percentage getting digital cable—to watch everything from Nickelodeon and Disney to VH1 and pay-per-view movies. They still consume a lot of traditional media, listening to radio stations that play classic rock, adult contemporary, and country music, as well as reading magazines that cover parenting, sports, and cars. But they're clearly more tech savvy than most other groups, downloading music from the Internet each week, and owning cell phones with many features. Increasingly, they order bundled service packages for phone, Internet, and cable service—because it's new, convenient, and cool.[20]

These useful segmentations can evolve using progressively more direct individual information to fine-tune the predicted behaviors. The individuals who are in the "Upper Mid Middle Age w/ Kids" segment could provide the business with specific ages and genders of their children in return for more relevant advertising, discounting, or direct utility to them as parents.[21]

Location-Based Intent and Content Sources

Location-based sources of information can take the form of mobile phone providers as well as other third-party services such as AT&T, Samsung, Apple, Waze, and Foursquare. Location-based information of individuals is valued by businesses as it enables far more relevant ads. Worldwide mobile advertising spending will reach 18 billion in 2014 and is expected to grow to 42 billion by 2017.[22] Knowing the location of an individual is very important for understanding the context of that individual's behavior. For a business, it communicates to the business that an individual is near one of its stores, engaging in a particular activity (sports arena), or in transit from one city to the next. Location-based information can fall into both categories of volunteered personal information: intentionally and incidentally. An individual may have downloaded a mobile app and explicitly agreed to share his or her information in exchange for some type of location-based utility such

How much do you care that only you and those you authorize should have access to this information?

% of adult Internet users who say it is important–or not–to them to control these types of information

■ very important   ■ somewhat important   ■ not too important

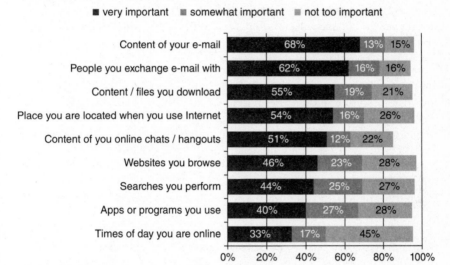

FIGURE 5.7 How Much Do We Care about Who Accesses Our Information?
Note: N = 792 for Internet users and smartphone owners. Interviews were conducted in English on landline and cell phones. The margin of error on the samples is +/– 3.8 percentage points.
Source: Pew Research Center's Internet and American Life Project Omnibus Survey, conducted July 11–14, 2013, on landline and cell phones.

as finding a restaurant, store, gas station, or point of interest. In this case, revealing an individual's location would be categorized as an intentionally volunteered location. Many times, individuals do not read the permissions aspect of their mobile applications or even understand that they are transmitting their location to their mobile phone. In this case, this would be considered incidentally volunteered location information.

Figure 5.7 indicates that 54 percent of individuals have sensitivity to revealing their location. This sensitivity is mitigated when an individual receives a reward or utility for revealing the information. In other words, individuals don't simply want to volunteer their location just to be sold something that may or may not be relevant to other aspects of their current personal location.

Location-based advertising (LBA) is a new form of advertising that integrates mobile advertising with location-based services. The technology is used to pinpoint consumers' locations and provide location-specific advertisements on their mobile devices.

MOBILE PHONE MANUFACTURERS   Mobile phone providers such as AT&T, Samsung, and Apple utilize location-based information from individuals to deliver added context for potential purchases or individual utility. In this example, we explore Apple's use of incidentally and intentionally volunteered location data.

Apple   Apple's users both incidentally and intentionally volunteer their locations on different devices—iPhones, iPod Touch, iPad, iPad Mini, Apple TV, Apple computers, and iTunes. Apple then sells this location information to advertisers. Individuals have the ability to opt out of "interest-based" from "iAd." Apple recommends that individuals not opt out of location-based ads, however, because they will not reduce the number of ads but will simply reduce the relevancy of the ads. Apple also takes this location-based information and combines it with other volunteered information such as occupation, language, zip code, area code, unique device identifier, and time zone for advertising. Apple also makes portions of an individual's personal information available to "strategic partners." Apple does aggregate its users' information to help protect personally identifiable information when monetizing the targeting of its subscribers. Apple's advantage is the clear diversity of its ecosystem with identities and attributions consistent across devices.

Individuals volunteer their location information via their devices using a combination of cellular, Wi-Fi, and GPS. If an individual's device does not have a clear line of sight to GPS satellites, the device determines the individual's location by using crowdsourced Wi-Fi3 and cell tower locations.[23]

Location-Based Service Providers

Location-based service providers specialize in helping businesses monetize available location-based information from individuals (e.g., Waze and Foursquare). Both service providers have distinct approaches to location-based advertising and utility.

WAZE   Waze is a location-based social networking website that produces a GPS-based geographical navigation application program for smartphones with GPS support. It provides display screens with turn-by-turn information and user-submitted travel times and route details. This information is location-dependent information that is downloaded over the mobile telephone network. Google acquired Waze for $1.1 billion in 2013. Waze offers its turn-by-turn navigation app for Android and iOS with intentionally volunteered crowdsourced traffic updates from individuals' mobile phones. Fifty million mobile phone users intentionally volunteer their road status in real time. Waze's expertise is also applied to real-time crowdsourcing of other location-based data such as police traps and accident locations. When Waze's real-time location information is combined with Google's Street View project (expenditure of $1 billion to $2 billion), the potential utility for individuals and businesses is significant. Google Street View is a technology featured in Google Maps and Google Earth that provides panoramic views from positions along many streets in the world. This adds to Google's quid pro quo of exchanging personal information with the individual for utility; that is, the more utility Google can provide, the more information the individual is willing to volunteer.[24]

FOURSQUARE   Foursquare is also a location-based social networking website for mobile devices. It offers differently than Waze, as Foursquare asks individuals to check in at venues using a mobile website, text messaging, or a device-specific application by selecting from a list of venues the application locates nearby. Foursquare bases its map intelligence on the Open-StreetMap (OSM) project, a collaborative project whose vision is to create a free editable map of the world. OSM is a crowdsourcing project that is created by individuals volunteering their information to the project. When individuals check in based on their location, they receive check-in awards with user points and occasionally "badges." Foursquare's 35 million users have volunteered their personal interests to create a database of 50 million points of interest (e.g., bars, restaurants, ice cream shops).

Other location-based companies such as Yelp, Yext, and Yellow Pages have location-based points of interest, but Foursquare's information is unique in that it is based on intentionally volunteered information via crowdsourcing with roughly four billion check-ins by individuals via their mobile apps. The other location-based companies basically know the venues and their addresses, but Foursquare knows how the venues are connected and the flow of the get-togethers at those venues. Foursquare's check-ins supply not only the name and address of the venue but also important contextual information such as whether friends are joining the individual and even where the party goes after getting together at this venue (e.g., "After we've had pizza at Frank's Pizza, we typically go for ice cream at Joe's Ice Cream Parlor").

Foursquare also offers an Amazon-like recommendation engine based on the individual's volunteered preferences (e.g., "People who eat at the sushi bar typically go across the street to get Starbucks coffee"). An individual who searches on Google for a restaurant will find less contextual information relative to Foursquare because of the volunteered "patterns" and "preferences" that Foursquare collects from its users. A search on Google will find all the pizza places, but Foursquare is more likely to find the most popular ones, saving the individual time sorting through the myriad of Google search results. This is utility to the individual and serves as more relevant and contextual information for advertisers.

Foursquare also has many third-party partnerships because of a developer-friendly application programming interface (API). Foursquare allows its partners—Path (photo-centric social network for one-to-one/ one-to-many private messaging), Uber (connects passengers with drivers of luxury vehicles for hire), Facebook's Instagram (online photo sharing and video sharing with digital filters), Twitter's Vine (create and post short video clips), and Yahoo!'s Flickr (image hosting and video hosting)—to utilize its location data in exchange for these partners supplying Foursquare with locations of social activity via location of posted photos and videos. If Foursquare receives many check-ins and travel tips and also sees that many people are posting Instagram photos along with many Uber requests for pickups, these contextual data points can indicate that a particular restaurant or defined area is popular with individuals or groups of demographically similar individuals.

Figure 5.8 shows a series of three screen shots from the Foursquare app. The first screen shot is the general navigation screen (check-in, friends,

FIGURE 5.8 Foursquare Screen Shots
Source: http://gizmodo.com/5502704/foursquare-shows-why-you-should-be-excited-about-windows-phone-7-apps.

society, settings, log out). The middle screen illustrates the general map listing as a result of the query. The third (far right) lists the ranked order of the search list by popularity.

Transaction Intent and Context Sources

The combination of Amazon ($61 billion revenue), eBay ($16 billion), and Walmart ($470 billion with $9 billion online) holds a tremendous intelligence on retail transactions.

AMAZON   Amazon does not explicitly sell transactional data to businesses but does monetize transactional data by selling advertisements on a cost per click fee basis. Amazon uses its historical transaction data to infer that certain individuals with similar or related interests from past Amazon behavior will more likely purchase the business's similar product. These ads will appear when the individual is engaged in certain activities on Amazon's website (e.g., detailed page, search, and browse activity; Buy Box; tower ads).

Businesses advertise on Amazon using the following process:

- Business uploads product catalog and sets a cost-per-click budget.
- Individuals see business's ads on Amazon.com.
- Individuals click on ads, which brings them to the business's website.
- Business pays for that individual's click on a cost-per-click fee basis.
- Individual may or may not purchase once on the business's website.

Amazon shares portions of other relevant customer information with other businesses affiliated with Amazon or its subsidiaries within the bounds of Amazon's privacy policy. This transactional data is rich in inferred intent. When Amazon's transactional data is combined with other personally volunteered information on Amazon, it drives a useful recommendation engine for individuals. The transactional information is combined with the following other volunteered personal information:

- Personally identifiable information:
  - Name
  - E-mail
  - Password
  - Communications
  - Personalized advertising preferences
  - Address book
  - One-click settings

- Payment settings
- Credit card information
- Promotional certificate
- Gift card balances
- E-mail notification settings:
  - Product availability alerts
  - Delivery alerts
  - Special occasion reminders
  - Newsletters
- Recommendations:
  - Recommended for You
  - Improve Your Recommendations
- Shopping lists and gift registries:
  - Wish Lists
  - Baby and wedding registries
- Seller accounts
- Your Profile:
  - Product reviews
  - Recommendations
  - Listmania lists
  - Reminders
  - Personal profile
  - Wish List

The types of intentionally volunteered personal information that best indicate future buying intent are the shopping lists and gift registries. These lists are the most explicit communications of what an individual will likely buy or wish to buy in the near future.

Amazon also shares aspects of its transactional data when initiating cobranded and joint offerings with specific businesses (e.g., Starbucks, OfficeMax, American Apparel, Verizon Wireless, Sprint, T-Mobile, AT&T, J&R Electronics, PacSun, Eddie Bauer, and Northern Tool + Equipment).[25]

EBAY   Like most companies, eBay collects and uses personal information to do a variety of business functions on its site as well as sharing information with other business partners.

It addresses personal information in four categories:

1. Collection
2. Usage
3. Disclosure
4. Communication preferences

Collection

- When a consumer registers and or enters information, eBay collects the personal information.
- It may combine this personal information with information from other companies and eBay entities.
- It uses cookies and other technology to track a consumer's online interaction with the site.

Usage

- EBay uses information to accomplish the consumer's requested services.
- It personalizes the site for the consumer, communicates with the consumer, and offers special eBay promotions.
- It enforces eBay terms and conditions, acts to prevent fraud, and maximizes site safety.

Disclosure

- EBay discloses consumer information to facilitate site transactions.
- It occasionally provides information to other companies that help provide eBay services.
- It shares limited information with law enforcement and others to help ensure the safety of eBay's community.

Communication preferences

- The consumers' volunteered preferences inform eBay of their preferred communication methods.

In addition, eBay also uses volunteered personal information for the following activities:

- Facilitate the service requested
- Resolve disputes
- Troubleshoot problems
- Process transactions
- Collect fees
- Measure the consumer's interest in eBay services
- Customize the eBay experience
- Enforce eBay's terms and conditions and as otherwise described at the time of collection[26]

WALMART   Walmart is rich in transactional data, with one million transactions occurring each hour. The average U.S. family of four spends over

$4,000 a year at Walmart, and one of every four dollars Americans spend on groceries is spent there.[27] The company has revolutionized the linkage between transactions in supply chain logistics. It shares the transactional data dimensions of when products are sold in real time to the businesses that stock its shelves.

The technical core of how Walmart records transactional data is through its registers, which are tightly integrated with the supply chain using Walmart's system, called Retail Link. Retail Link is essentially a decision-support system that bridges Walmart with its suppliers. Suppliers then get a detailed view of how their products flow through Walmart stores. Suppliers also have a detailed view of the inventory data prior to an actual transaction. Retail Link is also where purchase orders are executed between Walmart and the supplier. The result is that Walmart achieves a tremendous efficiency and lowering of the company's inventory costs. The transactional data is transmitted directly from the point-of-sale registers in real time to the manufacturers. Walmart and its suppliers then use the point-of-sale data to infer future consumer buying intentions and taste trends, gauge demand, and eliminate the need for warehousing, as the supply chain is based on just-in-time inventory. The power of controlling the intelligence around transactions allows the company to determine its contracts on price, volume, delivery schedule, packaging, and quality.

Walmart also sets its own profit margin for each supplier, which is an inversion of the traditional supplier-retailer model. Based on its transactional data and what that confers relative to future buying, Walmart then provides each supplier with a customized business plan. It then grades each supplier on weekly, quarterly, and annual report cards based on the supplier's execution against detailed strategic business planning packets. This eliminates consternation about demand forecasting or price negotiation between Walmart and suppliers. In many respects, Walmart has a far better understanding of the buying intent of the supplier's customers than the supplier does.

Walmart's knowledge of inferred demand based on transactional data allows it to drive even further cost-cutting and thus optimize profit margins.[28]

Video Intent and Context Sources

Understanding intent from video sources such as YouTube, Vimeo, and Hulu has its own nuances.[29]

In the ever-increasing digitization of the individual, the new standards for sourcing intent and context have expanded to meet purer behavioral digital wakes such as search engines, social networks, online display advertising, location services, transaction, and online video.

HARVESTERS   Harvesters of the indirect voice collect and mine data from an individual's interactions from the sources category. The harvesters of the indirect voice align along the following categories.

Search
- Chango, Magne+ic, Adroll, Simplifi, Retargeter, Hitwise, Yieldbot, AdGooroo, Google

Social
- Janrain, Sharethis, CrowdTrust, Gigya, GoChime, Syncapse, Add This, Colligent, Blab, Biz

Display
- Bluekai, Exelate, V12 Group, Biz, Quantcast, Cross Pixel Media

Location
- Local Response, GoChime

Transaction
- MasterCard, Visa, First Data, Cross Pixel, Cardlytics, American Express, Bluekai

Video
- Nielsen, Trendrr

BUYING ENGINES
Buying engines of the indirect voice are platforms enabling advertisers and agencies to target consumers based on that behavioral data. The buying engines of the indirect voice fall into the following categories.

Search
- Marin Software, Yieldbot, Acquisio, Kenshoo, Searchvision, Double-Click Search

Social
- Nanigans, Optimal, TBG, 140 Proof, Unified, Hootsuite, Socialflow, Adaptly, Facebook, X+1, Twitter, LinkedIn

Display
- Criteo, Adroll, Strug, Turn, Google, Tellapart, Utbrain, Magne+IC, Disqus, Chango, Nativo, Cellogic, Taboola, MediaMath, VarickMedia, TheTradedesk, DataXO, Sharethrough

Location

- PlaceIQ, Tapad, Jumptap, IAd, Gradient, Local Response, Adelphoc, StrikeAd, Session M, Adstruc, Adtheorent, Everyscreen Media, PayPal Media Network, Foursquare

Transaction

- Amazon, eBay, Walmart, Coupons, FatWallet.com

Video

- Videology, Visible Measures, Selectable Media, Collective, Adap.TV, BrightRoll, Spotxchange, TubeMogul

ANALYTICS Analytics for the indirect voice enable marketers and agencies to glean insights and optimize the results of their intent-based marketing buys. The major analytics players for cell phones are the following categories.

Search

- Google Analytics, WebTrends, Coremetrics (IBM), Omniture, comScore

Social

- Adobe, Tracx, Sysomos, CalmSea, Bottlenose, Awe.sm, Radian6, Nuvi

Display

- Google Analytics, Webtrends, Omniture, Encore, Chartbeat, C-3 metrics, Dg MediaMind, Coremetrics (IBM)

Video

- Pixability, TubeMogul, FreeWheel[30]

Notes

1. Albert Costill, "25 Things You Didn't Know about Snapchat," Search Engine Journal, February 28, 2014. www.searchenginejournal.com/25-things-didnt-know-snapchat/91169/.
2. Craig Smith, editor/owner, Digital Marketing Ramblings, "By the Numbers: The Hundred and 25 Amazing Facebook User Statistics," Expanded Ramblings.com, March 13, 2014. http://expandedramblings.com/index.php/by-the-numbers-17-amazing-facebook-stats/#.U87EsvldUoM.
3. Center for Information-Based Competition, 2014 research.

4. Albert Mehrabian, Institute of Judicial Studies, Handout 1, Albert Mehrabian Communication Studies. Albert Mehrabian is currently Professor Emeritus of Psychology, UCLA.

5. Google.com, "AdWords Trademark Policy," https://support.google.com/adwordspolicy/answer/6118?hl=en.

6. Bus100JLucas, Website Analysis, Google wiki. https://sites.google.com/a/email.vccs.edu/bus100jlucas/website-analysis; comScore, "comScore Releases March 2014 U.S. Search Engine Rankings," April 15, 2014. https://www.comscore.com/Insights/Press-Releases/2014/4/comScore-Releases-March-2014-U.S.-Search-Engine-Rankings.

7. Facebook.com. "Interacting with Ads, Personal Information Security." https://www.facebook.com/help/499864970040521/.

8. Cooper Smith, "Making Sense of FBX—The Facebook Ad Exchange That Is Becoming a Retargeting Giant," Business Insider, March 19, 2014. www.businessinsider.com/explaining-fbx-facebook-exchange-3-2014-3.

9. Facebook.com, "Facebook Advertising Guidelines, Advertising Philosophy, June 4, 2014. https://www.facebook.com/ad_guidelines.php.

10. Reuters, "Pinterest Lays Base for Money-Making Features with New Tool," Samachar.com, March 12, 2013. www.samachar.com/pinterest-lays-base-for-money-making-features-with-new-tool-ndmnNcajbbb.html.

11. Alexei Oreskovic, Reuters, "Pinterest Takes Huge Step Toward Finally Making Money with New Analytics Tool," Business Insider, March 12, 2013. www.businessinsider.com/pinterest-takes-a-huge-step-toward-making-money-2013-3.

12. Jim Edwards, "Ex-Facebook Exec Says Twitter Is Now a More Advanced Advertising Platform," Business Insider, September 11, 2013. www.businessinsider.com/facebooks-ad-exchange-v-twitters-ad-exchange-2013-9.

13. Dino Grandoni, "Here's the Answer to the Question Everyone's Asking about Twitter's IPO," The Huffington Post, September 12, 2013. www.huffingtonpost.com/2013/09/12/twitter-public-money_n_3916996.html.

14. Josh Bersin, "The 9 Hottest Trends in Corporate Recruiting," Forbes, July 4, 2013. http://en.wikipedia.org/wiki/LinkedIn. http://www.forbes.com/sites/joshbersin/2013/07/04/the-9-hottest-trends-in-corporate-recruiting.

15. "Product: You," Biz Brain. www.bizbrain.org/product-you/.
    Additional information can be found at:
    a. http://searchenginewatch.com/article/2095210/How-Google-Makes-Its-Billions-The-20-Most-Expensive-AdWords-Keyword-Categories.
    b. "Product: You," Biz Brain. www.investopedia.com/stock-analysis/2012/what-does-google-actually-make-money-from-goog1121.aspx.

    c. http://mashable.com/2013/08/28/online-ad-revenues/.

    d. www.huffingtonpost.com/lili-balfour/how-much-are-you-worth-to-twitter_b_4099327.html.

    e. www.forbes.com/sites/victorlipman/2013/05/01/the-worlds-most-active-twitter-country-hint-its-citizens-cant-use-twitter/.

    f. www.mediabistro.com/alltwitter/promoted-trends-earnings_b39637.

    g. www.mastersinit.org/digital-afterlife/.

    h. www.technewsdaily.com/16515-facebook-personal-information.html.

    i. www.biztechmagazine.com/article/2012/06/dollars-and-cents-behind-facebook-apps-infographic.

    j. www.washingtonpost.com/business/technology/facebook-earnings-report-the-details-are-in-the-ads/2013/10/30/ee6280be-418a-11e3-a624-41d661b0bb78_story.html.

    k. www.businessweek.com/articles/2012-05-18/nine-things-you-should-know-about-facebooks-ipo.

16. Military.com, "8 Questions Your Auto Insurer Will Ask." www.military.com/money/insurance/auto-insurance/8-questions-auto-insurer-will-ask.html.

17. Larry Kim, "The Most Expensive Keywords in Google AdWords," *The WordStream Blog*, July 18, 2011. www.wordstream.com/blog/ws/2011/07/18/most-expensive-google-adwords-keywords.

18. United States Senate, Committee on Commerce, Science, and Transportation, "A Review of the Data Broker Industry: Collection, Use, and Sale of Consumer Data for Marketing Purposes," Staff Report for Chairman Rockefeller, December 18, 2013. http://business.cch.com/ald/SenateCommerceDataBrokerReport.pdf.

19. Nielsen, "16 Kids & Keyboards," 2014 ConneXions® Segmentation System. www.claritas.com/MyBestSegments/Default.jsp?ID=37&id1=2611099&id2=16. Copyrighted information ©2014, of The Nielsen Company, licensed for use herein.

20. Nielsen, "05 Suburban Spenders," ConneXions® Lifestage Group. www.claritas.com/MyBestSegments/Default.jsp?ID=38&id1=2611099&webid=&id4=05&social=no. Copyrighted information ©2014, of The Nielsen Company, licensed for use herein.

21. *The WordStream Blog*, "The PPC Guide for Beginners, Part 4: Finding Your Keywords," August 14, 2013. www.wordstream.com/blog/ws/2013/08/14/ppc-guide-for-beginners-4.

22. Gartner, "Gartner Says Mobile Advertising Spending Will Reach $18 Billion in 2014," press release, January 21, 2014. www.gartner.com/newsroom/id/2653121.

23. apple.com, "iOS 6: Understanding Location Services." http://support
.apple.com/kb/HT5467; apple.com, "How to Opt Out of Interest-Based
Ads from iAd." http://support.apple.com/kb/HT4228.

24. Alyson Shontell, Business Insider, "Waze CEO Explains Why He Just Sold
His App to Google for ~ $1 Billion," Yahoo! Finance, June 11, 2013. http://
finance.yahoo.com/news/waze-ceo-explains-why-just-163425109.html.

25. Amazon.com, "Amazon.com Privacy Notice," March 3, 2014. www
.amazon.com/gp/help/customer/display.html?nodeId=468496.

26. ebay.com, "Privacy Summary," October 26, 2013. http://pages.ebay
.com/help/account/privacy-summary.html.

27. Dina Spector, "18 Walmart Facts That'll Make Your Head Explode," Business
Insider, February 21, 2013, www.businessinsider.com/incredible-facts-
about-walmart-2013-2?op=1.

28. Chris Petersen, "Walmart's Secret Sauce: How the Largest Survives
and Thrives," Retail Customer Experience, March 27, 2013. www
.retailcustomerexperience.com/blogs/walmarts-secret-sauce-how-the-
largest-survives-and-thrives/; Walmart, "Retail Link Overview." www
.wal-martchina.com/english/supplier/rl/rl.htm; Bill Saporito, "The Trouble Lurking on Walmart's Empty Shelves," *Time*, April 9, 2013. http://
business.time.com/2013/04/09/the-trouble-lurking-on-walmarts-empty-
shelves/; Sam Hornblower, "Always Low Prices," WGBH, *Frontline*.
www.pbs.org/wgbh/pages/frontline/shows/walmart/secrets/pricing
.html.

29. kbs+ Ventures, Darren Herman, Taylor Davidson.

30. Ibid.

CHAPTER 6

Today's Customer's New Voice
Vertical Industry Innovators

The customer's new voice has been picked up quickly by a group of business innovators who have decided to be the first and best in their industry to leverage the new willingness and ability of customers to exchange purchase intentions and context for extreme levels of product relevancy and customer experience. This group of business innovators can be thought of as vertical industry and horizontal (cross-industry) industry innovators.

Vertical Industry Innovators
- Automotive
- Communications
- Consumer products
- E-commerce
- Financial
- Health
- Insurance
- Retail stores
- Technology (consumer)
- Transportation
- Utilities

Industry Innovators (Vertical)

Today's consumer "information for utility and/or monetary exchange" models are rapidly evolving. The largest opportunity is in the intentionally volunteered information area. This holds the most promise for businesses that want to achieve extremely high levels of relevancy. Whereas the incidentally shared information will still need to be analyzed to create inferred buying intentions, intentionally volunteered information can be managed to generate actual buying intentions.

The following are examples for the first half of the current decade of leading firms making their first investments to enable individuals to intentionally and explicitly volunteer personal information directly to the business. In each case, the business has provided sufficient utility and an active or passive information sharing mechanism to compel and/or facilitate individuals to share intentionally volunteered personal information directly with the business.

- "I intend to buy X in the future; help me buy the best X at the best price."
  - Amazon, eBay, Zappos
- "Here's my smart object's activity data; advise me on product relevancy, pricing, and consumption."
  - Aviva, Colorado Springs Utilities, Southern California Edison, Oklahoma Gas & Electric, General Motors/Chevrolet, State Farm, Ford
- "Here's my location data; advise me of and/or coordinate my location-based products/services."
  - Mercedes-Benz, AT&T Mobility, Foursquare, Facebook, Yelp, Groupon, Google, Tesco, Jaguar
- "I have spent money in these things; show me where my future savings opportunities are."
  - Intuit
- "I want to buy X, Y, and Z on A, B, and C dates; manage my savings/spending to enable my purchases."
  - Bancorp
- "I am buying X, Y, and Z now; adjust my price to reflect competitive pricing."
  - Tesco
- "I intend to achieve this personal goal; help me achieve it with product/service suggestions."
  - Meredith (health, beauty), Intuit, Bancorp, North Face
- "I intend to do X activity; tell me how to do it, and then help me buy the supporting products wisely."
  - Lowe's, Procter & Gamble (P&G), Kraft, Home Depot, Meredith (retail, health)
- "Here are my personal tastes for this service; adjust my experience and environment accordingly."
  - Virgin Atlantic
- "I need to better manage my disparate service providers; help me better manage my service information and better leverage future service providers."
  - Microsoft's HealthVault, Bancorp, MasterCard, FIS's mFoundry

- "Here are my physical activity data and goals; help me achieve my goals compared to others."
  - Nike, Apple, North Face, Meredith
- "Here are my medical vital statistics and location; advise me on alerts and new services."
  - Verizon Communications
- "As I experience my personal and professional life, passively and pro-actively stream me relevant information and suggestions."
  - Google Glass, Jaguar[1]

The following examples are listed by industry sectors: automotive, communications, consumer products, e-commerce, financial, insurance, retail stores, technology (consumer), health, transportation, and utilities.

Automotive

The automotive industry can be characterized as focusing on major strategic initiatives to extend the customer's new voice through the personal "connected" smart vehicle.

FORD Ford Motor Company has realized that there is a tremendous opportunity to connect the individual, his or her car, and the world. The automaker has committed to exploring innovations relative to what happens when individuals can connect to their cars informationally as well as to a broader information infrastructure. Ford has taken a broad approach to actually creating an information infrastructure to enable this information, called OpenXC. OpenXC is an application programming interface (API) for an individual's vehicle. For an individual to leverage the API, a small hardware module would be needed to be installed in order for the app to read and translate metrics from a car's internal network. App developers can then start making vehicle-aware applications that have better interfaces based on information context, have minimum distraction to the individual while driving, and also can be integrated with other connected services. The end result—the individual gets more insight into the car's operations and can share that easily.

Ford has partnered with Bug Labs to create a standard way of creating aftermarket software and hardware for individual vehicles. This will allow Ford to tap into the broader free market of app developers. The premise is that every new car has many built-in computers and electronics, which produce an incredible amount of information when an individual drives the car. An individual will be able to choose from various independently developed apps in order to access the car's intelligence as well as broadly share this information with other individuals, groups, and organizations if they choose to do so. Ford has designed the API so it isolates the vehicle's hardware so it is protected from destroying the hardcoded systems that operate the vehicle. Ford's vision is that an individual will be able to leverage the vehicle's overwhelming volume of operational and diagnostic information as easily as people navigate their smartphones. To spur innovation and independent development in this area, Ford has launch an OpenXC developer platform for both software and hardware developers. According to Paul Mascarenas, Ford vice president and chief technical officer, "By connecting cars and trucks to wireless networks, and giving unheard-of access to vehicle data, entirely new application categories and hardware modules can be explored—safety, energy efficiency, sharing, health; the list goes on. OpenXC gives developers and researchers the tools they need to get involved." The app development space of hardware hacking is similar to the initiative at General Motors (GM)/Chevrolet with the MyStats initiative for the Volt vehicle. This will enable individuals to take the information that their vehicles produce and leverage the data for themselves or in groups. To accelerate these efforts, Ford reached out to the broader information ecosystem to leverage their beta tool kits. The first OpenXC beta tool kits were sent to universities such as the University of Michigan, MIT, and Stanford University, and to HCL Technologies in India.

At Michigan State University, an undergraduate team of students built an Android app using the OpenXC system to collect data from the Ford MyKey® system and integrated it into a centralized database with a visual report card format. Ford's MyKey system allows owners to program a key that sets safety restrictions for each driver (e.g., limit the top speed of a car or the maximum volume of the radio). The developed MyKey Report Card provides individuals with a report card of the driving habits of each of a car's drivers by collecting data from the vehicle using an Android phone or tablet. The individual driver not only can customize the data displayed on the report cards but can also specify report card delivery methods. An individual can set emergency notification options that send text messages or e-mail to another individual driver if a vehicle exceeds a specified threshold. The MyKey Dashboard (Android app) supplies driver data from the vehicle, displaying real-time data in a virtual instrument panel, and also shares it with a centralized database. The MyKey Report Card website was written in HTML5 and Java EE 6. The Android app uses an Android SDK and OpenXC vehicle interface, which enables an Android device to receive this data. To extend the university efforts, OSIsoft, a worldwide manufacturer of application software for real-time data infrastructure solutions, sponsored a hackathon to create an application using vehicle data from OpenXC in combination with its enterprise data analytics platform.

Ford's vision is that vehicle owners will have their experience extended by being able to access and share their individual driving data. Ford has divided the areas of innovation for its OpenXC platform into three categories:

1. Big data
2. Open-source innovation
3. User experience

Big Data   Ford is driving toward being a data-driven organization leveraging both internal and external data. Not only does it see this as a significant advantage toward product development and decision making, but it also sees the potential of sharing that vehicle intelligence with individual drivers to extend their driving experience. In turn, the individuals can consume the information themselves as well as share it with friends and potentially other organizations. Individuals can personalize their vehicles as well as make their vehicles more productive and efficient for their driving habits. In a broader societal context, by sharing their vehicle data, they can help their local community by sharing the data to reduce such things as congestion (by taking different routes at different times of the day) and even air pollution (e.g., drive times, driving patterns, vehicle efficiencies).

Open-Source Innovation   Viewing the car as an information platform, Ford and the individual driver can get access to real-time data. Ford gets the opportunity to potentially leverage that through rapid development of hardware and software applications. Individuals get to extend their experience through Ford's on-board and off-board applications using its SYNC in-car connectivity system utilizing its OpenXC platform.

User Experience   Information and connectivity to the vast amount of vehicle data can capture much more of the driving experience and thus be customized to enhance the total driver user experience. And individuals' driving information can be the mechanism for new ways to reduce driving fatigue and stress and also keep drivers more informed about all aspects of their driving.

Ford has had a long history of streaming data from such a complex product as a vehicle. Many vehicles require 20,000 to 25,000 parts to operate, and many of those parts produce their own data regarding fuel consumption, safety functionality, part performance quality, and operating emissions. Currently Ford gathers streaming data from more than four million cars with car sensors and remote management software. Much of this data is analyzed in real time, giving engineers a true glimpse at how each of the critical components of the car is functioning at any given time. Ford also provides telemetry of how the critical components are functioning in different road and weather conditions. In developing its Energi lineup plug-in hybrid cars, the automaker installed 74 sensors, including sonar, cameras, radar, accelerometers, temperature sensors, and rain sensors to monitor operation and performance. The Energi line of plug-in cars generates 25 gigabytes of data every hour. This data is streamed to the factory for real-time analysis, and a subset is returned to the driver via the mobile app.

Ford's MyFord Mobile app was designed for the Ford Focus Electric and allows individuals to manage vehicle functions via this mobile app. This app works in conjunction with MyFordMobile.com to provide individuals the best options for managing their vehicles' data based on their lifestyles. They can manage their vehicles' energy efficiency and economy, trip planning for the most eco-friendly route, battery charging, battery's state of charge and power usage, and remotely controlling charging and cabin temperature preconditioning. Individuals can also find a charging station, and change their charge settings dependent on on-peak/off-peak utility times for lower utility rates. Individuals can also prepare their cabin temperature to be at the desired temperature before they enter the car. They can also can analyze their driving based on their environmental impact (CO_2 saved and gasoline equivalent) and share this with the community. In addition, they can analyze their driving style from "zippy" (aggressive use of energy) to "Zen" (a more relaxed, conservative consumption). Individuals can also have a full range of community engagement tools to share their car performance statistics with local drivers (e.g., ranking of the furthest distance on a single charge). There is also a discussion board that offers uncensored, candid issues with the vehicles' operation and environment. Ford also encourages drivers to submit vacation scrapbooks. Individuals have the choice of engaging with personal information regarding their vehicle in three different ways:

1. "In Your Vehicle—Find EV-specific LCD display screens and functionality for real-time driving feedback and charging controls.
2. "At Your Computer—Use the MyFord® Mobile website to access vehicle information and control a variety of vehicle features.
3. "On Your Smartphone—Download the MyFord® Mobile app (Focus Electric or Plug-In Hybrid) to conveniently connect with your EV."[2]

In the testing environment, these cars generate 250 gigabytes of data per hour. The individuals are streaming to Ford not only smart vehicle data but also driving behavior. In 2004, Ford developed a self-learning neural network for its luxury grand tourer Aston Martin DB9. This neural network optimized engine performance not only for driving conditions but also for driver behavior. It could be debated whether this type of volunteered personal information is intentionally volunteered or incidentally volunteered personal information. The criteria would be whether the personal information flow is explicit and controlled (e.g., opt-in/opt-out choice) by the driver. Like most manufacturers, Ford also uses incidentally volunteered personal information from the Internet (e.g., social networks, search) to perform such analytics as sentiment analysis to understand individuals' context and buying intent.[3]

MERCEDES-BENZ   Mercedes-Benz launched "mbrace," which basically integrates your smart phone and/or computer, the Internet, and your vehicle. Mercedes-Benz presents the value proposition as added convenience, security, and safety. The first dimension is that it integrates social media, including Facebook and Google, and localized marketing services such as Yelp. The mbrace allows drivers to meet with other friends via localized Facebook telemetry to shop in Los Angeles or find a coffee shop in Chicago, or an ambulance in the middle of nowhere. It also allows drivers to monitor their vehicles when other people are driving such as children or a concierge/valet service, as well as integrate with medical or emergency services. There is a growing sense that the more connected an individual's car is with one's personal life and the resulting streamed information, the more apt people will be to buy the same brand and/or renew vehicle leases; that is, the "connected vehicle" equals the "connected and loyal individual."

GENERAL MOTORS/CHEVROLET   General Motors/Chevrolet's early efforts with OnStar were launched into a new digital conversation when Mike Roszak, the proud new owner of a Chevrolet Volt (plug-in hybrid electric car) decided to hack into the OnStar's applications supporting the Chevy Volt to start quantifying his own driving efficiencies with his new Volt. After checking in, he was able to now monitor driving efficiency information being sent from his Volt iPhone app to OnStar. He realized that this same information might have great utility for other Volt owners to compare each other's miles per gallon (MPG) results online. Mike then developed a basic website (Volt Stats) with the help of other forum members called GM-Volt.com, where Volt owners can post and track their vital driving statistics, such as miles per gallon (MPG), MPGe (MPG equivalent), and MPGcs (gasoline supplying all power). The site has turned into an efficiency competition where members compete for the top spots in these stats. Currently there are over 1,800 Volt drivers comparing individual driving efficiencies. The Volt itself was already very data rich with their Driver Information Center being displayed on their dashboard, giving drivers immediate feedback via OnStar performance information through its RemoteLink mobile app for iPhones and Android smartphones.

A small bump in the road came when OnStar's RemoteLink mobile app was being upgrading. The app that Mike had hacked into was now threatened to shut down the increasingly popular Volt Stats website. At this point, GM and OnStar realized the potential of Mike's work and stepped up their efforts to create a new public web API that would allow the OnStar data to be a platform for future personal vehicle data. This is quite a revolution from its origins as a service for luxury cars owners that integrated safety with an on-demand driver concierge service (e.g., if the airbag deploys, we'll know you're in distress and assist you). Individuals just had to hit the OnStar blue button to contact the call center. Today, 150,000 motorists have hit the blue button for help. What is not widely realized is that individuals are generating massive amounts of personal vehicle data that is collected by OnStar, from simple engine trouble codes to outside air temperature or even whether the gas cap is open. These personal vehicle data points not only support the functioning of the car but also get fed back into GM's quality management database to advance not only longer-term component quality initiatives but also immediate quality concerns that need to be addressed quickly—in some cases, addressing component quality issues prior to being included in assembly line processes.

GM and OnStar continue to develop other services leveraging this public API such as RelayRides. RelayRides is a peer-to-peer car sharing service. It allows private car owners to rent out their vehicles on a short-term basis via an online interface. Car owners can set their own prices, and the hosting company takes 25 percent. It has received $13 million in financial support from General Motors Ventures, Google Ventures, and others. Services like these are just the beginning, which gives individuals access to some of the remote control and telematics elements of RelayRides. Using technologies, OnStar can evolve into a broader foundation of object information beyond just automotive initiatives.

The potential of personal vehicle data goes far beyond just drivers keeping tabs on their miles per gallon. A powerful illustration of this is the new app that has been developed that allows Volt owners to check on the charging status of their Volt via their iPhone or Android. This allows them to manage the timing of the charging process to leverage off-peak utility pricing (i.e., integrating an individual's personal vehicle data to their utility company). To take this even a step further, using OnStar's software interfaces created for the V (OnStar's Advanced Telematics Operating Management System [ATOMS]), GM and OnStar are hoping to create new lines of business of such integration. Minimum requirements for this further expansion include securing the data. With the ATOMS system, the security validations are done through the back-office systems, which ensure that the data flowing from individual vehicles have minimum exposure. One of the new lines of businesses is looking at the possibility of partnering with utility companies to extend their "smart grid" services to Volt vehicles. They are prototyping applications that would enable the utility companies to send direct instructions to the car to control when it charges, thereby saving the car owner money and leveling electrical demand curves. The larger innovation opportunities could include creating a triadic connection between General Motors, local electric utilities, and the individual who owns and drives the vehicle; for example, all three of the entities could share relevant data for added efficiencies and utility.[4]

JAGUAR Jaguar incorporated location-based services in a recent mobile strategy specific to Canada. Jaguar's approach was threefold: local search data from Google AdWords, quick response (QR) codes to reach individuals in transit, and individuals' location data from their opt-in consent to the mobile app Poynt. Roughly 30,000 individuals have opted into Poynt's mobile app, whose utility is high as well as its requirement for personal information. Poynt integrates most of the individuals' personal data that resides on their phones. Individuals agree to allow Poynt to interact with the their search results, such as calls placed to businesses, mapping directions, viewing show times and movie trailers, or reserving a table at a local restaurant. The quid pro quo of personal utility is: High utility only comes from high degree of personal information sharing. This is a sliding scale. The Poynt mobile app is a good example of an application that requests a tremendous amount of trust in sharing from the individual to yield a high utility to that individual.[5]

Utility to the Individual
- Find the closest business.
- Find the closest cinema with your favorite movie playing.
- Find the closest restaurant based on your favorite culinary tastes.
- Find the cheapest gas in town.
- Find the most relevant events in your town based on personal information.
- Find relevant people based on reverse lookup and your personal contact database and history.
- Find the best offers relative to your personal preferences and history.
- Give the most relevant weather forecasts based on your activity.

Access to Personal Information Required
- Access to the individual's calendar:
  - All calendar events stored on the individual's device:
    - Includes the individual's friends and coworkers.
    - Includes confidential and sensitive personal information.

- Allows the app to add, remove, or change personal information.
  - Includes the individual's friends and coworkers.
- Allows the app to send messages and invitations to friends and co-workers from the individual's calendar.
- Contacts and contact history:
  - Allows the app to call phone numbers without the individual's intervention.
  - Allows the app to read data about the individual's contacts stored on the smartphone.
    - Analyze dimensions such as frequency of calls, e-mails, or other communication methods to specific individuals.
    - Allows apps to save the individual's contact data.
    - Allows the app to modify the data about your contacts stored on your device, including the frequency with which you've called, e-mailed, or communicated in other ways with specific contacts.
  - Allows the app to modify the individual's personal contacts.
  - Allows the apps permission to delete contact data.
- Other app activity on the individual's smart phone:
  - Allows the app to retrieve information about current and recently running tasks.
  - Allows the app to discover information about which applications are used on the device.
- Access to an individual's specific location:
  - General locations via cell towers, Wi-Fi, and an individual's specific location via GPS.[6]

Communications

The communications industry is at the epicenter of the customer's new voice with major players such as Google expanding their reach into interactive direct services, Verizon's forays into mobile health, Meredith transforming their traditional value model into direct information exchanges with customers, and AT&T mobility's expansion of their location-based offerings.

GOOGLE "Helpouts" is Google's initiative to enable individuals and any size businesses to buy and sell services via live video. Google is leveraging its existing video infrastructure to connect merchants and individuals on both an immediate and a scheduled basis. The service will allow sellers to create their own profiles and to leverage automated reputation management, scheduling, and payment processing. The service will be integrated with Google's powerful search and discovery tools for individuals.

Google's search and video infrastructure is at the heart of its evolving real-time utilities for both individuals and businesses. Google offers compelling information utilities that lead individuals to volunteer personal information. The more personal information an individual volunteers, the greater utility Google can provide. Google will leverage Marketplace, which is its online store designed to help individuals and organizations discover, purchase, and deploy integrated cloud web applications. These web applications integrate with Google's strategic apps (e.g., Gmail, Google Docs, Google Sites, Google Calendar, Google Contacts) and other third-party software. The unified interface facilitates integration across the strategic applications.

Google will also leverage "Hangouts" to deliver utility to individuals via live video. E-commerce and its respective transactions will be tightly integrated with Google Wallet. Hangouts is a Google networking utility that intertwines multimedia with one-on-one and group conversations leveraging photos, emoji, and video calls. The value exchange is that Google provides one integrated platform to individuals who want to leverage Google's powerful information utilities. In turn, Google gets an unprecedented view of the individual's personal information and exchanges with universal login/identity. Google has a view of an individual's photos and emoji, network friendships, and interactions across devices. Google's previous incarnation (Google Talk) supported invisible status whereas Hangouts does not.

Helpouts will cover a range of categories (e.g., computers, education, food, health, hobbies, and repair), and individuals can leverage it for professional assistance (e.g., teachers, counselors, doctors, home repair experts, cooking lessons, personal trainers, and hobby enthusiasts). Individuals would build to choose based on qualifications, availability, ratings, and reviews. Scheduling and paying for the services will be facilitated by Google's scheduling and payment infrastructure. Helpouts will be accessible from any device the individual chooses. The provider of services will have the option of offering Helpouts for free or charging for the service or session. If a fee is charged, both the provider and the individual will be required to use Google Wallet for the payment.

Before accepting payments, Helpouts will assist the provider in setting up a merchant account with Google Wallet. A transaction fee (e.g., 20 percent) will be applied to pay Helpouts. This includes credit card transaction and Wallet fees. Google's value exchange with the individual is that it will remove many of the traditional barriers the individual has historically experienced when searching for a seamless delivery of live (video) services; for example, a Japanese tutor from Japan could offer language training to students in the United States, a yoga instructor in California could provide classes to a stay-at-home moms in New Jersey, or an appliance repair professional could talk an individual through fixing a broken fan in the kitchen. Google may record sessions for three purposes:

1. Quality assurance purposes
2. In response to abuse reporting
3. Customer and provider retention

The individual can opt out of this quality assurance recording, which will void the 100 percent money-back guarantee. Google's money-back guarantee essentially states that if the individual is not completely happy with the experience, Google will first suggest that the individual request a refund from the provider. If the provider does not issue a satisfactory re-fund, and the individual has complied with Helpouts' terms of service and policies, Google itself will issue the refund.

As Google extends its value proposition of search to a deeper engage-ment of individuals and their personal information, it will likely intertwine its core search business and their businesses as well. Individuals could con-nect retailers and manufacturers to get recommendations and advice on specific product purchases. This would also naturally extend to the service aspects of a product. Once individuals search for a product on Google, they typically leave Google's universe and fulfill the actual need through retailers such as Amazon.

Google is also creating Google Glass as a wearable computer with a head-mounted display with the concept of producing a mass-market ubiq-uitous computer. From a customer's new voice perspective, this would be almost a totally passively shared information stream with which individuals could share some or all of their experiences based on their preferences. Google Glass will display information similar to a smartphone-like hands-free format that is integrated with the Internet via natural language voice commands. The initial users of Google Glass have commented that it's hard to conceive of how the streaming information that the individual provides can create such a highly relevant reciprocal information feed and return; that is, every behavior initiates a query and corresponding response. While this concept seems futuristic, this technology will likely be commonplace by the end of this decade and may define the future framework for per-sonally shared information. Individuals will ultimately have a firehose of personal information with a spigot control, which presumably will give the individual rewards and relevancy and the marketplace access to an incredi-ble quantity and quality of real-time personally generated information. Con-trast the information world of understanding whom an individual is friends with on Facebook versus understanding whom a Google glass wearer is associating with physically via facial recognition. Google is currently saying it is "symbolically" restricting apps and services that perform facial recognition on Google Glass.

MEREDITH CORPORATION   Traditional magazine publishers are challenged to redefine their medium, because advertisers are migrating to digital media. Meredith Corporation has been acquiring several digital properties, and has also been adding many web and mobile apps as its initial forays into the volunteered customer information ecosystem. One of these initiatives is through the website Allrecipes.com, where it connects with individuals based on their current and future buying aspirations relative to food items. The approach is to provide utility to the individual around managing and preparing personal recipes. They can store the recipes in their "recipe box," post reviews of other recipes, and consume their own recipes. From these recipes they can also create a shopping list, which gives an insight into future buying.

Meredith has also leveraged its powerful *Better Homes and Gardens* brand with the app "Must-Have Recipes from *BHG*" which brings individuals recipes inspired by its popular Red Plaid cookbooks. Individuals add their personal information such as notes and substitutes for each recipe to personalize the ingredients for their family's preferences. They can then organize their favorite recipes into groups in their recipe box. Based on individual shopping patterns, they indicate which stores they frequently shop at and create shopping lists by store or occasion. They also can indicate which ingredients can be acquired at which stores and then check them off their shopping list as they shop. Advertisers on the app can offer special bonus recipes based on what the individuals have indicated are their recipe preferences. The next logical step for innovation may be directly sharing personal information between Meredith, the stores themselves and the individual given the appropriate permissions and disclosures.

Perhaps the larger opportunity is Meredith's Shopping List app. This ties individual shopping lists to specials and coupons at local stores that the individual has indicated are frequented. Individuals can also use the Recipe.com Shopping List web app to add shopping items by voice, UPC scan via mobile phone, or basic text via phone/PC. This allows other individuals such as family members to add to the shopping list. The app tracks how much savings the individual experiences from the personally generated list. The app actually auto-groups the individual's shopping items by aisle (e.g., dairy, meats) for added time savings for the individual's physical shopping activity. All this personally shared data can be synchronized across multiple devices. An individual's shopping list can be e-mailed or printed as well as shared on Facebook. Meredith includes hyperlocal retail offers and shopping lists powered by its Grocery Server. Grocery Server is Meredith's U.S. grocery store database. The Shopping List app also ties grocery specials and coupons to the individual's shared shopping information. The hyperlocal offers reinforce the immediacy of local purchases and physical product confirmation.

Meredith also has its "Mom+" app, which extends its traditional magazines to be more interactive media where individuals can share photos and get recipes and related coupons via Facebook, Twitter, Pinterest, and e-mail. The app is integrated with QR codes, tags, and watermarks.

In addition, Meredith has partnered with Pfizer to create a "Healthy Living" app that synchronizes with Pfizer's Lipitor brand and Meredith's *EatingWell* magazine that helps individuals manage their cholesterol with recipes and heart-healthy tips. The *EatingWell* magazine reaches three million readers and its website has four million unique visitors per month. This "Recipes 2 Go" app is Pfizer's first consumer app in the United States for a prescription product. The intention of the app is to provide practical cholesterol management in sync with healthy recipes to help individuals manage lifestyle changes to support their cholesterol treatment regimens. The app actually filters recipes by cholesterol category and then assists individuals to the step-by-step recipes. Additionally, pictures can be magnified to give users a closer look at meals. In turn, Pfizer's sponsorship of the app enables it to promote Lipitor. Individuals can share their personal prescription information via the app and receive a $4 co-pay card that can be used on prescriptions. Once individuals provide their personal prescription information, they can store their prescription IDs inside the app for quick reference.

Meredith also has forays into the fitness world with its "Fitness Express Workouts" app in support of its fitness magazine. Individuals can share their trouble zones in the app (e.g., abs, arms, butt, thighs) to target their workouts accordingly. They can also opt for a full body workout. The app synchronizes the individual's information with appropriate cardio workout routines. The recommendations offer step-by-step instructions and images to show the individual how to perform the work. Individuals first categorize themselves into five potential categories and what the physical outcome will be (e.g., abs, upper body, lower body, total body cardio). The app logs each workout so individuals can keep track of their physical progress. The app is designed to function on personally volunteered information but also allows that personal information to be shared with others—friends, family, fitness buffs, or communities. This app also receives live Twitter feed and Facebook updates.

There also is a FamilyFun mobile app, which encourages individuals to volunteer their information as well as their families. The type of personal information that is volunteered extends broadly across the family's activities: eating, crafts, educational activities, children's activities, entertainment, and travel (by personal financial budget constraints).

Meredith also has a "How to Paint Anything" app from *Better Homes and Gardens* that provides a glimpse into future home improvement projects based on the individual's personal volunteered information. Not only does this give a glimpse into the individual's desire to perform simple painting projects but also would give a glimpse into other home improvement opportunities and accessories.

Meredith states that the information that is incidentally or intentionally volunteered can be utilized by third-party providers and advertisers.

VERIZON COMMUNICATIONS Verizon Communications is one of the key players in the mHealth space with its LifeComm system. Verizon began by viewing the customer's new voice as a new source of growth as it faced saturation in the U.S. market for mobile phones and landlines. Verizon is competing with companies such as AT&T and Apple that are also expanding into the volunteered customer information base by selling both devices and services.

Verizon recently acquired Hughes Telematics, vaulting deeper into the automotive technology market. Hughes markets products that offer GPS tracking, communications, and safety features in cars (e.g., streaming personal vehicle data for various services and alerts). Verizon is looking to integrate individuals and their personal data from their smartphone, their cars, and their homes. Hughes offers a variety of data and voice connections to vehicles that are monitored through its call centers. The system provides emergency services, location-based features, and vehicle diagnostics, which can easily be expanded beyond basic utilities to more high-touch personal data ecosystems and applications. Hughes telematics also operates Life-Comm, supporting the health industry and particularly caregivers streaming personal data on critical aspects of individuals who are in a higher-risk situation primarily because of their age or health condition. The LifeComm service was primarily designed to help active seniors maintain their independence while providing peace of mind for caregivers. This personal data application was adopted from Hughes's automotive solutions to provide emergency response and GPS location services for personal use (e.g., on-touch emergency calling, automatic fall detection).[7]

AT&T MOBILITY AT&T Mobility has partnered with brands such as Gap, Staples, Zales, Neiman Marcus, Duracell, Motorola, and Discover to introduce AT&T Alerts to notify individuals of location-based deals nationwide. AT&T's geo-specific deals leverage cell tower data without accessing the phone's GPS information to determine when an individual is located within a designated geo-fence (virtual perimeter around a store or event). In order for individuals to begin receiving discounts, rewards, and offers via text messaging, they must first sign up for AT&T Alerts in their settings and preferences as to how they will share their location relative to their interests, such as apparel and accessories, art and entertainment, electronics, children, pets, retail, restaurants/grocery, food and drinks, travel, automotive services, health and beauty, household items, or office/school supplies. AT&T commits that it will not use the individual's personal information outside the context of the AT&T Alerts program.

Consumer Products

Consumer products has one of the largest opportunities to leverage the consumer's new "direct" voice to transform decades of "once removed" communications/interactions/transactions to direct-to-consumer communications, that is, traditional model of CPG ↔ Retailer ↔ Consumer to consumer's new voice model of CPG ↔ Consumer.

HANES   Hanes has initiated a volunteered personal information campaign about what color panties women wear in exchange for a free set of panties.
The twist is that they are asking individuals (targeting women) to share their collective panties with the world via social media. There is a slightly salacious overtone to the campaign, giving it a bit of covert sexuality and female bravado. Hanes created a website that includes a color wheel where individuals are prompted to click on the appropriate panty color they are wearing or on the currently trending panty color ("Tweet on any tile below for a chance to win this week's colorful giveaway, curated by our style expert"). Hanes playfully taunts individuals: "What color are you wearing? That's right, we're asking. Dare to share, and you could win this week's colorful giveaway, curated by our style expert." The website then reveals a series of interesting Pinterest-style images that, when clicked on, rotate to reveal a predetermined humorous and edgy tweet based on the chosen panty color.
Here are examples of purple panty tweets:

- Inspiring purple panties turn any butt into a beaut.
- Purple is trending in New York City today.
- Violets are red; violet is under my blue jeans.
- I'm not afraid to tell; I'm no shrinking violet.
- I insist on amethysts.
- A star rises brightly in the purple sky, so no wonder it's the color I prefer.
- Say no to boring people—mauve over, boring underwear wearers.
- Having a boring day? Do what I'm doing—tell the Internet about your purple panties.
- Purple panties make the perfect creative muse.

- I don't think it's a coincidence that purple and perfect start with the same letter.
- This is just the start of my purple reign.
- My undies just aren't good; there are the grapest undies ever.
- Make less sense-vio-let me tell a secret.

Apparently, women are more willing to talk about their underwear; only 5 percent of the respondents have been men. Twenty-three percent of the respondents picked pink as their favorite color. Haynes used a very simple and clear value exchange to prompt individuals to share personal information of a fairly intimate topic. The website is simple, visual, and automated.[8]

COCA-COLA   Coca-Cola's "MyCokeRewards" is a customer loyalty marketing program. Individuals enter codes found on specially marked packages of Coca-Cola products on Coca-Cola's website. Codes can also be entered via texting them from mobile phones. These codes are assigned virtual points, which can be redeemed for prizes or sweepstakes entries. Coca-Cola also has a mobile app for MyCokeRewards that allows individuals to manage their points via their smartphones. Twenty million individuals can acquire points from anywhere; Coca-Cola's 15 U.S. brands with more than 230 products are eligible for redemption. By the very act of submitting their points, individuals volunteer their consumption volume, demographics, and geography. They also volunteer their product consumption behaviors and the affinity behavior between products (*Source:* Adage.com). One of the challenges of many consumer packaged goods campaigns that require volunteered personal information is to navigate the privacy laws, particularly when children are part of your market segment. MyCokeRewards drew criticism from the Center for Digital Democracy, an advocacy group that focuses on how food products are marketed to children. The group criticized Coca-Cola for collecting personal information from children as well as the implications for promoting adolescent obesity.[9]

NIKE   Nike is one of the forerunners in the wearable technology market. Credit Suisse estimates that the market could reach anywhere from $30 billion to $50 billion over the next three to five years. The market of wearable technology is the amalgamation of personal wearable accessories with embedded sensors, displays, and other digital technology, such as Nike's FuelBand series, Google's Internet-connected eyewear (Google Glass), and Apple's iWatch. *Barron's* reports that the wearable technology market is "a mega trend" that has hit "an inflection point in market adoption" and will have "a significant and pervasive impact on the economy."[10] Nike has focused on its Nike+ FuelBand SportsWatch GPS, Running App, and Sports-Band for generating personal physical information for an individual. These wearable technology products can be categorized into tracking personal physical activities all day—for example, steps, calories, active time, or specific activities like runs (e.g., distance, pace, duration). The SportsWatch's GPS and the Running App maps are tied to the individual's GPS location.

Nike encourages the participating individuals to earn NikeFuel points. NikeFuel is a tally of all the physical activities in an athlete's life (e.g., running, walking, basketball). Nike+ devices automatically measure the individual's physical activities and convert them into NikeFuel points. NikeFuel is a single standard of measurement so individuals can compare and compete against their friends and other athletes using this universal physical metric. NikeFuel offers a visualization of your physical progress. Nike has set up certain awards, trophies for individuals who have a certain level of NikeFuel points. The nascent industry of wearable technology (e.g., Samsung Galaxy Watch, Google Nexus Watch, Intel SmartWatch) is projected to be a billion-dollar industry for the coming years, with today's functionality in its infancy.

KELLOGG   Kellogg has created a mobile app called "Special K Plans" that allows individuals to create customized weight management plans based on their personal health data. This app was designed by nutritionists to help individuals reach the health and weight goals that are most important to them based on their specific requirements. Kellogg has also created contests such as the "2 Week Challenge" as well as allowing the individual to input personal events or weight goals to create a "line in the sand" for their weight-loss aspirations. Individuals can create a plan that assists them in maintaining current weight through access to daily menus and shopping lists. The individuals will update their own progress. Based on their progress, they will receive helpful advice and motivations based on their volunteered information. Through the information that the individual volunteers about his or her health and life, Kellogg gets a much broader glimpse into the goals of the individual as well as the future intent of the individual's behavior.

PROCTER & GAMBLE   Procter & Gamble (P&G) has approached volunteered consumer information on several different fronts. One of their initiatives is called the "Beauty Adviser." Beauty Adviser offers the individual assistance with choosing the right beauty product (consultations for cosmetics, skin care, and hair care), how to use the product, and the latest beauty news through a digital magazine. With P&G's Beauty Adviser app, individuals can scan a product bar code or search for a specific product to learn about the product's ingredients or even other individuals' reviews on the product. The app also allows individuals to share their articles and to post reviews and videos with other individuals on Facebook or e-mail.

In another initiative, P&G launched a mobile app "Always Me," which is a comprehensive menstrual period and ovulation tracker. This app was designed with input from women-focused website editors, bloggers, and female health experts to help women manage their cycles, and offers support and advice that are personalized by the individual's data input so as to help women stay connected with their bodies in a customizable way. One of the biggest benefits with Always Me is the fact that a woman can submit a question related to her menstrual cycle, and a health professional will provide a timely answer within 24 hours. Women are allowed to submit personalized, private questions for this expert Q&A function. Other utilities are a comprehensive, interactive tracker and calendar to help women manage their periods and cycles. P&G has made the personal data inputs discrete to allow the individual to make immediate and direct online purchases of Always feminine hygiene products from this mobile app. There are also built-in tips on topics ranging from how to better manage one's cycle, health matters, and exercise. In the process of creating this app, P&G provided a preview of the application to key health experts, including obstetricians, gynecologists, and female cycle experts. Influencers reviewed the application to test functionality and provided comments on their user experience.[11]

KRAFT Kraft has introduced the mobile app "iFood," which helps individuals in the kitchen. Kraft's iFood app brings simple food ideas to individuals based on their searches and personal food information. Based on the individual's input, the app delivers how-to videos, recipes, a recipe box, and a built-in shopping list. Kraft can then access not only current behavior of the individual but also future buying intent via the recipes and recipe box.

L'ORÉAL L'Oréal is the world's largest cosmetics and beauty company. It purchased Kiehl's, an American cosmetics brand retailer that focuses on premium skin, hair, and body care products. Kiehl's began geo-fencing in 2011 at its 44 stand-alone stores. Kiehl's later expanded its geo-fencing program to encompass 53 stores nationwide. Further expansion plans include geo-fencing for Kiehl's kiosks located in various department stores. The geo-fencing radius extends from half a mile in New York and other big cities to two miles in many suburban areas. Thousands of individuals have opted to share their GPS location information in order to receive Kiehl's alerts. Kiehl's added free product giveaways to add to individuals' value proposition for relinquishing their location information. Typically, adding an incentive to sign up for the location-based text alerts will increase the participation by up to twofold. Individuals are highly sensitive to the frequency of marketing messages they receive on their cell phones because of the highly personal nature of the device. Therefore, Kiehl's limits its text messages to approximately three mobile alerts every month on new products, seasonal and promotional offers, as well as special events. Limiting the number of text messages keeps the personal utility equation in balance and thus keeps the opt-out rates at a minimum.[12]

After applying the volunteered location information from the individual's smart phone relative to the geo-fencing radius, 73 percent of the individuals who had received a location-based text alert made a purchase after receiving the text. Kiehl's has observed that the response rate when individuals share their location information is much higher relative to comparable e-mail campaigns that are not location-based. Since the individual is closer to the store, the potential purchase has higher relevance and utility to the individual; the offer is made at the right place and the right time. Kiehl's promotes this program at checkout, on social sites, as well as through e-mail. One recent e-mail campaign resulted in 4,500 new opt-in users. A survey revealed that 81 percent of the individuals remembered receiving the text alerts and 77 percent would be more likely to visit Kiehl's as a result of receiving the text message. The next steps are to integrate the individuals' shared location information relative to the geo-fencing radius into Kiehl's customer relationship management (CRM) system. This will enable Kiehl's to more effectively leverage the individuals' shared location information from this program.[13]

NORTH FACE   The North Face is an American outdoor product company specializing in outerwear and equipment. Its initial move into leveraging the customer's new voice started with geo-fencing in 2010. The North Face geo-fenced its physical stores as well as outdoor gathering places such as parks and ski resorts. It implements this geo-fencing by asking individuals to sign up for the North Face "Summit Signals" text messages. Individuals agree to receive messages personalized to their location regarding information about relevant gear, local events, educational tips on outdoor activities, and special offers. Here are three examples of Summit Signals' short message service (SMS) messages:

1. TNF: If u explore in the most severe conditions, take cover in a Plasma Thermal Jacket. It'll keep u warm & dry in high altitudes. Get urs @ TNF Downtown Seattle.
2. TNF: You've trained. You're ready. The TNF Boulder Marathon is this Sunday, Sept. 19. Run a 10K, a half or a full marathon. Register @http://bit.ly/DD3OK.
3. TNF: If you hike & you run—thru puddles, streams & dry terrain alike, we've got the shoe for you: Alkaline GTX XCR. Tell us ur size @TNF Portland.[14]

The North Face's program is opt in and requires individuals to volunteer their phone number and gender, and to indicate the number of texts they wish to receive per week. It would also send text messages regarding promotions (e.g., free water bottle with a purchase) and information about new product arrivals since the company's apparel and gear are primarily seasonal items. In addition to store promotions, branded texts would be sent related to when individuals enter the geo-fence around outdoor recreational areas for a particular event such as a marathon or ski competition. The Summit Signals program also includes condition alerts for such things as snow, wind, and trail conditions via mobile apps.

The Summit Signals program has proven to be a valuable CRM tool for the North Face. Not all messages promote a specific call to action, but rather they build brand equity and loyalty among existing customers by engaging them with information and events sponsored by the North Face that encourage them to get outdoors, driving unplanned purchases down the road for the products necessary for those activities. Specific program response rates are not public information, but the company has expanded the program to all 37 of its retail locations nationwide in the past year and makes several messages available via its different types of geo-fenced locations each month.

The North Face also has a mobile app called "TracKING," which is a performance mobile tracking app that helps individuals track their runs and hikes. It creates a library of their unique routes that they can share with their friends (e.g., Facebook). Individuals can also set up competitions among their friends as well as share tracked routes. The North Face also adds prizes for these types of competitions. In addition, it feeds the individual all relevant wiki points of interest near where the individual is running or hiking. The North Face also built in a personal data dashboard to monitor progress. Within the individuals' dashboards, they can monitor their own performances, community results, contest information, and competition prizes. Utility to the individual includes:

- Upload all of your favorite trails, hikes, and runs to create a personal performance library.
- Discover new and interesting spots on your routes via wiki points.
- Get voice prompts on distance achieved.
- Challenge friends to top you, or outperform them on their own routes for universal bragging rights.
- Geolocate your routes to the wikisphere so the community can learn more about their significance.
- Share your results with your entire Facebook community.
- Compete in weekly contests to earn special prizes.
- Make new friends with a shared passion for exploration.

E-Commerce

Rapid innovation is occurring every day in the e-commerce space fueled by the customer's new voice. By the very nature of e-commerce, companies like Amazon and eBay can transform and disrupt entire industries when they drive levels of product relevancy and customer experience to levels unobtainable in the traditional model where direct exchange of purchase intentions and context was not feasible or even possible.

NETFLIX Netflix is a provider of on-demand Internet streaming media. It has more than 25 million users, with roughly 30 million plays per day. Individuals consume more than two billion hours of streaming video with over four million ratings per day and three million searches per day. By the nature of its business, Netflix asks that individuals volunteer their media consumption behavior—for example, rewinds, fast forward and pause, time of day and week—as well as make known their geolocation data and device information (e.g., smartphone, television, tablet, game consoles, Blu-ray players, set-top boxes). Netflix adds this to the metadata from third parties, such as Nielsen and social media data from Facebook and Twitter, to understand an individual's consumption behavior better.[15]

ZAPPOS Zappos.com, the largest online shoe store, was acquired by Amazon.com in 2009. Zappos's mobile apps have the typical information that you'd expect from a progressive online store: make returns from inside the app, returns support, save searches, zoomable high-definition product images, "Keep Me Logged In" feature, notifications for when an individual's desired products come back in stock, and social media product sharing (e.g., Facebook, Twitter, e-mail, and text message). The initial volunteered personal information dimensions of the mobile app are helpful to both Zappos and the individual. Zappos allows individuals to place their preferences as shopping filters (e.g., color, type of fabric). Conversely, Zappos.com launched its new fashion management system (FMS), which will inject personal fashion knowledge into individual preferences. Zappos's fashion management system will intervene with individuals when they are about to create a fashion tragedy, such as socks with sandals; the system will actually block the purchase. Zappos's focus groups showed that an overwhelming 93 percent of men who wear socks with sandals are less attractive to their spouses.

AMAZON Amazon.com, a multinational e-commerce company based in the United States, is the world's largest online retailer. Amazon generates a great deal of incidentally volunteered information simply through the tremendous volume of transactions that purchases create. Amazon can then infer propensities to future purchases based on historical buying behavior; for example, a camera purchase suggests future camera accessory purchases. Its goal is to augment these types of propensity analytics around buying behavior by more fully engage the individual into revealing future intent of related or unrelated purchases. One of Amazon's early forays into this type of capability is the Amazon Windowshop mobile app. In this app, Amazon is attempting to extend its sophisticated online buying analytics by creating a far more interactive experience with its customers being able not only to have more control over their buying information but also to indicate future buying intent with such features as the Wish List. The Wish List is targeted at asking individuals to place their desired future purchases in their Wish List in their app. When they do so, Amazon no longer needs to infer from behavior patterns but can act on explicitly volunteered information either through incentives such as free shipping or further discounts.

EBAY   EBay has started a service formally called "Garden by eBay" and casually referred to as "eBay garden." This service lets individuals test, review, and interact with new features that eBay is developing. The service is designed to allow individuals to volunteer their reactions and new product ideas and features that would heighten the eBay experience for the individual. One of the ideas that eBay is testing on Garden by eBay is called "Stuff by eBay," which is an easy way to organize all of an individual's purchases from eBay and other online merchants. Purchases would be linked through the individual's e-mail, and the purchase records, return policies, and shipping status would be centralized in one place. Shipping status would also be centralized. EBay commits that the individual's volunteered information will stay private and never be shared. It also has "eBay Local Shopping," which relies on the individual to volunteer their location in order for eBay to check local availability and prices of items from more than 50,000 stores across the country.

"Giftologique" asks individuals to share personal information relative to potential gifts they will give now and in the future to family and friends. Giftologique guides the individual through a series of questions where the individual volunteers the demographics of friends and family as well as likes and dislikes based on product and price categories. Giftologique also allows individuals to "pin" promising ideas to their "maybe list" for future purchases.

"Discover eBay" asks individuals to share their likes and dislikes so eBay can personalize their shopping experience. They can tell eBay which product categories they like or do not like as well as "like or dislike" products for indicating preferences. EBay assigns an "Activity Score" that counts the number of actions the individual has taken in the prior 14 days that will volunteer specific personal preferences. The higher the amount of personal shared information, the more personalized the shopping experience will be. EBay then uses this personal information to augment its predictive engines for both positive and negative inputs. It has also invested in firms like GSP,

Hunch, and Milo, to have a closer connection with individuals' incidentally and intentionally volunteered information. For example, Hunch combines algorithmic machine learning with user-curated content to connect affinity to items on the web, from fashion to food. Hunch's predictive ability will take an individual's shared messages and feedback scores and combine them with other dimensions such as keywords and clicks to create a more relevant experience for individuals.

"SecretGuru" is another eBay move into leveraging the customer's new voice in the category of collaborative consumption marketplaces. Secret-Guru is a concierge-style service where individuals buy time from professionals in activities ranging from cooking to business mentoring and beauty. EBay has made a name for itself as a well-known marketplace for individuals selling physical goods, and now has created a parallel site based on the idea of hiring services. "Gurus" get their own pages on the site, which is uniform and templated. These gurus can describe what they do and why they are the best choice for individuals who desire a particular task or job. Those who are interested in hiring gurus contact them through the site for additional inquiries, negotiations, and assignments. Examples of gurus' advertising services are:

- Banish bad clothes days forever.
- Have fun with making gorgeous cupcakes.
- Paint the town!
- Create your own graffiti.
- Discover your unique body constitution.
- Wardrobe detox.
- Learn how to make Indian food the easy way.
- Taste luscious chocolate.
- Immerse yourself in the world of whiskey.
- Spreading the fairy paint.
- Try your hand at designing shoes.
- Your personal five-star chef for the night.
- Beer on a budget.
- Learn how to make delicious artisan breads.
- Learn to make sushi food with style.
- Need some help planning the perfect party or corporate event?[16]

Financial

MASTERCARD MasterCard's primary entrance into leveraging the customer's new voice space is MarketPlace where MasterCard MarketPlace searching for offers for the individual by one's location. MarketPlace categorizes offers by category: new, national, and local. MasterCard has mobile apps like "ATM Hunter," Google Wallet, PayPass, and MasterCard Easy Savings. Google Wallet is an app that turns the individual's mobile phone into their virtual wallet. The Google Wallet mobile application for Android allows consumers to use all U.S.-issued credit or debit cards. Tapping your phone at checkout sends your payment via MasterCard PayPass—no need for paper money or cumbersome change. For the small business market, MasterCard has released a MasterCard Easy Savings program that gives rebates on small business purchases automatically, which are applied to the monthly card statement without coupons or codes. MasterCard was also a financial backer of mFoundry, which provided mobile financial services by offering personal finance management software platforms. Individuals could then have a more active role in managing their individual finances and information across disparate financial entities. FIS acquired mFoundry in 2013.

BANCORP Bancorp's Simple.com enables individuals to be much more active in understanding, managing, and controlling their own financial data. Its goal is to replace an individual's traditional bank. Simple.com offers an individual's financial budgeting tools like Mint, but does not aggregate accounts at other banks, credit cards, and loans into a single view. It categorizes an individual's transactions in real time with all financial activity readily searchable. Its reports give individuals detailed analysis of their finances over time. They set up their own financial goals in order to save money over a certain time. Simple.com also allows individuals to set aside money for their different spending categories and goals. It refers to an individual's real balance as a "Safe to Spend" balance based on an individual's future goals. Simple's approach is to enable an individual to view all savings as transactions relative to discrete individual financial goals. Individuals input their own spending goals (e.g., "I want to buy a $500 camera in three months") to the rigor of saving, and would then set up a standard automatic transfer to savings toward that goal. This gives an individual's savings explicit buying context and intent. The individual sets up the time period and spend amount (i.e., goal), and Simple lays out the incremental deductions every day to allow the individual to reach that goal. This savings rate is all in the context of the individual's "Safe to Spend" amount. Mint is more focused on organizing and categorizing individuals' spending relative to their stated financial goals. Simple is more focused on an individual's discrete, personal spending goals and savings required to achieve those goals.

FIS FIS is a global provider of technology and services to the financial services industry, serving more than 14,000 clients in over 100 countries. FIS recently acquired mFoundry, which was funded by MasterCard, Bank of America, Motorola, PayPal, and Intel) and provided mobile financial services by offering personal finance management software platforms. MFoundry suggests that if individuals are empowered to take a more active role in managing their finances and information supporting their financial activities, they benefit by having more of a holistic view of their financial assets, liabilities, and budgets based on their individual goals. The financial institution benefits in the following ways:

Strengthen customer loyalty
- New insurance and investment account openings increased by 8 percent and 7 percent, respectively.
- Direct deposits increased 3 percent.
- Average balance increased 45 percent.
- $8 average per account overall balance benefit.

Improve cost savings
- Fifty-two percent decrease in interactive voice response (IVR) call volumes
- Twelve percent decrease in live agent call volumes
- Fifteen percent decrease in check writing
- $6 average saving per account through channel efficiency and service gains

Drive top-line growth
- Eight percent increase in quantity of debit transactions
- Nine percent increase in value of debit transactions
- $14 average revenue lift from increased transactions
- Up to $100 of additional user revenue from various mFoundry mobile features

INTUIT Intuit's Mint.com is a web-based personal financial management service that extends typical online banking applications and personal finance management software by providing useful information and smart, specific recommendations for saving or making more money based on each user's individual purchase history. Mint's information engine is based on the patent-pending categorization technology that automatically identifies and organizes transactions made in an individual's bank, credit, investment, brokerage, or retirement account. Individuals who have used this software have saved over $2,000 on average through better information about their transactions.[17] It then uses a proprietary search algorithm that finds savings opportunities that are unique relative to the information that has been input. Once individuals begin populating their various financial data across industries, they can navigate the site under four different categories: banking, investments, insurance, and credit scores. Under each category, you can enter your intentionally volunteered personal information and Mint.com will search for the best value relative to the information you provide.

In the banking category, there are five subcategories: credit cards, checking, savings, certificates of deposit (CDs), and home loans. In the investments category there are brokers, rollovers, and individual retirement accounts (IRAs). Under insurance, there is auto and life insurance. And credit scores allow you to access your credit score from Experian.

Mint's primary service allows members to track bank, credit card, investment, and loan transactions and balances through a single user interface as well as make budgets and goals, which gives a view into the future financial state the individual desires. To encourage innovation from developers, Intuit has opened its APIs to its financial data service. It also recently began offering its product to financial institutions on a white-label basis. Currently, Mint has 12 million users. Intuit also offers "FinanceWorks" through other financial institutions, which enables individuals to manage their finances (e.g., checking, savings, credit cards, loans, and investments) that they have with disparate financial institutions within their current bank or credit union. FinanceWorks offers individuals account aggregation and account organization for budgeting and expense categorization. Individuals can manage such items as spending, bill paying, and tax-deductible expenses. FinanceWorks also enables an individual to plan for future spending and savings with an eye toward long-term financial goals. This gives the institution a glimpse into the future intent and goals of an individual's financial information beyond just the institution's transactions.

Health

The healthcare industry has a vast opportunity to utilize the "Patient's" new voice to not only create a higher quality of life for every aspect of healthcare through real-time connections between patients in the industry. This type of "new voice" has the potential of redefining health diagnostic and techniques, patient communications, as well as training healthcare workers. There is also a significant opportunity to greatly reduce costs due to the accuracy and real-time nature of connecting a patient, healthcare practitioners, researchers, and patients with mobile health technologies such as mobile patient monitoring rapidly evolving mobile phone health apps.

MICROSOFT   Microsoft's vision for HealthVault is to be a trusted place for individuals and their families to gather, store, use, and share their personal health information online. Microsoft sees the utility for individuals volunteering their personal health information as falling into four categories:

1. **Organize an individual's family health information.** Microsoft's vision is that there will be great utility for individuals and their families to volunteer health records so they can be organized and available online. Keep track of all the details, whether you are managing complex health issues or just want to stay on top of your family's wellness. This app allows an individual to track such things as medications, allergies, health history, fitness, blood pressure, lab results, and conditions and illnesses, along with X-rays, scans, and other images as well as other kinds of health and wellness data. For example, a mother could use HealthVault to prepare her kids for such activities as sports teams and summer camps by keeping track of the children's medical records in a family account. This alleviates the need for a pediatrician's office to fax records (e.g., immunization history) each time a child enters another sport or activity. This enables the individual to capture the medical information once and effortlessly use it again and again without dealing with other siloed medical information at individual doctors' offices or hospitals.

2. **Be better prepared for doctor visits and unexpected emergencies.** Individuals can be better prepared for emergency situations by making sure that their most important health information is available for emergency responders. Individuals would create their own emergency profiles for themselves and their family. When individuals have their entire important health information in one place, they would be able to leverage doctor visits more effectively simply by having access to it. Personal health information tends to be scattered because there are multiple doctors involved. If a mother is managing her own and her children's health information, simply having all of the up-to-date medications and allergies lists, as well as recent vital health statistics such as blood pressure, blood glucose, and weight in one place would have tremendous utility for her.

3. **Create a more complete picture of an individual's health.** From a HealthVault perspective, the individual is the most logical integration point of one's medical information. From this perspective, if an individual can channel all the lab results, prescription history, and visit records from a myriad of labs, pharmacies, hospitals, and clinics to the personalized HealthVault record, the individual will be assured that this information will be readily accessible for the next request. An individual can also add his or her own electronic copies of medical information and/or images. If an individual has a chronic condition that requires electronic monitoring, the patient can stream the monitored

data directly to the HealthVault. All of his or her personal health input can be done via the web or mobile app.

4. **Achieving an individual's fitness goals.** An individual can input personal weight and fitness goals in a weight management dashboard that tracks weight, activity, and diet with individually set goals that can be actively monitored. An individual can also stream wearable smart device data directly to his or her HealthVault fitness profile. Individuals can also share their progress via social media to celebrate their weight, activity, and calorie achievements.

GOOGLE HEALTH AND ONPATIENT Google also started a similar service called "Google Health" in 2008 focused on providing individuals with a convenient method for centralizing their health records and then matching them up with other medical resources such as pharmacies and doctors. Google decommissioned the service in 2011. A new venture called "OnPatient" began as a new public health record service from DrChrono Inc., which attempted to continue and improve upon what Google Health had started. An individual could use the iPhone mobile app OnPatient to allow the doctor to scan the individual's Passbook QR code, which then gave the doctor access to the medical record once verified. DrChrono has taken this a step further, so, instead of just giving the patient a place to store medical records created by other medical professionals, the service emphasizes recording medical information by the patients themselves via smartphones and apps. The data collected then gets processed to enable them to find the right doctors, schedule appropriate appointments, send secure messages between individuals and medical professionals, as well as track health spending.

Insurance

The rapid evolution of real-time sensing devices enabled by microelectromechanical devices has the potential to transform the insurance industry for real-time monitoring and assessment of actual risk exposure. These devices have the opportunity to transform the industry once tied to traditional actuarial data.

STATE FARM State Farm Insurance is a group of insurance and financial services companies operating in the United States. The group's main business is automobile insurance. State Farm's customer's new voice initiative is entitled "Drive Safe and Save—Empowering Your Drive." This emphasizes the control factor of volunteering intentionally streamed vehicle information (i.e., "Take control and receive a discount up to 50 percent off your auto insurance"). State Farm communicates that if you are a good driver, you'll be able to control how much you can save on your auto insurance by installing one of the three vehicle communication services and agreeing to intentionally stream the data. This data contains driving behaviors such as miles driven, routes, vehicle speed, and even whether drivers and their occupants wore seat belts. Some of the vehicle communication devices also record acceleration, braking, turns (left and right turns), time of day the vehicle was driven, and whether the driver drove 80 miles per hour or faster.

This type of volunteered personal information could either create a discount or potentially increase the insurance rate. For example, the less time the vehicle is driven, the more the driver would save on insurance, as well as the more safely the vehicle is driven the more the driver would potentially save on insurance. What is interesting about this approach is that it can be an active driving characteristic calculation. The driver can actually monitor each of the driving factors to see how a change in any of the driving factors affects the insurance premium. This allows drivers to actively modify their driving characteristics to improve their grades and increase automobile insurance savings.

With the proliferation of usage-based customer information in the insurance industry (usage-based insurance [UBI]), it is just one of the first industries to tap into these personal data streaming capabilities. One of the key business benefits of this customer intelligence approach is that this volunteered data will be an excellent source for new product development and services for insurance customers—insurance products that weren't even possible without this streaming customer intelligence. This real-time stream also enables real-time testing and rapid product development. Will this type of real-time direct consumer data ultimately replace actuarial processes? This is an excellent example of how direct-from-consumer intentionally volunteered customer information could potentially supplant the historical predictive analytics approaches and augment or replace the actuarial tables and analytics (i.e., real-time actual data rather than a historical proxy). In terms of managing risk and claims costs, this usage-based data approach will revolutionize the process by which insurance companies manage risk and the associated costs. It will also enable them to develop a much more sophisticated pricing structure and as a result improve profitability as well as differentiating products by individuals, not just markets. As a true win-win, individuals will also be able to manage their insurance costs by managing their driving dimensions and iteratively improving their driving habits. Low-order data (data about an inanimate object versus personal data) from a customer's new voice type platform will build credibility for State Farm to migrate to high-order personal data (i.e., about me).[18]

AVIVA   Aviva is a British multinational insurance company headquartered in London. It is the sixth-largest insurance company in the world and has 43 million customers in 21 countries. Aviva has developed an app that is designed to save safe drivers money on their car insurance, with the marketing message that "it's only fair that you pay an individual price based on how well you drive." By using the app, drivers could pay up to 20 percent less for their car insurance. Aviva's app is free and downloadable to a driver's smartphone using the phone's built-in GPS tracking. Added features allow drivers to clock the first 200 miles of a journey, where they can collect different driving skill badges and share their progress on Facebook and Twitter. At 200 miles, Aviva Drive will give an individual driving score between 0 and 10 (10 being the safest). The app will show how the driver's score compares to the national average. The driver is also able to compare the driving score against friends' scores on Facebook. Aviva then uses drivers' scores to give them feedback on their driving and to calculate potential discounts they've earned on their car insurance.

Retail Stores

Retail stores have the limitless ability to create unheard of levels of product relevancy and customer experience when their customers have the ability to directly communicate purchase intentions and preferences in real time either while in the store, online, or in the seamless movement between the two shopping environments.

WALMART   Walmart is extending the in-store shopping experience with its mobile app (Scan & Go) targeted at personalizing the individual's shopping experience through such things as in-store navigation and money-saving opportunities. It also allows individuals to scan and bag their groceries as they shop. This enables them to manage their shopping budget with a running total prior to checking out. Walmart's mobile app won 2012 Mobile Retailer of the Year from Mobile Commerce Daily and 2012 Mobile Excellence Awards. Walmart's mobile app encapsulates its slogan "Save money. Live better" with a mobile app that enables individuals to automate their shopping experience at home, in Walmart stores, or anywhere in transit. Walmart is also centralizing the use of the mobile app with exclusive mobile-app-only shopping events. This is an efficient way for Walmart to communicate its price "Rollbacks" initiatives dynamically rather than relying on an individual to haphazardly discover them by physically walking through the store. Walmart promotes its "Value of the Day" price initiatives to the mobile app as well. Individuals can also browse their local store ads, scan barcodes and QR codes, check inventory and prices, and order refills and view $4 prescriptions.

When an individual checks for product availability and pricing, the mobile app also serves up affinity to items viewed by other shoppers. This augments the retail practice of placing affinity items in the same physical proximity. The item searched on as well as the affinity items also provide relevant information to the shopper (e.g., no artificial flavors and colors, naturally gluten-free food, kosher. It's a mutually beneficial cross-sell opportunity. The app requires that individuals give access to their hardware controls to scan bar codes and QR codes. The individual is also asked to give permission regarding the accounts on the device in order to send notifications. Walmart also adds a shipping bonus that enables free shipping when an individual sends an order to a Walmart store. The mobile app also enables $0.97 shipping on select products. Quite possibly the biggest mutual benefit for the example would be giving individuals the ability to check out of the store themselves. Walmart will experience significant checkout cost efficiencies, and the customer will benefit from the checkout efficiency as well.

HOME DEPOT   Home Depot has several initial projects for volunteered personal information. One is its mobile app, which, while having most of the standard features of other mobile apps, allows individuals to browse and shop both in-store and online. From a shared information perspective, Home Depot encourages individuals to create their own shopping lists, which give an indication of future purchases. It also asks that individuals share their locations to assist with local availability of products, and that they share which workshops they may be attending, which gives an indication of future product purchases as well.

Another initiative that Home Depot has invested in is "eHow." This is an online how-to guide with over a million articles and 170,000 videos offering step-by-step instructions. These how-to guides and videos are created by paid freelance writers and are organized by product category. Home Depot will fund specific categories that it wants to drive product interest in and then track the "likes" and activity of these how-to sessions. Home Depot branded these how-to articles and videos with the Home Depot badge.

Home Depot's major foray into volunteered customer information was in 2012 when it purchased Redbeacon.com, which provides a service for individuals who are looking for a trusted service professional to accomplish a particular task—for example, "I want a reputable plumber to text me an offer to fix my sink (see picture) this Saturday." Anthony Rodio, CEO of Redbeacon, states that Home Depot's strategy extension from do it yourself (DIY) to do it for me (DIFM) is an incremental value proposition for both its customers and its business fundamentals. He describes Redbeacon as the "Bat-Signal" for individuals who need help with their home projects. Professionals find Redbeacon valuable because their skill set is more craftsperson oriented than business oriented. Redbeacon provides a ready-made business infrastructure to engage with clients. Much of household engagement for DIFMers is with the woman of the household (i.e., chief householding officer).

Redbeacon prescreens and approves suggested service professionals with its own Home Service Guarantee. Redbeacon provides a service for individuals who are looking for a trusted service professional to accomplish a particular task. Redbeacon prescreened, approved, and backs up the suggested service professional by its own Home Service Guarantee.

Redbeacon does use e-mail as the primary form of communication but also facilitates individuals and professionals to trade contact information easily so they can talk with each other over the phone. The company also has created a built-in interface so the professionals can ask relevant questions about the potential job before quoting a price or offering to come on-site to visually determine the characteristics of the job.

Redbeacon's utility to professionals is compelling. Professionals can also set their own service perimeter, which is part of the basic professional application process. They can change this service perimeter at any time to make it as wide or as narrow as they prefer. Redbeacon charges professionals $29.99 a month for unlimited relevant requests by individuals for jobs. Professionals also earn points by purchasing the job's materials at Home Depot, at a rate of two points for every $1 spent. Their monthly subscription fee starts them off each month with 300 points. Professionals who purchase a moderate amount of a job's materials from Home Depot are likely to earn back their monthly $29.99 subscription fee with one job.

Much of Redbeacon's utility to individuals is time savings (e.g., making many phone calls, searching online review lists, gathering disparate price estimates, and research on what jobs should cost in their area of the country). The other time savings is that they are not overwhelmed with a large number of responses. The maximum number of responses is four, and the individual typically gets the first response within 10 minutes of submitting a request.

Redbeacon's additional utilities for both individuals and professionals are:

- Preapproved for high-quality service:
  - Redbeacon prescreens and preapproves all the service professionals in the individual's community:
    - Interviews each professional
    - Verifies their profile information
    - Checks licenses, background, and service history
- Taking Redbeacon's Pro oath:
  - Service professionals who pass Redbeacon's prescreening process are required to take the Redbeacon oath:
    - Arrive on time
    - Come prepared
    - Courteous and trustworthy
  - Once professionals agree to the oath, Redbeacon certifies them as Pros.

- Redbeacon scores:
  - The Pro's score is calculated by a combination of:
    - Quality of work
    - Level of detail included in profile
    - Customer ratings
    - Responsiveness to customer needs
- Reviews from real customers:
  - Redbeacon provides Pro reviews from Redbeacon customers. Each Pro has an average star rating based on these customer reviews.
  - Individuals can also screen additional reviews from other sources such as Google, Yahoo!, and Yelp.
- Three strikes rule
  - Once Pros take the Redbeacon oath, they're expected to deliver a high level of service every time. Each time they fall short of that oath, they receive a strike on their record. A service professional who receives three strikes is excluded from Redbeacon's service recommendations.

The Redbeacon process has six steps:

- Step 1: Individual makes a request (takes about 30 seconds).
  - What services the individual needs (e.g., maid, plumber).
  - Key details of the job (with photos if possible).
  - When and where the job needs to be done.
  - Preferred contact method for quotes (e.g., e-mail, text, phone).
- Step 2: Redbeacon's technology matches individual's job with Pros.
  - Finds qualified, local, Redbeacon-approved Pros.
  - Checks their availability for the individual's project.
  - Confirms reputations with reviews and related work history.
  - Verifies they've taken the Redbeacon quality service oath.
- Step 3: Redbeacon sends quotes to individual.
  - Redbeacon sends the individual four competitive quotes.
  - Individual picks the preferred Pro and price.
- Step 4: Pro is booked through Redbeacon site.
  - After the individual reads the reviews, Pro's profile, and Redbeacon score, he or she makes the service decision and submits a credit card to book the service professional. By making a booking through the Redbeacon site, the individual receives:
    - Redbeacon guarantee
    - Scheduling assistance
    - End-to-end customer care
- Step 5: When the job is complete, payment is through Redbeacon.
  - Pro submits invoice through Redbeacon.

- Individual can add a tip or just let the credit card be automatically charged for the agreed-upon rate after 24 hours.
- Step 6: Redbeacon is the individual's advocate after the fact.
- Redbeacon holds the professional accountable to the service oath—that the job is done right.

The Redbeacon model may be the harbinger of the future incarnation of home improvement stores and many other retailers. Individuals will send up the "Bat-Signal" with their mobile device for a particular need (e.g., home improvement projects) and the store with the best service infrastructure. Interactions will be predominantly video-based with retailer staff and their circle of certified professionals. Any physical interaction will be done with the individual taking a physical product at a distribution center. The concept of physical stores with a full range of merchandise will belong to a bygone era. Interactions between individuals and retailers will be transparent with simple feedback, as will interactions of both the retailer and the professional.[19]

LOWE'S Lowe's' vision is to redefine home improvement through mobile apps. This entails giving individuals a more integrated way to their personal information with Lowe's information to plan, build, buy, and explore their current and future next home improvements. Individuals can create their own shopping lists, view their purchase history, and store their individual information on their MyLowe's card for access anywhere they travel. Individuals now have much more control and access to their information relative to their home improvement activities. The information that is stored on the card and the app facilitates returning items to the store. It also tracks in-store purchases and gives the individual paying an immediate reference point. The individual can also input buying triggers such as air filters for the furnace. The MyLowe's card/app also allows individuals to input personal information to create a home inventory, to input their shopping lists for easy access, and to list storage for future reference. The MyLowe's card app enables all this information to be easily integrated and accessed for purchases via the mobile phone. Other personal information utilities are streaming how-to videos, as well as a full image library of those products for decorating and remodeling.

TESCO Tesco is a British multinational grocery and general merchandise retailer headquartered in the United Kingdom. It has several initiatives surrounding the customer's new voice space. ClubCard, Click and Collect, and Real Food all have aspects of individuals volunteering personal information to realize utility around the shopping experience. The Tesco ClubCard is the customer loyalty card. By signing up to Tesco's ClubCard, individuals

reveal their identity and other personal information in exchange for receiving points for every £1 they spend either shopping at Tesco or using other
Tesco services, such as Tesco Finance. Individuals receive extra points for
taking advantage of special offers. They also typically receive one Green
ClubCard point for every carrier bag they reuse as part of Tesco's green initiative. More than 15 million individuals have made a decision that sharing
their personal information was worth the rewards of the Tesco ClubCard.
Tesco's mobile app extends the shopping utility even further to individuals
who agree to share their location information with Tesco in exchange for
the following utility:

What Individuals Get	What Individuals Give
Finding nearest Tesco store	Basic contact information
No longer need the physical ClubCard	Location
Order and amend the individual grocery list	Grocery lists
Browse recipes by course or cuisine	Shopping preferences
Shop via smartphone	Access to device functionality

An extension of Tesco's utility is its Price Promise where an individual's
shopping basket items (in-store, online, or mobile) are checked against
pricing from Tesco's competitors (e.g., Asda, Sainsbury's, Morrisons). If the
individual's comparable shopping basket is cheaper at a competitor, Tesco
will give the shopper a voucher for the difference in price up to a certain
amount. The individual gets notified either in-store, via e-mail, or via mobile
phone.

Once the individual installs Tesco's mobile app, the person agrees
to share the location using the phone's GPS or network location sources
(e.g., cell towers, Wi-Fi). The individual also allows the mobile app to
take pictures and videos with the camera automatically without asking
permission each time, as well as being able to control the smartphone's
vibrator for Tesco alerts. Another aspect of Tesco delivering utility to
individuals in exchange for the individual sharing future buying intent
is Tesco's Real Food program and magazine implemented via a mobile
app. Real Food is an interactive recipe magazine with all ingredients being able to be purchased directly within the mobile app. The recipes are
also visual, with pictures and how-to videos. Tesco also has a Click &
Collect shopping service for a small fee. The individual orders groceries
online, from home, or from the mobile app, and arranges a particular
time slot to pick the groceries up at a drive-through facility. Tesco's plan
is to implement geo-fencing for the service so Tesco receives a notification when a Click & Collect customer enters a certain radius of the

pickup area. When the customer arrives at the collection pickup point, the grocery order can already be pulled and waiting to be loaded into the vehicle.

MEIJER   Meijer Inc., a Midwestern chain of supermarkets, implemented geo-fencing to offer individuals real-time shopping lists displayed according to the aisle they are currently on. Coupons and weekly specials also appear as well as a dynamic shopping list based on their location in the store, a time saver. Meijer's aisle sensors pick up the individual's aisle location and integrate that with the shopping list that the person had previously prepared online. Meijer's mobile app then reorders the individual's shopping list based on the aisle location, which speeds up the shopping process. Meijer integrates geo-fencing with its mPerks rewards program. An individual can search and clip digital store and manufacturer coupons from the mPerks website or from the Meijer mobile app. In addition, shoppers are rewarded when they purchase through the mPerks rewards program. At checkout, they receive instant savings on the coupons and rewards that they digitally clipped. They receive special shopping discounts once they reach a certain spending level in a specific Meijer department. They can earn up to three rewards at a time, and track their progress using the meter on each reward. In addition to savings, when revealing their identity through the mPerks program coupled with revealing their location data, individuals can leverage the following:

- Receive digital savings coupons via mPerks
- Individualize how they save with mPerks rewards
- Locate the fastest route to any physical Meijer location
- Browse sale items
- Check off items on the individual's digital list
- Search and find products on a store map
- Search, browse, and save recipes (indicate future shopping intent)

An added revenue stream for many retailers is that brands are willing to pay for advertising for some of the selected promotions.

The benefits for the business include:

- **Expanded individual engagement.** Businesses can engage with individuals in real time while the individuals create their shopping lists at home or while in the store.
- **Expanded individual intelligence.** The business can leverage individuals' buying intents, past purchases, and exact location within the store by sending them messages, offers, or coupons to enhance their shopping experience.

- **Individual's location.** The business will know the individual's location at any time in order to send location- and context-specific buying suggestions.
- **Future buying intent.** Individuals will share their shopping lists that contain specific products at exact product locations within the store.
- **Expanded shopping cycle time efficiency.** Businesses can present an exact map of the inside of the store that includes aisle locations, store facilities and services, and product locations. All of this information includes the associated contextual information and routing/navigation assistance.
- **Increased shopping basket size.** By the retailer presenting the most efficient path through the store to select products, added time is created for the individual to purchase additional items.
- **More effective individual analytics.** The shopping activity creates data and heat maps of where the individuals spent their shopping time, what they actually purchased, and which deals were most effective.[20]

Technology (Consumer)

The prolific expansion of personal technology is boundless given the massive portable computing power and the resulting stream of personal utilities that mobile devices and wearable technology are generating. The key will be to inspire the sharing of information that is created with businesses in order to especially increase the rewards and utilities of the starting value proposition of personal technology.

SONY   Sony's SmartWatch is based on the Android operating system where an individual can discreetly communicate electronic updates from text messages, e-mails, Facebook, and Twitter. Applications can be downloaded from Google Play. An individual can connect a smartphone to a SmartWatch to access and control music from the phone.

APPLE   One of Apple's strategic initiatives is to integrate calls, texts, maps, and music into the individual's vehicle dashboard via a modified version of Apple's iOS. This is a natural follow-on, as 95 percent of vehicles currently have existing integration for music playback and control with current iOS devices. This new version of Apple's operating system will allow individuals to make and receive calls, play music, listen to and dictate texts, and navigate with Apple Maps.

Apple's Siri will be packaged with the system to allow for easy, intuitive voice controls. Siri is an intelligent personal assistant and knowledge navigator that uses a natural language interface to answer questions, make recommendations, and perform actions by delegating requests via a variety of web services. Siri's design capabilities are focused on adapting to an individual's preferences over time and then personalizing the recommendations based on the individual's behavior. Siri integrates navigation services such as OpenTable, Google Maps, MovieTickets, and TaxiMagic. Siri is based on voice recognition technology from Nuance and various service partners that allows individuals to make reservations at restaurants, buy movie tickets, or get a cab by dictating instructions in natural language to Siri.

In order to use the immigration aspects of the new iOS capabilities, individuals agree to volunteer certain aspects of their behavioral information (e.g., calls, music consumption patterns, navigation services) in return for the utility of these respective services. Apple announced an initial list of automobile manufacturers to launch this eyes-free capability: BMW, GM, Mercedes-Benz, Land Rover, Jaguar, Audi, Toyota, Honda, and Chrysler. Apple filed for a patent for an in-car remote control system that will likely integrate its voice-commanded Siri services with the hands-free button on automakers' steering wheels.[21]

Apple's iWatch will soon hit the market with a 1.5- to 2-inch screen, concentration on an individual's biometric data, and deep integration with Apple's existing iOS devices. The iPhone will also serve an important "secure user" identification likely tied to an individual's unique physiological identifier (e.g., retina, voice). The iPhone will focus on its kinetic-energy-gathering abilities to open up new possibilities in the health care industry for biometric monitoring (e.g., heart rate, pedometer). This type of functionality for smart watches is just in its infancy.[22]

SAMSUNG One of Samsung's core strategies is to evolve its smartphones into being more of a music player. Samsung partnered with Jay-Z, the 43-year-old rapper, to allow Samsung Galaxy smartphone users to download Jay-Z's "Magna Carta Holy Grail" three days before the album was publicly available. The Galaxy smartphone users faced several technical issues such as servers being overloaded with the overwhelming demand, as well as a perceived privacy invasion relative to the information that was required by the mobile app—GPS location of the phone, phone call IDs, ability to "modify or delete the contents of your USB storage," and "a full network access." Music business practitioners suggested that possibly the smartphone locations would be harvested to better understand where Jay-Z fans listen to the music and as a result better communicate with them.[23]

Perception is reality, and Samsung's requirement that Galaxy users provide personal information, including their age, location, phone records, and social media information, was perceived to be too much "volunteered" personal information relative to the value of the downloadable album. Samsung preordered a million copies of "Magna Carta Holy Grail" to distribute as part of this reported $20 million partnership. This highly public release amplified the fans' negative reaction to the privacy intrusion, and as a result the advocacy group Electronic Privacy Information Center (EPIC) asked the U.S. Federal Trade Commission to investigate the app for privacy violations. EPIC stated that "Samsung failed to disclose material information about the privacy practices of the App, collected data unnecessary to the functioning of the Magna Carta App, deprived users of meaningful choice regarding the collection of their data, interfered with device functionality, and failed to implement reasonable data minimization procedures," in a statement obtained by the *Los Angeles Times*. Samsung acknowledged the complaint, and has publicly stated that the complaint is baseless. "Samsung takes customer privacy and the protection of personal information very seriously. Any information obtained through the application download process was purely for customer verification purposes, app functionality purposes and for marketing communications, but only if the customer requests to receive those marketing communications."[24]

The lesson learned here is that the value proposition for trading individuals' personal information should be tested to determine the sensitivity relative to the reward. Regardless of specific regulations or industry practices, the perception of asking for too much personal information relative to the perceived value of the reward is the true litmus test. The proactive approach would be to test the requested personal information requirements against a sample group prior to launching the mobile app relative to the specific reward (e.g., album download). This is particularly the case for such a high-profile marketing campaign.

Transportation

The transportation industry has a tremendous need and opportunity to be far more engaged with their customers relative to real-time relevancy and customer experience. This simple example of Virgin America being able to completely tailor their service to the exact personalization requirements of the customer is just the beginning of what the transportation industry can do in terms of achieving extreme levels of customer experience and operational efficiencies.

VIRGIN AMERICA   Virgin America extends the utility of understanding an individual's travel preferences by partnering with rental car service Silvercar to integrate car preferences such as climate control, radio station preferences, seat-positioning settings, itinerary destinations, and favorite restaurants directly into the rental vehicle prior to pick up. The Silverstone mobile app allows individuals to input all of their personal travel preferences, which are then implemented in a vehicle that is equipped with navigation, satellite radio, and a Wi-Fi hot spot. Virgin America will offer the service to its "Elevate" members for a seamless and connected travel experience from air to ground. Members can earn 2,500 Elevate points on their first and fourth Silvercar rentals plus four points for every dollar spent with Silvercar.

Virgin Atlantic has historically established itself as catering to an increasing population of tech-savvy individuals. Once individuals share their personal preferences via the app and then arrive at the destination airport, they simply scan a QR code located on the windshield of the rental car to unlock the vehicle and drive to their destination with all the personal travel preferences programmed into the vehicle (source: PRNewswire.com). More important, individuals have significantly more control over their travel experience just by bypassing paper contracts and physical lines. All Silvercar rental vehicles come with free in-car Wi-Fi, Sirius XM satellite radio, and Bluetooth. Once travelers have completed their journey, they receive their rental car receipt via their smartphones.[25]

Utilities

The awareness of our limited natural resources and the desire to be "green" for both businesses and consumers has coincided with the ever-evolving connected consumer and their new voice to work together with utilities to create the utmost in utility efficiencies working together for a win-win, that is, an ultra-efficient grid for the utility provider and a lower cost utility for the consumer.

COLORADO SPRINGS UTILITIES   Utilities are also an excellent example of the customer's new voice. Colorado Springs utilities offer electric, natural gas, water, and wastewater services that can be monitored daily via automated meter reading (AMR), which represents the technological advancement in previously manual meter reading. This is particularly important in areas where conservation is of the utmost importance, and it requires both the utility and the individual to coordinate conservation efforts for mutual benefits. Armed with this information, individuals can take appropriate action to lower their utility bills as well as synchronize usage with water restriction time frames, monitor potential leaks, and explore rebate options. One of the primary benefits of real-time streaming customer usage data is that the near real-time monitoring of utility consumption provides almost instantaneous diagnostics and status data for everything from water usage to gas and electricity usage. This can then be analyzed in a central database for more efficient billing, troubleshooting, and analytics. This AMR technology renders antiquated the practice and expense of periodic physical trips to read a meter. As with other volunteered customer information, it replaces estimates based on past or predicted consumption with actual real-time consumption data. The individual's streaming utility data then creates the platform for an information partnership between the utility providers and the individual to better control the use and production of electric energy, gas usage, or water consumption.

SOUTHERN CALIFORNIA EDISON   Southern California Edison's SmartConnect® enables individuals to proactively manage their electricity costs with smart meters integrated with online tools before the final bill arrives. The online tools include a budget assistant and usage charts to aid individuals in tracking their energy use to maximize their cost savings and reduce their carbon footprint. SmartConnect allows individuals to drill down to daily usage and billing information with near real-time energy usage data. This usage information puts the individuals in control of how and when they use energy based on their lifestyle and budget. In addition, Southern California Edison offers usage incentives that the individual can take advantage of based on grid usage. These "Save Power Days" incentives are applied to the individuals' bill credits. In turn, this enables Southern California Edison to more effectively, efficiently, and reliably manage the delivery of electricity services. When Southern California Edison and individuals integrate their information and efforts, there is the potential to reduce emissions as well.

OKLAHOMA GAS & ELECTRIC   Oklahoma Gas & Electric (OG&E) is creating a Positive Energy® smart grid to improve energy efficiency for itself and the individuals consuming electricity. The smart grid is a secure wireless network with two-way, real-time communication with a new meter installed on the outside of an individual's home. The new smart meter enables OG&E to remotely read, connect, and disconnect service, which creates operational efficiencies that will be passed on to the individual as energy bill savings. The system allows individuals to monitor their energy use and electricity cost information from any location via the secure website at www.myOGEpower.com. This enables the individual to make better decisions as to how and when to use the electrical power to save energy and utility expense. OG&E enables this savings opportunity for the individual within the initiative it calls "smart hours" or Variable Peak Pricing (VPP). It works on the premise that electricity costs more to generate and use during peak periods of high demand. Also, other factors such as weather conditions and the time of year could potentially drive electrical rates higher.

With the information provided from the smart grid, individuals can pattern their electrical usage when costs are lower and/or off-peak. For example, during the summer cooling season, peak hours are 2 to 7 P.M. weekdays, with prices varying based on demand. Every day, individuals are sent an alert notifying them of the next day's peak electricity price via their phone, text, e-mail, or all three. Consumers also have choices to shift their electricity use to other off-peak hours, such as weekends for laundry; use the dishwasher and do cooking later in evenings or in the mornings; turn off lights, TVs, and computers when not in use; precool the home before 2 P.M. and then turn up the thermostat after 2 P.M.; and shut off pool and hot tub pumps during peak hours. OG&E is forging an information partnership. Its vision is to create better-informed customers, which will in turn assist it in making better mutually beneficial utility decisions. OG&E has branded this "Positive Energy Together®." Individuals now have control over their usage information to lower their energy bills with optional rates that are based on the time of day they use energy.

Notes

1. Center for Information-Based Competition, 2013–2014 research.
2. "MyFord® Mobile FAQs." https://phev.myfordmobile.com/content/mfm/en_us/site/help.html.
3. Mark van Rijmenam, "Ford Drives in the Right Direction with Big Data," SmartData Collective, July 6, 2013. https://smartdatacollective.com/bigdatastartups/132521/ford-drives-right-direction-big-data.
4. Sean Gallagher, "GM Introduces New Mobile Device: 4G LTE cars," Arstechnica.com, January 6, 2014. http://arstechnica.com/gadgets/2014/01/gm-introduces-new-mobile-device-4g-lte-cars/; Sean Gallagher, "OnStar Gives Volt Owners What They Want: Their Data, in the Cloud, "Arstechnica.com, November. 25, 2012. http://arstechnica.com/information-technology/2012/11/onstar-gives-volt-owners-what-they-want-their-data-in-the-cloud/.
5. David Murphy, "Jaguar Campaign Gets to the Poynt," mobilemarketing magazine.com, March 1, 2011. http://mobilemarketingmagazine.com/jaguar-campaign-gets-poynt/.
6. Google Play, Description of Poynt mobile app. https://play.google.com/store/apps/details?id=com.poynt.android&hl=en.
7. Zorica Kristic, "Hughes Telematics Announces Keith Schneider to Expand Role and Become President of Its Lifecomm Subsidiary," Hughes Telematics, June 2, 2011. https://healthcaretechnologymagazine.com/HTM/index.php/en/healthcare-it-news/item/970-hughes-telematics-announces-keith-schneider-to-expand-role-and-become-president-of-its-lifecomm-subsidiary; Sherri Snelling, "For Caregivers, New Tracking Technology Offers Peace of Mind," nextavenue.org. November 30, 2012. http://www.nextavenue.org/article/2012-04/caregivers-new-tracking-technology-offers-peace-mind.
8. Rebecca Cullers, UndercoverColor.com. "Ladies, Hanes Wants to Know the Color of Your Panties and They Double Dog Dare You to Tell Twitter," Adweek.com, August 2, 2013. www.adweek.com/adfreak/ladies-hanes-wants-know-color-your-panties-151627.

9. Jeff Chester, Center for Digital Democracy, and Kathryn Montgomery, American University, "Interactive Food and Beverage Marketing: Targeting, Children and Youth in the Digital Age," report from Berkeley Media Studies Group, May 2007, http://digitalads.org/documents/digiMarketingFull.pdf; MyCokeRewards wiki. www.mycokerewards.com/home.do.

10. Tiernan Ray, "AAPL, GOOG, BRCM Tops in Credit Suisse's 'Wearables' Weltanschauung," *Tech Trader Daily* (blog), *Barron's*, May 17, 2013. http://blogs.barrons.com/techtraderdaily/2013/05/17/aapl-goog-brcm-tops-in-credit-suisses-wearables-worldview/.

11. Giselle Tsirulnik, "Procter & Gamble Lets Women Discreetly Buy Feminine Hygiene Products via Mobile," mobilemarketer.com, November 15, 2010. www.mobilecommercedaily.com/pg-lets-women-discreetly-purchase-feminine-hygiene-products-via-mobile.

12. Dana Mattioli and Miguel Bustillo, "Can Texting Save Stores?, 'Geofencing' Lets Retailers Offer Deals to Nearby Customers, Fight Price-Shopping," *Wall Street Journal*, May 8, 2012. http://online.wsj.com/news/articles/SB10001424052702303978104577362403804858504.

13. Chantal Tode, "Kiehl's Exec: 73pc of Opt-in Customers Make a Purchase after Receiving a Text Alert," Mobile Commerce Daily, September 21, 2012. http://www.mobilecommercedaily.com/kiehl%E2%80%99s-exec-says-geotargeting-improves-results-for-text-messaging.

14. Christopher Heine, "North Face Tests Geo-Fencing, Will Consumers Bite?," ClickZ, October 13, 2010. www.clickz.com/clickz/news/1741930/north-tests-geo-fencing-consumers-roped.

15. Will Richmond, "Netflix's 2 Billion Streaming Hours in Q4 Blows Away Competitors," VideoNuze, January 4, 2012. http://gigaom.com/2012/01/04/419-netflixs-2-billion-streaming-hours-in-q4-blows-away-competitors.

16. Ingrid Lunden, "eBay Is Now Selling Live Services, Launches Secretguru as a Beta Pilot in the UK," TechCrunch, October 2, 2012. http://techcrunch.com/2012/10/02/ebay-is-now-selling-live-services-launches-secretguru-as-a-beta-pilot-in-the-uk/.

17. Intuit.com, "Frequently Asked Questions," https://financeworks.intuit.com/quickenweb/locale/en_US/help/faq-di-toc.html; Mint.com, "Frequently Asked Questions." https://www.mint.com/privacy/faq/; https://www.mint.com/help/.

18. State Farm Mutual Automobile Insurance Company, "Drive Safe & Save." https://www.statefarm.com/insurance/auto/discounts/drive-safe-save?; Charles Nguyen, "State Farm's Usage-Based Insurance Program Grows Rapidly," Online Auto Insurance News, January 24, 2013. http://news.onlineautoinsurance.com/companies/state-farm-ubi-car-insurance-98853.

19. Eric Love, "How to Save Money at Home Depot," eHow. www.ehow.com/how_4559750_save-money-home-depot.html; Redbeacon, "Frequently Asked Questions." www.redbeacon.com/about/faq/; HomeDepot.com, "FindTrustedProsforaBetterHome."www6.homedepot.com/redbeacon/index.htm.

20. Rachael King, "Stop & Shop's Smart Use of Mobile Devices," *CIO Journal* (blog), May 9, 2012. http://mobile.blogs.wsj.com/cio/2012/05/09/stop shops-smart-use-of-mobile-devices/; Dana Mattioli and Miguel Bustillo, "Can Texting Save Stores?" *Wall Street Journal*, May 10, 2012. http://online.wsj.com/news/articles/SB1000142405270230397810457736240380 04858504.

21. Richard Read, "Leaked: Images of Apple's 'iOS in the Car' Hit the Web," The Car Connection, January 22, 2014. www.thecarconnection.com/news/1089839_leaked-images-of-apples-ios-in-the-car-hit-the-web; Stephen Edelstein, "Apple CarPlay iPhone Integration to Debut in Geneva: Video," Motor Authority, March 3, 2014. www.motorauthority.com/news/1090649_apple-carplay-iphone-integration-to-debut-at-2014-geneva-motor-show.

22. Mikey Campbell, "Analyst Ming-Chi Kuo: Apple 'iWatch' Mass Production Pushed back to November," AppleInsider.com, July 10, 2014. http://appleinsider.com/articles/14/07/10/apple-iwatch-mass-production-pushed-back-to-november-analyst-says.

23. Jon Blistein, "Jay-Z's 'Magna Carta Holy Grail' App Under Investigation by Privacy Group," Rolling Stone, July 16, 2013. www.rollingstone.com/music/news/jay-zs-magna-carta-holy-grail-app-under-investigation-by-privacy-group-20130716.

24. Huffington Post, "Jay-Z's Samsung App under Investigation for Privacy Violations," July 17, 2013. www.huffingtonpost.com/2013/07/17/jay-z-samsung-app-investigation-privacy-violations_n_3610221.html.

25. PR Newswire, "Virgin America Launches Service to San Diego," Virgin America, February 12, 2008. www.prnewswire.com/news-releases/virgin-america-launches-service-to-san-diego-56894372.html; David Port, "Smartphone-Enabled Car Rental Aims to Make Life Easier," Entrepreneur, June 20, 2013, from the May 2013 issue of *Entrepreneur*. www.entrepreneur.com/article/226341.

CHAPTER 7

Horizontal Industry Innovators

Consumer-direct knowledge markets are the evolution of the digitization of our personal world, and the corresponding commercial world has created distinct sharing markets and economies. The following are among the major markets:

1. Collaborative consumption
2. Quantified self
3. Wearable technology
4. Mobile health
5. Internet of Things (individual and industrial)
6. Sensor technology
7. Virtual reality
8. Augmented reality

Collaborative Consumption (Sharing Your Stuff)

Collaborative consumption is an economy where individuals share access to products or services, rather than purchase their own products or service delivery. Most often they are enabled by technology and communities.

The most prominent names leveraging the collaborative consumption models are eBay and Craigslist. Emerging marketplaces of collaborative consumption include social lending (e.g., Zopa), peer-to-peer accommodations (e.g., Airbnb), peer-to-peer travel (e.g., LocalGuiding), peer-to-peer tasks (e.g., TaskRabbit), travel advisers (e.g., Locish), car sharing (e.g., Zipcar, RelayRides), commuter-bus sharing (e.g., RidePal, GoGet CarShare), and parking space sharing (e.g., ParkatmyHouse).

The concept of collaborative consumption is not new. It is the emergence of the enabling technologies that has given it a new form and function. Further renewal of collaborative consumption stems from the financial crisis of 2007–2010, which incentivized individuals to rethink how they could maximize their current personal assets as well as leverage underutilized assets via peer-to-peer marketplaces (e.g., share other individuals' assets, create new jobs and income streams).

The concept has recently been championed by Rachel Botsman and Roo Rogers in their 2010 book *What's Mine Is Yours: The Rise of Collaborative Consumption* (HarperBusiness). They describe collaborative consumption as "a new socio-economic 'big idea' promising a revolution in the way we consume." Botsman and Rogers state that collaborative consumption is actually a social revolution that allows individuals to "create value out of shared and open resources in ways that balance personal self-interest with the good of the larger community." They further explain that the concept of trust across multiple marketplaces constitutes the new currency of the collaborative economy, but state that "reputation capital" creates a massive positive disruption in where power, influence, and trust reside.

Collaborative consumption can be segmented into three market types:

1. **Product service markets.** Individuals pay for the benefit of using a product without needing to purchase the product. This type of system disrupts traditional industries that are based on an individual purchasing a particular product for its lifetime use without sharing the use of this product with other individuals (e.g., DVDs, tools, cars, books, homes).

2. **Redistribution markets.** This market enables individuals to sell used products that they no longer want to other individuals who have a need for the particular products. Redistribution markets can entail either outright donation, swapping, or pure selling (e.g., clothing).

3. **Collaborative lifestyles.** This system enables individuals with similar needs or interests to collaboratively share less tangible assets such as time, space, skills, and money (e.g., broker relationships for individuals with service providers).

Examples of collaborative categories are:

- Bartering
- Bike sharing
- Book swapping
- Carpool/ride sharing
- Car sharing
- Clothes swapping
- Club theory
- Cohousing
- Collaborative workspace
- Coworking

- Crowdfunding
- Fractional ownership
- Garden sharing
- Home exchange
- Local exchange trading systems (LETS)
- Peer-to-peer lending
- Peer-to-peer renting
- Product service system
- Seed swap
- Taxi sharing
- Time banks
- Virtual currency

Note: Local exchange trading systems (LETS) enable individuals to exchange goods and services without traditional money but rather with local LETS currency.

Typical categories include accommodations, animals and pets, arts and crafts, buildings and do-it-yourself, business and children, clothing, fancy dress hire, food, gardening, health and personal, home and domestic, interior design, sports and leisure, transport, and tuition/education. Benefits from collaborative consumption range from reducing carbon foot prints, to basic saving costs from borrowing and recycling products, to increasing happiness and contentment due to positive social interactions.[1]

Collaborative Consumption Time Line

1995: eBay, Craigslist founded.

1999: CouchSurfing (Fenton e-mailed 1,500 students at the University of Iceland asking for a couch to sleep on and received 50 responses).

2000: Zipcar begins in Boston based on European business model.

2003: CouchSurfing.com website is launched.

2007: Chegg (used textbook marketplace) launches at Iowa State University.

2008: Bag Borrow or Steal begins; Recycled Bride (used wedding attire and accessories); Airbnb (sharing accommodations); TaskRabbit (hyperlocal marketplace for neighbors to buy and sell tasks).

2009: Rent the Runway (service for women to rent stylish designer gowns for events).

2010: LooseCubes (marketplace for sharing office space).

2011: Zaarly (hyperlocal buyer and seller marketplace); Zipcar goes public; Getaround (peer-to-peer car sharing).

2012: Craigslist has 50 million U.S. users and 30 billion page views per month; Zipcar has 650,000 members and cars in 28 North American states and provinces.

Collaborative communication marketplaces are predominantly safe and effective, but there are some misuses, as with any marketplace. While there are checks and balances built into most collaborative consumption marketplaces, collaborative interactions can still go awry. An Airbnb host communicated that her apartment was used as a meth lab and her identity was stolen after renting using Airbnb. Since the incident, Airbnb has added a protection element (safety page) with a $50,000 host guarantee to cover damage such as vandalism.

Facebook accounts are often used as validation steps that offer a reasonable level of security but still have vulnerabilities. Scaffold cofounder Sam Rosen explains that there are three levels of identity validation:

1. You are who you say you are.
2. You are generally a good person.
3. You are a good person within the given marketplace.[2]

Big players such as Google will also be entering the collaborative market services with offerings such as Helpouts. Helpouts will enable individuals as well as small and large businesses to buy and sell services via live video using Google's pervasive video infrastructure. The ability to connect merchants and individuals on both an immediate and a scheduled basis via video will be a compelling commerce capability. Added to this capability will be the ability for merchants to create their own commercial profiles and to leverage reputation management tools as well as scheduling and payment features, while offering extensive search and discovery tools for individuals.

Google's live video infrastructure will increasingly be leveraged to provide a common enabler for an increasing list of real-time products and services. This live infrastructure will also be integrated with other current and evolving Google products, such as the virtual wallet and payment service Google Wallet.

EBay is also moving down this collaborative consumption path with its concierge-style SecretGuru service, which offers merchants a range of services directly to individuals, from business mentoring to beauty tips (www.secretguru.co.uk/how-it-works.php).

One of the rationales behind both eBay and Google entering the collaborative consumption marketplaces (more typically the home of, e.g., Zaarly, TaskRabbit, and Live Ninja) is that they can't go head-to-head in pure product-based markets with a giant like Amazon that has an existing extensive network of fulfillment centers and distribution warehouses.

For both eBay and Google, collaborative consumption marketplaces offer a wide diversity of markets, such as computers, education, food, health, hobbies, and repair. One can then imagine services on Helpouts ranging from health consultations and fitness classes to appliance repair support and cooking lessons.

Education is clearly one of the important categories for Google, as it is well-suited for video delivery. Google is partnering with several other well-known brands (e.g., One Medical Group, Sears, Weight Watchers, and Alliance Française) to offer education services related to existing product and service offerings. Google is also supporting collaborative services for smaller individual merchants and individuals such as yoga instructors and personal trainers who can offer services either for free or paid.

Google's offerings are tremendously expanding the traditional barriers of offering live services, because of the removal of the constraint of physical proximity—for example, a French tutor in Paris offering language training to students in China, a yoga instructor in Los Angeles offering classes to housebound seniors in Arizona, or a plumber in Ohio walking a homeowner through a toilet repair in Indiana.

Google's dominance in its core search and AdWords business is a natural fit for integrating the act of individuals and businesses searching for products and services to online video recommendations and advice on product purchases, installation, and use. This capability may help Google stem the trend of individuals increasingly turning to Amazon for product information and reviews.

It is not only Google's dominance but its technical sophistication in the underlying search algorithms and its advertising sophistication that give it an upper hand when competing with the reach and proficiency of smaller collaborative consumption start-ups (e.g., LiveNinja, PowHow, Live Moka, InstaEdu, Shmoop). Other collaborative consumption start-ups such as Angie's List, Udemy, Skillshare, TaskRabbit, CreativeLive, and Curious may have less overlap with Google's initial core collaborative marketplace, but still there is an overlap of common elements that Google could compete against.[3]

Quantified Self

Quantified self (QS) is a trend to use technology to collect information about an individual's daily life. This includes inputs to one's body, physical and emotional states, and physical and mental relative performance. Examples of inputs could range from a person's diet to the air one breathes. Examples of emotional states could range from mood to blood oxygen levels. Examples of performance could range from conventional subject matter tests to running a marathon. Many of these inputs are voluntarily shared by the individual with purposes ranging from pure socialization to needing guidance to improve the quality of the inputs. Quantified self utilizes technology that enables self-monitoring or self-sensing incorporating wearable sensors (e.g., EEG, ECG, video). Another more holistic quantified self approach that incorporates wearable computing capabilities is known as "life-logging."

The opportunity for businesses is to tap into the quantified self movement with product and service relevancy. The key will be to develop utilities or rewards to the users of quantified self technology that will motivate them to share their performance data in exchange for added benefits to them. This intimate set of performance behavioral data that is generated by quantified self devices will be shared at the discretion of the consumer who is using these devices. For the appropriate business, this could be a real-time stream of actual behavioral data that the business could utilize to improve its products or simply maximize its current performance. The key will be to add sufficient motivating utility that prompts a consumer to unlock this intimate, real-time data.

The following are some examples of quantified self devices and applications:

- **Fitbit.** Fitbit is a device to track an individual's physical activity awake or asleep. Individuals can wear the device all day because it is portable enough to fit in pockets, pants, shirts, or bra, or on the wrist when lying down or asleep. The data is automatically collected when the device is near a wireless device. The display has various visualization choices for physical and sleep activity. Individuals can also view their data on their new mobile website. Fitbit can also track an individual's diet as well as exercise and weight.
- **Digifit.** The Digifit ecosystem is a full suite of Apple apps that record heart rate, pace, speed, cadence, and power of your running, cycling, and other athletic endeavors. Data can be uploaded to the well-established training sites Training Peaks and New Leaf. The ecosystem is split up into the Digifit, iCardio, iRunner, iBiker, iSpinner, and iPower apps. To utilize the full functionality of the app, you must purchase the Digifit Connect ANT+ dongle and an advanced functionality app.
- **MoodPanda.** MoodPanda.com is a mood tracking website and iPhone app. Tracking is very simple: You rate your happiness on a 0 to 10 scale, and optionally add a brief Twitter-like comment on what's influencing your mood. MoodPanda is also a large community of friendly people, sharing their moods, celebrating each other's happiness, and supporting each other when they're down.
- **MoodScope.** MoodScope is a web-based application for measuring, tracking, and sharing your mood. Moods are measured using an online card game, and can be shared automatically by e-mail with friends, with the idea that these activities can raise mood in and of themselves.

The mood log can be charted to see progressions and as a way to identify events that may have influenced your mood.

- **Zeo personal sleep coach.** This consists of a wireless headband, bedside display, set of online analytical tools, and an e-mail-based personalized sleep coaching program.
- **RunKeeper.** RunKeeper is a mobile application available on iPhone and Android to track your runs: distance, duration, speed, and calories consumed. The mobile application uses GPS to measure your distance. It also has several features to motivate you to run: (1) you can preset exercise intervals and distances; (2) it allows you to listen to music while running; (3) a voice informs you about the progress of your run; and (4) it stores a history of your runs. The mobile interface shows you a list of your runs, while the website has fitness reports with visualizations of your runs.
- **Momento.** Momento is an iPhone journal writing app. It allows you to make entries using text or photos, and enables you to tag them with people from your address book and locations from the GPS as well as category tags. In addition to what you capture on the phone itself, the app can automatically include events from web services, including Twitter, Facebook, Flickr, and others. Any web service that provides an RSS or Atom feed can be included. The app also has export and backup features.
- **DailyMile.** DailyMile is social workout-sharing site geared toward currently active people who want to give and get encouragement from the community. Users can add workouts manually—with photos and videos—or upload workouts from devices. Workouts will automatically be mapped. DailyMile integrates with Garmin devices, Nike+, iPhone, and Android. DailyMile syncs easily with Twitter and Facebook. Signup is free. Users can easily see others' workouts and post encouragement, similar to commenting on friends' posts on Facebook.
- **Klout.** Klout is a metric for overall online influence. Klout gives a score ranging from 1 to 100, with higher scores representing a wider and stronger sphere of influence online. Klout uses over 35 variables on Facebook and Twitter to measure True Reach (the size of your engaged audience, including only active accounts), Amplification Probability (the likelihood that your content will be commented on or retweeted), and Network Score (the influence level of your engaged audience).[4]
- **Bellabeat.** Enables expectant mothers to share their unborn babies' heartbeats and experience with friends, family, and other future moms.
- **Basis—fitness tracker, sleep analytics.** Basis captures critical aspects of individual sleep: REM sleep, deep sleep, light sleep, tossing and turning, interruptions, and duration. To help the individual understand the implications of the sleep qualities, Basis provides a personalized sleep

dashboard with a summary of the sleep metrics as well as a Sleep Score to benchmark sleep quality.

■ **Sony's life-tracking Core.** Sony's Core is focused on tracking a health-conscious individual's activity. It integrates with the individual's social entertainment activities as well. Core tracks such things as how long an individual sleeps, his or her photos, as well as the music listened to. Core also tracks how often an individual interacts with particular friends. Core sends sensor data updates to the individual's phone, which is mashed together with social and entertainment information as part of Sony's life-logging package.

■ **Sensoria's new smart sock.** Sensoria Fitness smart sock tracks in real time an individual's activity type and level, pace, cadence, stride length, distance, calories burned, and how well an individual exercises; it coaches runners in real time.

■ **The Dash.** Consisting of wearable fitness sensors built into an individual's existing headphones, the Dash is a pair of Bluetooth in-ear headphones that also provides performance tracking via built-in health and body sensors. The Dash has passive noise cancellation, pass-through audio transparency, and an ear bone transduction microphone that eliminates background interference. The Dash works with a connected smartphone or the Dash's built-in four gigabytes of storage to load songs directly. It also is a full activity tracker, with built-in heart rate, oxygen saturation, and energy-expenditure monitoring.

■ **Stir Kinetic Desk.** The Stir Kinetic Desk is a desk that moves with the individual as he or she works at the desk. Go from a seated to a standing position with a simple double tap on the touch screen. The Stir Kinetic Desk's software adapts to the individuals workstyle and knows when the individual arrives, stands, and burns extra calories. It also learns about the individuals patterns and preferences. In its active mode, the Whisperbreath feature gradually moves the desk up and down. It also invites the individual to change positions. It also has a subtle, tactile reminder to breathe deeply.

■ **Lumo Back—posture-saving device.** Lumo Back is a posture and activity sensor. It monitors an individual's posture and coaches the individual to improve posture throughout the day. It is worn comfortably underneath or over clothes. The sensor gently vibrates when the individual slouches. When synchronized with a compatible mobile device (e.g., smartphone), Lumo Back tracks the individual's daily activities such as steps taken, time spent sitting, calories burned, as well as sleep habits.

■ **MyFitnessPal.** A MyFitnessPal.com account gives individuals access to a food and exercise database so they can log in their food and exercise. The searchable food database has over 3,932,000 food items. Individuals can create their own personal food database by adding their own foods and recipes. They can log in not only their meals but also their exercise. There also are discussion forums to learn from others, share tips, and receive and give encouragement. Individuals can also create a personalized diet profile customized to their weight loss goals. My-FitnessPal also supports popular diets such as Atkins, the South Beach Diet, and the Zone.

- **Trace.** An action sports motion tracker with app for quantified-self surfers, skaters, and skiers, Trace works with sophisticated GPS and inertia sensors all tied into AlpineReplay, the largest network of skiers and snowboarders on the web with 43 countries, 1,400+ resorts, 460,000 ski days, and 5.1 billion feet of vertical jumping with over 2.5 million jumps. Trace's algorithms calculate speed, distance, jump height, and rotation. Individuals can then post their statistics on leaderboards to compare their performances against those of friends or anyone else in the world (i.e., Fitbit for extreme sports).[5]
- **Prep Pad.** This kitchen scale connects to an iPod via Bluetooth to provide individuals with their food's nutritional value. The individual places the food on the 9-inch pad, enters the type of food by either selecting it (can be voice-activated) or scanning it via a bar code. The Prep Pad will compare the nutritional value of the food in question with USDA recommendations and the individual's personal diet plan settings.
- **Lapka Organic.** This USB-shaped block contains a probe that measures the level of nitrates in an individual's food to determine if it was produced organically or with synthetic fertilizers. The iOS app communicates to the individual how acceptable (or not) the levels of nitrates are.
- **HAPIfork.** This smart fork monitors how fast an individual eats, vibrating and lighting up when you take too many bites in too little time. If you're really into tracking, you can plug the utensil into your computer to synchronize your information to a full web dashboard.
- **TellSpec.** This device will detect allergens by simply waving it over the food and will also read nutrients, calories, and ingredients in foods and beverages.

Many of these examples can also be categorized as wearable technology.

Wearable Technology

Wearable technology, wearable devices, tech togs, or fashion electronics are clothing and accessories incorporating computer and advanced electronic technologies. The designs often incorporate practical functions and features, but may also have a purely critical or aesthetic agenda.

Wearable technology is related to ubiquitous computing—ever-present technology that is interwoven in everyday life and frictionless in any interaction or transaction.[6]

The opportunity for businesses is similar to that of the quantified self movement. The key will be to develop utilities or rewards to the users of wearable technology that will encourage them to share their activity data in exchange for added benefits to them. Whether it is personal biorhythms or workout performance, this type of data would be invaluable to many businesses that are trying to either improve their product development, optimize their current use of the product, or simply improve the experience of the product. Particularly for experience improvement, the nature of a real-time data feed would be invaluable to optimize a product's effectiveness and experience.

The major categories for wearable technology are smart watches, cameras, e-textiles and clothing, mHealth (mobile health), fitness and activity trackers, and augmented reality (AR) glasses.

There has been a continually increasing number of wearable technology companies, many of which are well-known brands such as Adidas, Boston Scientific, Eurotech, Fitbit, Garmin, Google, Jabra, Jawbone, Johnson & Johnson, Medtronic, Meta Watch, Motorola Solutions, Nike, Pebble, Plantronics, Polar Electro, Recon Instruments, Samsung, Sony, and Zephyr Technology.

Table 7.1 is a more complete list of the proliferation of wearable technology companies.

The calculator watch, introduced in the 1980s, was one original piece of widespread worn electronics.

Mobile Health

The widespread adoption and use of mobile technologies is creating tremendous opportunities to improve an individual's health and health care in general. Health professionals are finding consumer-driven mobile health to be more engaging and less costly. The utility for intentionally sharing their health information is clear—it enables people to lead healthier lives and be more engaged as a patient in their medical treatments.

Mobile medical applications (MMAs) can help individuals manage their own health and wellness, encourage healthy lifestyles, and enable access to individuals' own medical information when and wherever they need it.

According to industry estimates, 500 million smartphone owners globally will be using a health care application by 2015. By 2018, 50 percent of the expected 3.4 billion smartphone and tablet owners will have downloaded mobile health applications. These individuals include health care professionals, consumers, and patients.[7]

TABLE 7.1 WEARABLE TECHNOLOGY COMPANIES

Clothing/Footwear/Glasses

Adidas	Fairytale Fashion
Aetrex	Fantich and Young
Agent of Presence	Fashioning Technology
Alina Designs	Fibretronic
Alphyn Industries	FIFT
Apira Science	Figtree Factory Studios
Bagir	Firebox
Baidu	Fraunhofer IPMS
Bergans	fūl
Biodevices	GlowFur
BIOTEX	Go Gloves
Black Milk	Halston
Blacksocks	hi-Fun
BladeRunner	Hot Pop Factory
Bogner	Hyginex
Boost Products	Infineon
Brando Workshop	Innovega
Brother	IntelligentM
BS-Glow	Interactive Wear AG
Burton	Inventables
Celio	io
Chrome Industries	Jezign
Columbia	Kenpo
Conergy	Klymit
Conscious Clothing	Koyono
Continuum Fashion	Laser Laces
Craft Technology Group	Levelwear
CuteCircuit	Levis
Dano	Lodenfrey
Diana Lin Design	Loop.pH
Dior	Lost Values
Ditto	LumiGram
DNA2Diamonds	Luminex
Dope+Drakkar	Lux et Deco
Dots Gloves	Machina
Dropshades	Macy's
Dunhill	Maplin
Enlightened	Marchon3D
EroGear	Marks & Spencer
Evolved Footwear	Max Virtual

(continued)

TABLE 7.1 (*Continued*)

Micro'be' Fermented Fashion	Ross + Doell
Mobile Warming Gear	Rothco
Moondial	Roxy
Music and Sons	Sakku
Myvu	Scott-E-Vest
Nalini	SenseBridge
Nieuwe Heren	Sessions
Noon Solar	ShadowTS
Nordic Gear	Shady Beats
Norrøna Lofoten	Shieldex
Novonic	Simpack
Nvidia	Smart Fabrics
NYX Clothing	Smart PJ's
Nyx Devices	SmartLife Technology
O'Neill	SMI
O2	Solarc
Oakley	Solas Fashion
Olympus	SOLE Footwear
ONO Running	SolePower
Orange UK	Solid Gray
Orbital Outfitters	Soyntec
Patagonia	StrideLite
PDD	Studio 5050
Pensar	Studio Roosegaarde
Pivothead	Studio Swine
PixelOptics	Sunload
Polaroid	SunnyCam
Pratesi	Swany
QIO Systems	Syte Shirt
Quirky	Targus
Quute Illumina	TeamLab
RallyPoint	Technical Illusions
Ray Kingston Inc.	Telepathy One
RealD	Texsys
Reebok	Thanko
Regal	ThinkGeek
Replay	Timbuk2
Republic	ToBe Technology
Re-Timer	Tobii
Reware	Triumph International
Rosner	T-Sketch

TABLE 7.1 (*Continued*)

Tumi	Gotwind
UniFirst	Headflat
Uranium	Hointer
Urban Tool	iHome
V-Dimension	iLoveHandles
VectraSense	IMEC
Vergence Labs	Incipio
Voltage	Indiegogo
Wearable Tech Expo	Instagram
Westcomb	International Fashion Machines
Wool & Prince	Intertech Pira
Woolrich	iPazzPort
Wrangler	iWorm
XS-Labs	iZettle
Zeal	Kanguru
Zegna	KeyGlove
ZionEyez	Klingg
	Konarka
Components	Lambda Labs
AEGLO	Lion Hound Technology
Ainste	Livescribe
AnyGlove	MakerBot
AOptix	Mbient Lab
Autodesk Research	Microcontinuum
BagJack	Microvision
BEARTek	Mobis
Belkin	Nanomars
Bitbanger Labs	Odersun AG
Cell-Mate	Pentax
Chaotic Moon	Peratech
Clear Blue Hawaii	Pharad
CommBadge	Photojojo
Double Robotics	Plantronics
EcoXGear	Powerbag
Eleksen	ROHM
Eurotech	Sinch
Everquest Design	SmartWallit
Fitright Industrial	SolarShopper
Genius	TerraCycle
Global Solar	Top Floor
GoPad	Variable Technologies

(*continued*)

TABLE 7.1 (*Continued*)

Verbatim	Finis
Versetta	Fitbit
Voltaic	Fitbug
VoyVoy	Flat-D
Wacom	Frog Design
WEEL Technologies	Gadgets
Xsens	Garmin
Zeiss	GeoPalz
	Glowdoggie
Gaming/Augmented Reality/	Goose Design
Virtual Reality	Grathio Labs
Aiken Labs	Green Goose
ARAIG	HAPILABS
ASTRO Gaming	Haruyama Trading Company
Atheer	Heapsylon
Hasbro	HeartMath
Oculus	Hexoskin
Peregrine	Hitachi
Thalmic Labs	Honda
Thought Technology	Huggies
TN Games	Instep Nanopower
Vuzix	Intellego Technologies
XpanD	InteraXon
Zappar	i-Rule
	Jawbone
Fitness/Health/Pets	Ki Fit
Affectiva	Kinsa
Alivecor	Koga
Amiigo	Lark
Basis	LUMO BodyTech
Blazewyygear	MC10
BlueQ Wireless	Ministry of Supply
BodyMedia	Mio
Byte Works	Misfit Wearables
Cambridge Concepts	New York Times
Codoon	Nintendo
Crave	NuMetrex
Dew Motion	Oxford Metrics Group
Dreamtrap	Parlee Cycles
Durex	Pavegen
electricfoxy	Perfect Third

TABLE 7.1 (*Continued*)

Phyode	Hercules
Polar	iLogic
Polar Electro	iTreq
Proteus Digital Health	iWorld
Ridogulous	Jaybird
Sakakibara-Kikai	Jays
Sanyo	KEF
Scosche	Klipsch
ShaveTech	Lifepod
Snaptracs	Liquid Image
Somnus	Looxcie
SSI America	Lullabelly
Tecnalia	Marshall
Textronics	Memoto
Tomorrow Incorporated	Monster
Under Armour	Nokia
Varvara	NXT
Volt Heat	Perfusion Technology
Wellcore	Philips
Withings	PlayButton
Zansors	Rampant Gear
Zeo	Sensorcom
	Singbox
Headphones/Media Players/Cameras	Skullcandy
Aftershokz	Sleepsonic
Beats by Dre	SOL Republic
BiGR Audio	Sonic Impact
Boomphones	Sony
Bose	Sound Asleep
Bowers & Wilkins	SoundBrace
Cardiio	Sprayway
Cowon	Stressed and Depressed
Cozy Tunes	Turtle Beach
Denon	Ultrasone
Epson Moverio	V.I.O.
Fadigear	V-Moda
FlashWear	
GoPro	**Medical**
GRO Design	Argo Medical
G-Tech	Asahi Kasei
Halo	Asthmapolis

(*continued*)

TABLE 7.1 (*Continued*)

Avery Dennison	Tanizawa
Axio	Taser
Bebionic	TitanArm
Berkeley Bionics	Ugobe
Bionic Vision Australia	VIKING
BTS Bioengineering	Zephyr
Cyberdyne	
Ekso Bionics	**Multiple Offerings**
Emotiv	Adafruit Industries
Equipois	Brookstone
FIK	Budweiser
First Warning Systems	Canon
Focus Labs	Casio
GTX Corp	Crescent
iRhythm	Disney
Med Sensation	Eton
NeuroFocus	Fujitsu
Neurosky	Gadgets and Gear
Neurowear	Google
NewYu	Hammacher Schlemmer
PLX	iKey
ReSound	iMainGo
Second Sight	Kickstarter
Silent Call	Kopin
Sonitus Medical	La Tete Au Cube
Sotera Wireless	LG
SRI	Microsoft
Touch Bionics	Motorola
Venture Heated Clothing	Motorola
	NASA
Military/Law Enforcement/Safety	NEC
Agilite	Nike
AKKA	NXT
Amendment II	Vodaphone
BAE Systems	Walmart
Civil Rights Defenders	
Elbit Systems	**Sports**
General Dynamics	Active Mind Technology
Hyperstealth	Alago
Lockheed Martin	aquapulse
Skeletonics	Camelbak

TABLE 7.1 (*Continued*)

Chaval Response	Xara
Cool Shirt	Zanier
Craghoppers	
Danfoss PolyPower A/S	**Watches**
Eclipse Solar Gear	Acer
EXO2	Agent Watches
Gears	Alfred Dunhill
Gerbing	Allerta
GolfSense	Apple
High Sierra	Bia
Hövding	Breitling
Instabeat	Cabestan
Jansport	Cadence
Kombi Sports	Central Standard Time
M-BOYE	Chinavasion
Navispace AG	Citizen
NLO Moto	Cookoo
Noxgear	defakto
O-range	Devon Works
Osiris	Emopulse
Pearl Izumi	Fonderie 47
Picard	Fossil
POC	Foxconn
Quiksilver	Futaba
Reevu	GEAK
REI	Hallmark
Reusch	Harry Winston
Rip Curl	HEX
Sensosolutions	Hoptroff
Siemens	House of Marley
SmartSwim	HP
Solestrom Swimwear	Hublot
spnKIX	I'm Watch
Spyder	inPulse
Surfanic	Kaventsmann
Toast	Kempler & Strauss
Tourmaster	Limmex
VAUDE	Meta Watch
Velocomp	Mr Jones Watches
Volcom	Mr Jones Watches
WarmX	Mutewatch

(*continued*)

TABLE 7.1 (*Continued*)

Neumitra	Timex
NZN Labs	Tokyoflash
Pebble	TomTom
Phosphor	Urwerk
Plastic Logic	Vachen
Razer	VEA
Romain Jerome	Vigil Monitoring
Royale	WearIT
Runtastic	Whatever Works
Samsung	WIMM
Seiko	Xylobands
Sprout	Ziiiro
Suunto	Zoomboard
Swap	ZShock

The range of mobile apps continues to grow for health professionals, with applications ranging from radiation emergency medical management (REMM), which gives health care providers guidance on diagnosing and treating radiation injuries, to two other mobile medical apps that can assist in diagnosing cancer or heart rhythm abnormalities. There are also medical apps that could function as a central command for a glucose meter used by an insulin-dependent diabetic patient.

The real benefit to consumers is that they can continue to live their daily lives while health care practitioners and researchers can do real-time monitoring of their vital signs as well as directly providing care.

Whereas the initial mobile health initiatives were focused on the industrialized nations, the rapid increase in mobile phone penetration in lower-income nations has opened up a tremendous opportunity to extend greater health care and guidance to a larger segment of developing countries.

The following are examples of mobile health applications:

- Help patients with diagnosed psychiatric conditions:
  - For example, post-traumatic stress disorder (PTSD), depression, anxiety, obsessive compulsive disorder.
  - Maintain behavioral coping skills by providing a "skill of the day" behavioral technique or audio messages that the user can access when experiencing increased anxiety.
- Provide educational information, reminders, or motivational guidance to smokers trying to quit, patients recovering from addiction, or pregnant women.

- Alert (GPS enabled) asthmatics of environmental conditions that may cause asthma symptoms, or alert an addiction patient (substance abusers) when near a pre-identified high-risk location.
- Motivate patients using video and video games to do their physical therapy exercises at home.
- Prompt individuals to enter which herb and drug they would like to take concurrently, and provide information about a summary of what type of interaction was reported.
- Help asthmatics track inhaler usage, asthma episodes experienced, location of user at the time of an attack, or environmental triggers of asthma attacks.
- Prompt individuals to manually enter symptomatic, behavioral, or environmental information, the specifics of which are predefined by a health care provider, and store the information for later review.
- Provide patient-specific screening, counseling, and preventive recommendations from well-known and established authorities based on patient characteristics such as age, sex, and behavioral risk factors.
- Use checklist of common signs and symptoms to provide a list of possible medical conditions and advice on when to consult a health care provider.
- Guide individuals through a questionnaire of signs and symptoms to provide a recommendation for the type of health care facility most appropriate to their needs.
- Record the clinical conversation a clinician has with a patient, and send it to the patient to access after the visit.
- Allow individuals to initiate a prespecified nurse call or emergency call using broadband or cellular phone technology.
- Enable individuals or caregivers to create and send an alert or general emergency notification to first responders.
- Keep track of medications and provide patient-configured reminders for improved medication adherence.
- Provide individuals with a portal into their own health information—that is, access to information captured during a previous clinical visit or historical trending and comparison of vital signs (e.g., body temperature, heart rate, blood pressure, or respiratory rate).
- Aggregate and display trends in personal health incidents (e.g., hospitalization rates or alert notification rates).
- Enable individuals to collect blood pressure data and share this data through e-mail, track and trend it, or upload it to a personal or electronic health record.
- Provide oral health reminders or tracking tools for individuals with gum disease.
- Provide prediabetes patients with guidance or tools to help them develop better eating habits or increase physical activity.

- Display images or other messages in a timely fashion for a substance abuser who wants to stop addictive behavior.
- Individuals can log, record, track, evaluate, or make decisions or behavioral suggestions related to developing or maintaining general fitness, health, or wellness, such as those that promote or encourage healthy eating, exercise, weight loss, or other activities generally related to a healthy lifestyle or wellness.
- Provide dietary logs, offer calorie counters, or make dietary suggestions.
- Provide meal planners and recipes.
- Track general daily activities or make exercise or posture suggestions.
- Track a normal baby's sleeping and feeding habits.
- Actively monitor and trend exercise activity.
- Help healthy people track the quantity or quality of their normal sleep patterns.
- Provide and track scores from mind-challenging games or generic "brain age" tests.
- Provide daily motivational tips (e.g., via text or other types of messaging) to reduce stress and promote a positive mental outlook.
- Use social gaming to encourage healthy lifestyle habits.
- Calculate calories burned in a workout.
- Track or manage patient immunizations by assessing the need for immunization, consent form, and immunization lot number.
- Provide drug-drug interactions and relevant safety information: side effects, active ingredient as a report based on demographic data (age, gender), clinical information (current diagnosis), and current medications.
- Enable health care provider (during visit) to access patient's personal health records that are hosted on either a web-based or other platform.[8]

Internet of Things

The Internet of Things (IoT) is the new environment where everyday objects can be connected to the Internet and participate together on an interconnected system. Cisco estimates that 50 billion devices and objects will be connected to the Internet by 2020.[9] When consumers connect their everyday objects to the Internet of Things, a tremendous opportunity exists both for the consumer and for the business that manufactures those everyday objects. At the consumers' discretion, they can share an array of important information about the functionality as well as experience higher utility with value-added services that the manufacturer could provide if connected. The business could collect an array of highly valuable operational data from the devices as well as extend their value proposition with value-added utility. This information exchange can extend also to governments, education, finance, and transportation.

Utility can also extend past the stovepipes of vertical industries and organizations to bring a higher aggregate utility to all parties involved. Instead of a fire alarm emitting just a localized beep, the fire alarm could turn off the gas supply to your home or gas appliances while emitting a parallel alarm to your home, mobile phones, local fire department, and alarm manufacturer.[10]

- Our physical bodies (connected sensors):
  - Check babies or children (e.g., http://mimobaby.com/).
  - Give medication reminders (e.g., www.vitality.net/glowcaps.html).
  - Track physical activity (e.g., https://www.alohar.com/developer/learnmore.html).
  - Optimize medication effectiveness (e.g., www.proteus.com/).
  - Monitor aging family members (e.g., http://beclose.com/beclosesystem.aspx).
  - Minimize on-site doctor's visits (e.g., www.preventice.com/products/bodyguardian/).
- Our homes (monitor and manage to reduce monthly bills and resource usage):
  - Improve heating efficiency.
  - Monitor status of appliances (e.g., Is the oven off?).
  - Find lost personal items (e.g., car keys, glasses, mobile phones).
  - Provide more effective and efficient home lighting.
  - Provide alerts for disasters (e.g., basement flooding).
  - Manage houseplants' watering and nourishment.
- Our cities (engage with data produced from cities and neighborhoods):
  - Provide more efficient waste removal.
  - Find places and parking more quickly.
  - Give pollution warning alerts.
  - Use electricity more efficiently.
  - Achieve streetlight efficiencies.
  - Individuals share knowledge back to cities and neighborhoods.
- Businesses (optimize operations, boost productivity, and save in resources and costs):
  - Improve maintenance and repair.
  - Predict versus real-time monitoring.
  - Monitor critical assets.
  - Monitor critical safety equipment.
  - Monitor manufacturing quality and consistency.
- Environment (more effectively managing our environment):
  - Monitor pollution levels.
  - Track water quality and consumption.
  - Protect wildlife more effectively.
  - Receive advanced warnings on physical disasters.

- Monitor environmental variables.
- Monitor damaging and illegal environmental acts (e.g., poaching and deforestation).[11]

In an industrial context, the Internet of Things has far-reaching economic implications. A report by General Electric on industrial applications for intelligent machines says that efficiency gains for systems of just 1 percent could result in 15-year savings of:

- $30 billion worth of jet fuel for the airline industry
- $63 billion in global health care savings with more optimized treatments, patient flows, and equipment use in hospitals
- $66 billion savings in fuel consumption for the global gas-fired power plant fleet[12]

Triangulated Personal Information

The Internet of Things is not just about connecting devices; it is also about having those connected devices collaborate and interact. Examples of companies focused on this type of collaboration are Sen.se, Arduino, and ThingWorx3, and there are others. The objective is to allow consumers to easily retrieve knowledge and functionality of things on a day-to-day basis without sitting at a computer or querying a human being. This is the vision of ubiquitous computing that would ultimately extend to every home, car, business, building, and system around the world.

Ultimately the Internet of Things will allow one or a series of triangulating physical objects to create extreme utility for the individual (e.g., alarm clock, coffee brewing, shower time, public transit schedule, personal address, home temperature).[13]

The triangulation of personal information ushers in a new dimension of directly sharing that information with the goal of making an individual's life easier as well as potentially providing financial rewards in exchange for a business increasing its insights and efficiencies.

Sensor Technology

Sensor technology is rapidly evolving to become part of a consumer's everyday life. As the consumer's life gets increasingly more digitized, sensors will be at the heart of the transformation. The majority of the information that is generated by the sensors will ultimately be shared at the discretion of the consumer. As consumers become increasingly engulfed in sensor technology as a vehicle to better their lives, businesses will have an unparalleled opportunity to understand a consumer's life in intimate detail if the consumer feels that sharing this sensor data will make life easier and at the same time feels safe about the information he or she is sharing. If a snapshot is taken of the current sensor technology of today, the following list provides a small glimpse into just the beginning of what sensor technology can capture and communicate.

Acoustics, Sound, Vibration
- Geophone
- Hydrophone
- Lace Sensor (a guitar pickup)
- Microphone
- Seismometer

Automotive, Transportation
- Air–fuel ratio meter
- Blind spot monitor
- Crankshaft position sensor
- Curb feeler, used to warn driver of curbs
- Defect detector, used on railroads to detect axle and signal problems in passing trains
- Engine coolant temperature (ECT) sensor, used to measure the engine temperature
- Hall effect sensor, used to time the speed of wheels and shafts
- Manifold absolute pressure (MAP) sensor, used in regulating fuel metering
- Mass flow sensor, or mass airflow (MAF) sensor, used to tell the engine control unit (ECU) the mass of air entering the engine
- Oxygen sensor, used to monitor the amount of oxygen in the exhaust
- Parking sensors, used to alert the driver of unseen obstacles during parking maneuvers
- Radar gun, used to detect the speed of other objects
- Speedometer, used to measure the instantaneous speed of a land vehicle
- Speed sensor, used to detect the speed of an object
- Throttle position sensor, used to monitor the position of the throttle in an internal combustion engine
- Tire-pressure monitoring sensor, used to monitor the air pressure inside tires
- Torque sensor, torque transducer, or torque meter, used to measure torque (twisting force) on a rotating system.
- Transmission fluid temperature sensor, used to measure the temperature of the transmission fluid

- Turbine speed sensor (TSS) or input speed sensor (ISS), used to measure the rotational speed of the input shaft or torque converter
- Variable reluctance sensor, used to measure position and speed of moving metal components
- Vehicle speed sensor (VSS), used to measure the speed of the vehicle
- Water sensor or water-in-fuel sensor, used to indicate the presence of water in fuel
- Wheel speed sensor, used for reading the speed of a vehicle's wheel rotation

Chemical
- Breathalyzer
- Carbon dioxide sensor
- Carbon monoxide detector
- Catalytic bead sensor
- Chemical field-effect transistor
- Electrochemical gas sensor
- Electronic nose
- Electrolyte–insulator–semiconductor sensor
- Fluorescent chloride sensors
- Holographic sensor
- Hydrocarbon dew point analyzer
- Hydrogen sensor
- Hydrogen sulfide sensor
- Infrared point sensor
- Ion-selective electrode
- Microwave chemistry sensor
- Nitrogen oxide sensor
- Nondispersive infrared sensor
- Olfactometer
- Optode
- Oxygen sensor
- Ozone monitor
- Pellistor
- pH glass electrode
- Potentiometric sensor
- Redox electrode
- Smoke detector
- Zinc oxide nanorod sensor

Electric Current, Electric Potential, Magnetic, Radio
- Current sensor
- Daly detector

- Electroscope
- Electron multiplier
- Faraday cup
- Galvanometer
- Hall effect sensor
- Hall probe
- Magnetic anomaly detector
- Magnetometer
- Micro-Electro-Mechanical Systems (MEMS) magnetic field sensor
- Metal detector
- Planar Hall sensor
- Radio direction finder
- Voltage detector

Environment, Weather, Moisture, Humidity

- Actinometer
- Bedwetting alarm
- Ceilometer
- Dew warning
- Electrochemical gas sensor
- Fish counter
- Frequency domain sensor
- Gas detector
- Hook gauge evaporimeter
- Humistor
- Hygrometer
- Leaf sensor
- Pyranometer
- Pyrgeometer
- Psychrometer
- Rain gauge
- Rain sensor
- Seismometers
- Snow Telemetry (SNOTEL)
- Snow gauge
- Soil moisture sensor
- Stream gauge
- Tide gauge

Flow, Fluid Velocity

- Airflow meter
- Anemometer
- Flow sensor

- Gas meter
- Mass flow sensor
- Water meter

Ionizing Radiation, Subatomic Particles
- Bubble chamber
- Cloud chamber
- Geiger counter
- Neutron detector
- Particle detector
- Scintillation counter
- Scintillator
- Wire chamber

Navigation Instruments
- Airspeed indicator
- Altimeter
- Attitude indicator
- Depth gauge
- Fluxgate compass
- Gyroscope
- Inertial navigation system
- Inertial reference unit
- Magnetic compass
- Magnetohydrodynamic (MHD) sensor
- Ring laser gyroscope
- Turn coordinator
- Variometer
- Vibrating structure gyroscope
- Yaw rate sensor

Position, Angle, Displacement, Distance, Speed, Acceleration
- Accelerometer
- Auxanometer
- Capacitive displacement sensor
- Capacitive sensing
- Free fall sensor
- Gravimeter
- Gyroscopic sensor
- Inclinometer
- Integrated circuit piezoelectric sensor
- Laser rangefinder
- Laser surface velocimeter

- Light detection and ranging (LIDAR)
- Linear encoder
- Linear variable differential transformer (LVDT)
- Liquid capacitive inclinometers
- Odometer
- Photoelectric sensor
- Piezoelectric accelerometer
- Position sensor
- Rate sensor
- Rotary encoder
- Rotary variable differential transformer
- Selsyn
- Tachometer
- Tilt sensor
- Ultrasonic thickness gauge
- Variable reluctance sensor
- Velocity receiver

Optical, Light, Imaging, Photon
- Charge-coupled device
- Colorimeter
- Contact image sensor
- Electro-optical sensor
- Flame detector
- Infrared sensor
- Kinetic inductance detector
- LED as light sensor
- Light-addressable potentiometric sensor
- Nichols radiometer
- Fiber-optic sensors
- Optical position sensor
- Photodetector
- Photodiode
- Photomultiplier tubes
- Phototransistor
- Photoelectric sensor
- Photoionization detector
- Photomultiplier
- Photoresistor
- Photoswitch
- Phototube
- Scintillometer
- Shack-Hartmann

- Single-photon avalanche diode
- Superconducting nanowire single-photon detector
- Transition edge sensor
- Visible light photon counter
- Wavefront sensor

Pressure
- Barograph
- Barometer
- Boost gauge
- Bourdon gauge
- Hot filament ionization gauge
- Ionization gauge
- McLeod gauge
- Oscillating U-tube
- Permanent downhole gauge
- Piezometer
- Pirani gauge
- Pressure gauge
- Pressure sensor
- Tactile sensor
- Time pressure gauge

Force, Density, Level
- Bhangmeter
- Force gauge
- Force sensor
- Hydrometer
- Level sensor
- Load cell
- Magnetic level gauge
- Nuclear density gauge
- Piezoelectric sensor
- Strain gauge
- Torque sensor
- Viscometer

Thermal, Heat, Temperature
- Bolometer
- Bimetallic strip
- Calorimeter
- Exhaust gas temperature gauge
- Flame detection

- Gardon gauge
- Golay cell
- Heat flux sensor
- Infrared thermometer
- Microbolometer
- Microwave radiometer
- Net radiometer
- Pyrometer
- Quartz thermometer
- Resistance temperature detector
- Resistance thermometer
- Silicon bandgap temperature sensor
- Special sensor microwave/imager
- Temperature gauge
- Thermistor
- Thermocouple
- Thermometer

Proximity, Presence
- Alarm sensor
- Doppler radar
- Motion detector
- Occupancy sensor
- Passive infrared sensor
- Proximity sensor
- Reed switch
- Stud finder
- Touch switch
- Triangulation sensor
- Wired glove

Sensor Technology
- Active pixel sensor
- Back-illuminated sensor
- Biochip
- Biosensor
- Capacitance probe
- Carbon paste electrode
- Catadioptric sensor
- Digital sensors
- Displacement receiver
- Electromechanical film
- Electro-optical sensor

- Fabry–Pérot interferometer
- Fisheries acoustics
- Image sensor
- Image sensor format
- Inductive sensor
- Intelligent sensor
- Lab-on-a-chip
- Leaf sensor
- Machine vision
- Microelectromechanical systems
- Photoelasticity
- Quantum sensor
- Radar
  - Ground-penetrating radar
  - Synthetic aperture radar
- Radar tracker
- Sensor array
- Sensor fusion
- Sensor grid
- Sensor node
- Soft sensor
- Sonar
- Staring array
- Transducer
- Ultrasonic sensor
- Video sensor
- Visual sensor network
- Wheatstone bridge
- Wireless sensor network

Other Sensor Technologies
- Actigraphy
- Analog image processing
- Atomic force microscopy
- Atomic gravitational wave interferometric sensor
- Attitude control (spacecraft)
  - Earth sensor
  - Horizon sensor
  - Sun sensor
- Catadioptric sensor
- Chemoreceptor
- Compressive sensing
- Cryogenic particle detectors

- Dew warning
- Diffusion tensor imaging
- Digital holography
- Electronic tongue
- Fine guidance sensor
- Flat panel detector
- Functional magnetic resonance imaging (fMRI)
- Glass break detector
- Heartbeat sensor
- Hyperspectral sensors
- Interferometric reflectance imaging sensor (IRIS) (biosensor)
- Laser beam profiler
- Littoral airborne sensor/hyperspectral
- Long-range reconnaissance and observation system (LORROS)
- Magnetic resonance imaging (MRI)
- Millimeter wave scanner
- Moire deflectometry
- Molecular sensor
- Nanosensor
- Nano-tetherball sensor
- Omnidirectional camera
- Optical coherence tomography
- Phase unwrapping techniques
- Positron emission tomography
- Push broom scanner
- Quantization (signal processing)
- Range imaging
- Scanning superconducting quantum interference device (SQUID) microscope
- Single-photon emission computed tomography (SPECT)
- Smart dust
- Special sensor microwave imager/sounder (SSMIS)
- Special sensors—ions, electrons, and scintillation (SSIES) thermal plasma analysis package
- Structured-light 3D scanner
- Sun sensor, attitude control (spacecraft)
- Superconducting nanowire single-photon detector
- Superconducting quantum interference device (SQUID)
- Thin-film thickness monitor
- Time-of-flight camera
- Triangulation and LIDAR automated rendezvous and docking (TriDAR)
- Unattended ground sensors[14]

The evolution of sensors into the consumer's life will be inevitable as long as sensors improve the quality of life of the consumer. They will ultimately replace many of a consumer's day-to-day activities such as locking the doors when leaving the home or ordering milk when it is low. They will pervade every aspect of the consumer's life and offer businesses the opportunity for high levels of integration if the discretionary data sharing is viewed by the consumers as making their lives easier and they feel safe sharing their personal sensor-enabled information.

Virtual Reality

Virtual reality (VR) is focused on creating a computer-simulated world that individuals can interact with. The experience goal is to make it difficult for the individual to tell the difference between what is real and what is not. Achieving a successful virtual reality experience is typically done through wearing a virtual reality helmet or goggles, such as Oculus Rift.

More specifically, VR is a virtual environment simulated by a computer that can mimic physical presence in places in the real world or imagined worlds. Most current virtual reality experiences are visual with sound. More advanced "haptic" systems are based on tactile feedback technology using sense of touch by applying forces, vibrations, or motions; the feedback better simulates the target environment. Currently, haptic systems are most common in medical, gaming, and military applications.

The choice of virtual reality environments by consumers opens up a new world of opportunity for businesses to understand the needs and wants of consumers at an entirely new level. When consumers are able to design their desired virtual reality environment and then communicate that to the business, the opportunity for either product development or real-time experience enhancement is significant. It presents a whole new level of understanding consumer intentions and context. As technology evolves in terms of processing power, image resolution, and communication bandwidth, consumers will be able to simulate virtually any environment, which will create new consumer insights and new opportunities for business.

Virtual reality has many different uses in the consumer's world (e.g., creation of motion pictures, displaying fine art, music experience, therapeutic applications, training, manufacturing, and even urban design). The best-known piece of consumer virtual reality is gaming. Typically, virtual reality is delivered through head-mounted displays (HMDs) with several released in the early to mid-1990s (e.g., Virtual Boy by Nintendo, iGlasses by Virtual I-O, Cybermaxx by Victormaxx, and the VFX-1 by Forte Technologies).

As VR evolved, other iterations appeared such as virtuality (gaming) and fairly limited VR systems for video arcades focused on racing, flight, and shooter games, which are still popular today. These types of narrow VR systems only simulate certain aspects of a virtual reality environment. Other examples include Wii Remote, Kinect, and PlayStation Move/PlayStation Eye, which track and send motion input from players through the gaming console.[15]

Today, one of the largest environments for consumer sharing is mobile phones over social networks. Businesses tap into this consumer information sharing to understand and leverage the business opportunities that this creates. Virtual reality may be the platform that consumers use in the future to share over social platforms such as a future iteration of Facebook. Facebook actually purchased the virtual reality headset company Oculus VR for $2 billion in 2014. Facebook regards virtual reality as the major platform of tomorrow for social networking. Facebook CEO Mark Zuckerberg stated, "Mobile is the platform of today, and now we're also getting ready for the platforms of tomorrow." He went on to say that "Oculus has the chance to create the most social platform ever, and change the way we work, play, and communicate."[16] Virtual reality author Mychilo S. Cline predicts that virtual reality will be increasingly integrated into our daily lives as much as performing simple posts on Facebook is now.

Augmented Reality

Augmented reality (AR)'s design goal is to blend virtual reality and real life. Individuals interact with virtual contents in their real world and are able to distinguish between the two worlds.

To distinguish AR from VR, with AR individuals continue to stay in touch with their real world while interacting with introduced virtual objects around them. Individuals using VR are isolated from the real world within a substitute world that is completely digitally fabricated. In their current forms, VR might function more effectively with video games and social networking in a virtual environment (e.g., Second Life, PlayStation Home).

In terms of maturity, augmented reality is marginally ahead of virtual reality, as several AR products already exist in the marketplace. The marketplace has seen an increased number of AR hardware from Google (e.g., Glass), and plans from Microsoft to launch something similar with its $150 million purchase of wearable computing assets.

Relative widespread adoption of both AR and VR may be linked to how well each platform integrates with everyday life. This may give AR a slight commercial advantage because the world that AR provides does not completely remove individuals from their everyday lives.[17]

When businesses apply augmented reality to engage consumers in their product, they create a much more complete picture of the consumer's intent and context. The following are 10 examples of where consumers will voluntarily immerse themselves in a product or service, which will actually provide direct information about how they intend to experience this product in the future. This is a completely new level of direct information input for businesses.

1. **Topshop Kinect dressing rooms.** Typically, physically trying on clothes can be arduous and an unpleasant experience for many consumers. Topshop has partnered with Kinect to create an augmented reality dressing room for consumers. This dressing room allows consumers to virtually try on clothes without having the physical constraints of real-world fittings.

2. **Shisedio makeup mirror.** Many women struggle with finding the right type of makeup for their particular complexions or a particular occasion, coupled with the fact that they can't return makeup after they have tested it. Shisedio's augmented reality makeup mirror captures an image of a consumer's face and then applies its latest cosmetic products to that image.

3. **American Apparel color-changing app.** Clothing retailer American Apparel is known for its colorful product collections, and now has extended that to an augmented reality tool to help consumers find the most relevant product in the most relevant color. Consumers can now scan the item in the store to see the product in different colors as well as read reviews by other consumers who have previously purchased the same item. This represents just the beginning iteration of virtual reality tools that can be used to incentivize consumers to visit physical stores if that is the store's desired outcome.

4. **De Beers "Forevermark Fitting."** Choosing an expensive diamond ring for a loved one can often be a difficult task. "Forevermark Fitting" from De Beers is an augmented reality download that allows consumers to try on De Beers's Forevermark collection virtually to view how different jewelry would look in different types of lighting relative to the consumer's skin tone.

5. **IKEA AR catalog.** IKEA launched an augmented reality catalog to enable consumers to visualize how specific pieces of furniture would look inside their home in the context of their current decor. The app also measures the size of the IKEA products relative to the surrounding room and fixtures to offer a real-world perspective on physical fit in the consumer's home.

6. **Sayduck furniture visualizer.** Sayduck released a similar mobile app that assists consumers in visualizing how its products and fixtures fit

and blend with their current home decor. The app displays the products in question by projecting a digital replica though the camera on a smartphone. The consumer can position the products at different angles to see how a product sits in the home.

7. **IBM AR shopping app.** IBM's research revealed that 58 percent of consumers desire product information in-store before purchasing a product, and 19 percent of consumers will browse mobile devices during shopping. In the context that 92 percent of all retail volume is in-store shopping,[18] consumers expect the same levels of personalization that they experience while shopping online. Scientists at IBM Research are working to achieve this by creating new augmented reality mobile shopping apps that will give in-store consumers instant product details and promotions through their mobile devices.

IBM's new app will provide consumers with a highly relevant shopping experience with real-time product comparisons and special offers as they physically move through the store. In other words, if consumers volunteer their exact physical location in the store, they will receive the utility of product comparisons as well as special offers relative to their real-time product experience.

This AR implementation is accomplished by capturing the images via the video camera on a consumer's smartphone or tablet. The product or row of items is then identified using advanced image processing technologies. Once the product is recognized by the app, the product will be ranked by a set of criteria (e.g., price, nutritional value). The app identifies appropriate loyalty rewards or similar incentives. The app will also be able to suggest other complementary products relative to the product being viewed by the consumer. For example, a consumer who is looking for breakfast cereal could specify a low-sugar cereal that is also highly rated by fellow consumers and is sale priced. As the consumer scans the cereals with the mobile device, the AR shows which cereals meet the criteria as well as relevant financial rewards such as same-day coupons.

In other words, the business offers a situational-specific utility and reward by using directly volunteered personal information from the consumer's smartphone. This is the current and evolving future of AR and directly volunteered personal information, which creates a win-win between business and consumer. On a broader scale, this directly volunteered personal information enables the retailer to better organize products in the store and adjust operational business practices to optimize the consumer experience. IBM's head of retail research, Sima Nadler, suggests, "What we're seeing is the blurring of the physical and the virtual." AR creates the environment that holds the promise for merging online and in-store shopping experiences. AR enables the transformational piece of bringing us from a world where consumers have been classified by broad demographics, which radically limited the extent of shopping personalization. Now, AR's promise for the shopping future will be one where the shopping experience will be a real-time iteration between the exchange of direct personal information and extreme relevance in shopping experience, utility, and reward.[19]

8. **Converse Shoe Sampler.** Converse's Sampler iPhone app applies augmented reality to allow consumers to virtually try on their trainers by aiming their smartphone camera at their leg. Consumers select a Converse trainer from the Converse catalog app and view the trainer on their foot. If they like what they see, they can opt to buy the particular trainer online. The business benefits by having consumers volunteer their likes and dislikes by their behavior of which shoes they view through their mobile app. The consumer benefits by the convenience and ease of viewing the shoe virtually as opposed to going through the physical buying process.

9. **Burberry Beauty Box.** Burberry Beauty Box store in Covent Garden (UK) allows consumers to select their skin tone and then place different polishes on the bar to show the consumers what the polishes look like in real life against their nails. This is a relatively simple example but illustrates the simplest of personal information exchange: "Show us the physical attributes of your nail, and we will compare our colors to your particular nail."

10. **Moosejaw X-Ray app.** The Moosejaw X-Ray app shows the consumer different levels of layered sweaters and jackets worn by the models. The consumer scans the models with a smartphone and then the AR app progressively can remove layers of clothing depending on the desired layer of clothes to view on the model. It would be categorized more in the dimension of novelty apps rather than pure utility.[20]

The essence of directly volunteered personal information in the context of augmented reality is to reveal a higher level of personal information relative to a direct shopping experience for the consumer. This unlocks new levels of utility and reward for the consumer as well as the opportunity for extreme relevancy on the part of the business.

New Customer Information Industry (Consumer as Stakeholder)

A new set of innovators has recognized the growing need for individuals to have more ownership and control over the personal information they create and share. The uniqueness of this new set of innovators is that their products and services exist with the consumer as the primary shareholder versus the traditional monetization of consumer data with the organization or business as the primary shareholder. This supports the growing trend of consumers taking more ownership and control of their personal data with the eventual state of managing and monetizing their information as one of their primary personal assets. This new set of innovators is actually creating a new industry around consumer direct information sharing that supports the new and evolving personal data ecosystem industry.

Harvard University's Berkman Center for Internet & Society has been a major advocacy group in this new personal data ecosystem industry. Its ProjectVRM (VRM stand for vendor relationship management) is an initiative that creates a new category of enablers for individuals to forge a new independence with businesses as well as a better vehicle to engage with those businesses. Doc Searls initiated this project roughly a decade ago as a fellow at the Berkman Center. VRM was viewed as an individual's natural counterpart to the existing customer relationship management (CRM) industry, but with the individual as the shareholder as opposed to businesses as the shareholders in the CRM industry.

VRM tools provide individuals with a more active role in the information components of their interactions with businesses relative to traditional CRM practices where the business is the most active participant. CRM traditionally has been focused on classic marketing activities of targeting, capturing, and acquiring customers. The concepts of VRM give similar tools to the individual, with the individual being the "professionalized" agent in the interaction or transaction.[21] Doc Searls has guided the VRM project for much of its existence.

The Berkman Center says, "The primary theory behind ProjectVRM is that many market problems (including the widespread belief that customer lock-in is a 'best practice') can only be solved from the customer side: by making the customer a fully empowered actor in the marketplace, rather than one whose power in many cases is dependent on exclusive relationships with vendors, by coerced agreement provided entirely by those vendors."[22]

The opportunity for businesses is to evolve capabilities that leverage the services that this new personal data ecosystem industry is creating for consumers. These new capabilities will support not only the consumer's new willingness and capabilities to directly share far more personal information but also their management and control of their information as their personal asset.

The new consumer-direct industry has created a broad array of software and services, such as "intentcasting" (defined as services used to broadcast an individual's buying intentions), privacy protection, databases, messaging, personal data and relationship management, transaction management, and trust-based or trust-providing systems and services.

Project VRM categorizes the development work in the VRM space in the following structure:

- Software and services
  - Intentcasting
  - Privacy protection
  - Databases
  - Messaging
  - Personal information management (aka PIMs; Personal Clouds, Stores, Lockers and Vaults)
  - Transaction management
  - Trust-based or -providing systems and services
- Service providers or projects built on VRM principles
- Infrastructure
  - Concepts
  - Hardware
  - Hardware
  - Standards, frameworks, code bases, and protocols
- People (analysts and consultants)
- Consortia, organizations, workgroups
- Meetups, conferences and events

Software and Services

- **TaskRabbit.** TaskRabbit is an online and mobile marketplace that allows individuals to outsource small jobs and tasks to others in their neighborhood. Individuals name the task they need done and the price they are willing to pay, and a network of preapproved TaskRabbits bid to complete the job.[23]
- **LiveNinja.** LiveNinja provides individuals with a convenient way to find and book chat sessions with experts, gurus, intellects, and specialists on anything the individual wants to learn. LiveNinja is based on a live video chat marketplace that provides individuals with direct and personalized access to service providers or individuals with expertise on a particular subject. Individuals can either find experts or sell their own expertise.[24]
- **Care.com.** Care.com provides services used by families to find caregivers. The site attracts 1.3 million unique visitors per month.[25]
- **AskForIt.** AskForIt is an individual demand aggregation and advocacy site (e.g., "We want cable TV providers to offer à la carte channels"). The individual's role is to ask for things he or she desires, and AskForIt will crowdsource other individuals who have similar "Asks." The individual

then takes this Ask and socializes it with friends via Facebook, e-mail contacts, and Twitter followers. Each Ask receives a dedicated page with a common port, share tools, and a counter to help the individual keep track of progress. Other individuals can join the original "Asker" to help support the sought-after goal. AskForIt assists individuals by optimizing their asked pages to have higher ranks in Google, Bing, and other search engines to optimize exposure and to improve the crowd-sourcing of the Ask. AskForIt also promotes the Ask through Facebook, Twitter, and other channels. AskForIt also drives traffic to its website to support the Asks. When an Ask begins to get traction, AskForIt acts as an advocate to represent the individual to those who have the power to make the Ask happen. AskForIt reserves the right not to advocate any Ask that is contentious, frivolous, seemingly impossible, or unrealistic.[26]

- **Body Shop Bids.** This is intentcasting for auto body work bids based on uploaded photos ("I want to receive bids on repairing my car based on my photos and report"). Body Shop Bids empowers individuals by enabling personal requests for information (PRFIs) and PRFPs. The first step is for an individual to upload photos and submit a damage report, which is done by using the smartphone app or the website. The individual then requests bids from local body shops based on the damage report and photos submitted. The body shops then respond to the individual's personal request for proposals within 24 hours. Once the bids are received by Body Shop Bids, the individual is e-mailed a link to view them in a standard format. The individual then selects the bid that is most desirable and schedules the repair online. Body Shop Bids then notifies the body shop.[27]

- **Intently.** Intentcasting "shouts" for services ("I'm looking for a newborn photographer to take natural shots of my six-week-old this weekend"). Intently is intended to connect individuals and businesses to accomplish certain tasks via mostly services by "shouting."
  Examples include:
  - Asked golf clubs in their area for membership pricing and selected the club based on price and how responsive and helpful the club was during the process.
  - Asked venue providers in the area for availability and price to hold a surprise birthday party. The first venue provider that replied won with a combination of price and service.
  - Wrote 40 job applications to companies in a specific sector and location. The applications produced an interview.
  - Asked for a wedding photographer. The winning photographer won the business because the photographer "clicked" with the buyer.
  - Asked about buying a mattress with the criterion of it being delivered on Saturday. The first supplier to reply positively won the business.

- Asked for advice about what health foods would remedy a stomach issue. The first health store to reply was helpful, and the individual bought items from that health store.
- Asked for a bed and breakfast at the last minute. The first supplier replied in five minutes and met the individual's budget.[28]

Neil Harris is the founder of Intently. Harris explains that its focus is predominantly in the service sector. Its experience has been that the model works best when there are multiple suppliers that could satisfy individuals and the individual is comfortable with delivering a request to all of the suppliers that can satisfy the request. In the Intently model, an individual will directly indicate what service is required to roughly 20 relevant suppliers. If the individual's request is in a distinct sector (e.g., hiring a venue, hiring a photographer), then typically five suppliers respond within a few hours. In this example, two of the five will indicate they have the ability to service the request and three will opt out. Of the two suppliers that have indicated they can service the request, there is a 90 percent probability that the individual will select one of the suppliers and complete the transaction. Therefore, a supplier that can service a request has a 50 percent chance of success with the individual. The factors that directly influence the supplier success rate are:

- Response time
- Completeness of response (addressing all points)
- Meeting individual's pricing requirements
- Meeting individual's service quality requirements

An overarching key to a supplier's success is to address the rational requirements of the individual, as well as to treat the individual as a human being from the first interaction—building rapport, responding personally, delivering excellent customer service, and treating the buyer (and his or her needs) as unique and special. Here's an example of an initial dialogue:

- Individual: "Hi there, I'm looking for a good newborn photographer to take some natural shots of my six-week-old Samuel this weekend. Can you help? Thanks, Vicki."
- Unsuccessful Supplier: "I am available. Please take a look at my website for prices."
- Successful Supplier: "Hi, Vicki, congratulations on the birth of your son—how exciting for you! I have two little boys myself and they are such fun. Regarding newborn photography, it's one of my favorite areas—here's a link to a session I did this year: [link to photos]. I am available on Saturday and Sunday afternoon this weekend. I can come to your home or you are welcome to come to my studio (presumably you'd prefer me to come to your home for the most natural

shots). Please let me know if you'd like to go ahead. Best regards, Melanie.[29]

All of these Intently examples start with a "shout" created on the website. Intently then searches for a range of people and businesses that may be interested in responding (this takes less than a minute). The individual then chooses who to send the shout to. When the service provider responds, the individual uses Intently to interact and ultimately close the deal. Intently's value proposition is that it saves the individual time by reaching out to multiple interested parties with only minimal effort on the part of the individual. An individual using Intently is anonymous except for one's visible name. At a certain point in the interaction, the individual may choose to share personal information with the prospective responding service provider. Individuals can also share "shouts" with friends and colleagues. Intently's service is free to the individual but there is a charge for sellers. For sellers, Intently monitors when users ask for a certain service and then matches them up with the ask.

- **OffersByMe.** This site has intentcasting for local offers ("I'd like to have a good steak dinner this Friday with two friends within 10 miles of my house"). OffersByMe operates by asking the individual what his or her buying intent is and then finds two local businesses that match the individual's criteria (i.e., personal request for proposal [PRFP]). OffersByMe differentiates itself from online coupons and daily deal approaches because typically these approaches have little idea who the individuals are and what they really want relative to their budgets. With OffersByMe's approach, the predominately irrelevant offers of the couponing approach don't occur.

  OffersByMe also distinguishes itself by managing offers as opposed to deals for the individual. The rationale is that the daily deals approach many times prompts a purchase that is compelling because of its money-saving opportunity but may have marginal relevance. The offers approach is based on products or services that the individual has actually targeted.

  OffersByMe is implemented via a mobile app that the individual works within 30 categories and hundreds of stores to find a particular offering that is relevant. Examples:

  - "I am looking to spend $50 on Italian food."
  - "I am looking to spend $40 for a massage."
  - "I am looking to spend $100 to join a gym."
  - "I am looking to spend $_____ on _____."

  Adam Goldberg from OffersByMe states that its business model focuses on location-specific services. Currently, OffersByMe has more than 450 businesses signed up in the Columbus, Ohio, area. OffersByMe focuses on targeted offers to individuals based on their stated wants and needs. Once the individual has made a request, OffersByMe offers only that individual a specific offer that is typically good for redemption only for that current day. This differentiates it from more of a mass-mailing offers approach (e.g., Groupon). This allows a highly targeted and relevant offer to the individual as well as giving a business more control of when and where the offer is utilized by the individual. This also adds further protection for the business by not cannibalizing its existing business. For example, a restaurant can better target a desired customer on a desired day, such as slow Thursdays, with OffersByMe's approach.

Goldberg has observed that the best win-win scenario for a business and an individual is when the individual has a high purchase frequency as well as flexibility to switch between suppliers. For example, individuals who desire plumbing services may need them only once a year whereas a person might like to eat Mexican food every Friday night. Therefore, OffersByMe's business model is best focused on businesses such as restaurants, beauticians, movie theaters, and bowling alleys. OffersByMe reaches conversion rates of 20 percent to 30 percent, as 95 percent of its model is based on "direct from individual" data (i.e., individuals communicating exactly what they want). More mass-marketing-based couponing (e.g., Groupon) utilizes predominately indirect data sources and as a result has a far lower conversion rate. Particularly for repeat customers, the conversion rate diminishes to roughly 0.1 percent.

One of the biggest challenges for both the individual and the business in this location-based offers model, when individuals are volunteering not only what services they desire but also their location, is delivering the offer and/or reminders when they are in proximity to their stated needs. If they are sitting at home or at work, streaming offers to them for a restaurant 20 miles away would be perceived as low relevancy even though they have indicated their interest in the restaurant. Proximity significantly increases relevancy. If it is a densely populated area, proximity-based intelligence of a cell phone is oftentimes limited to roughly 500 meters with cell tower triangulation. Engaging the GPS capabilities of the cell phone aids in this location equation but has a noticeable drain on a mobile phone's battery life. Oftentimes, movement of 500 or even 250 meters is enough, but it's not predictable or reliable.

The other challenge in managing discount offers is managing the demographics (i.e., low-end bargain seekers). This is where the balance between the individual's needs and the business's profitability requirements should be managed effectively (e.g., high-end restaurants that end up with only one-time bargain seekers on busy days, whereas affluent customers would patronize the restaurant with or without the offer). Another powerful advantage of location-based offers using "direct from individual" data is that when the individual actually utilizes the offer, the business has the opportunity to become far more knowledgeable about the new customer. In the case of restaurants, most times the restaurants have little knowledge of who their best customers are without these "direct from consumer" offers and apps.[30]

■ **Prizzm.** Prizzm is a social CRM platform rewarding customers for telling businesses what they want, what they like, and what they have problems with—that is, demand-based advertising ("I want relevant offers in my shared areas of interest in sports and travel for my current location; and every offer you send me I will rate, which will either allow you to keep sending me offers or shut your offers off completely"). Prizzm asks that individuals indicate what their interests and wants are in their particular location. The individuals then rate the ads they receive until the resulting ad stream is highly relevant. This intentionally volunteered personal information approach circumvents many of the negativities associated with traditional online advertising mechanics, such as behavioral tracking, selling that personal behavior, spam, and irrelevant ads.

Individuals who use Prizzm own their profiles and their personal data. They store their preferences, likes, and products or services (things they intend to buy) in their profiles. Prizzm commits to never reselling, licensing, or broadcasting their personal profiles and data to any party without the individual's explicit permission. The individual retains ownership over this data and can edit it at any time. The interactions and profiles are anonymous by default.[31]

■ **Thumbtack.** Thumbtack finds services from trustworthy local service providers ("I want a highly reviewed personal trainer experienced with 60+ females twice a week"). Thumbtack works in three steps:

■ Step 1: The individual communicates his or her service needs.
■ Answers a few simple questions.
■ Step 2: The individual receives quotes within 24 hours.
■ Thumbtack contacts available professionals.
■ Thumbtack e-mails individual up to five quotes.
■ Each quote is customized to the individual's needs.
■ Step 3: The individual compares quotes and hires the best professional.
■ Quotes are compared by prices, reviews, and service profiles.[32]

■ **Trovi.** PRFP/intentcasting; matching searchers and local vendors (Oregon/Arizona) ("I want a purple couch delivered this Sunday for under $1,000 and I want to buy it locally"). Trovi addresses the inherent weaknesses when an individual uses the search ecosystem to search for a local product or service. Paid ads for national stores surface higher in the search rankings not because of local relevance to an individual's search but because of a paid bias.

- *Example:* A local sofa store may show up 10 pages into the search rankings whereas a paid advertisement (e.g., IKEA) may be ranked number one or two.

Trovi asks individuals to communicate what products they want through their phone/tablet/computer (e.g., what they want, where they want it, when they want it, how much they are willing to pay). Trovi matches the request to the vendor inventory and then displays the products on the individual screen. Special offers, coupons, and any other any deals the vendors are offering are also displayed. TrovI's approach also benefits the vendors as the big national brands don't automatically appear higher in the rankings. The displays are truly about relevance to the individual.[33]

- **eSnipe.com.** ("I want to buy this Canon camera on eBay with minimum bids right before the auction closes.") This is a service that assists individuals in professionalizing their online buying, particularly for online auctions; eSnipe is designed to allow eBay buyers to automatically bid at the very end of an auction. The price each individual enters is the maximum that customer is willing to pay for the item being bid on. "Snipers" often win when the price is less than the maximum bid.[34]

- **Übokia.** PRFI/intentcasting based on images of items ("I want a formal gown, size 8, black, strapless, DKNY or Dior"). Übokia asks individuals to post what they are looking for, and then they wait for sellers to respond to them. The individual can specify the relative proximity, condition, and price of the desired item.

    Übokia also has üGroups where individuals can join with other individuals looking for similar items in similar categories. In their local area, they can buy, sell, and trade in a trusted environment (e.g., frugal moms of Denver, restaurant owners, vintage auto enthusiasts).

    Übokia also allows you to add a "want it" button on Pinterest. Individuals just need to click and drag the "want it" button into their browser's bookmark bar and then use it with their "Pin it" button. Übokia's "want it" button works on Firefox, Safari, Chrome, and Internet Explorer.[35]

- **Zaarly.** PRFP/intentcasting/buyer-centric marketplaces for local communities ("I want to buy a custom-made mahogany armoire locally for under $3,000"). Zaarly storefronts (created by local sellers) provide individuals a handpicked community of the best local service providers to the individual's location:

    - *Buying:* Individuals browse local listings for desired items based on reviews and descriptions. They place an order with a credit card in a secure environment that is backed by a $10,000 guarantee. The individual and the seller "chat" back and forth to finalize desired delivery nuances. Individuals have the option of making the seller one of their favorites of their "neighborhood."

- *Selling:* Sellers can set up their own Zaarly storefront with a custom URL. They list their skills, services, and experiences. These listings are then connected with local people. Zaarly guarantees credit card payments, and offers no-hassle refunds without complicated fees or insurance policies.

Zaarly is based on local buying of certain U.S. cities (e.g., New York City, Kansas City, Seattle, Los Angeles, and San Francisco).

Individuals who are selling will post anonymously and will accumulate reviews based on their track record for completing tasks and their payment history. Zaarly's "request" model for individuals has facilitated $40 million in transactions in the United States with half a million users.[36]

- **Airbnb.** Individual to individual (I2I), sharing economy, PRFI ("I want to stay in north Maui in an oceanfront condo with my family from January 12 to 24"). Airbnb is an online service that enables individuals (i.e., hosts) to rent unoccupied living spaces and other short-term lodging to other individuals. Airbnb has over 250,000 listings in 30,000 cities and 192 countries. Individuals can list anything they desire to rent to other individuals such as private rooms, entire apartments, castles, boats, manors, tree houses, tepees, igloos, and private islands.

Hosts register online and can create a personal online profile before listing a property. Every property is listed with feedback, recommendations, and ratings from previous guests.

Airbnb creates a trusted environment with multiple components.

- Airbnb verifies IDs with all guests and hosts by connecting to their social networks, scanning their official IDs, and confirming the personal details.
- Airbnb posts the profiles and reviews.
- When you book reservations on Airbnb, you can earn reviews that appear on your Airbnb profile. Reviews are written by real Airbnb users who have booked reservations on the site and want to let the community know of their experiences. If you don't have any reservations planned yet but want to allow friends to vouch for you, check out references.[37]

Privacy Protection
- **Abine.** DNT+, DeleteMe, PrivacyWatch: privacy-protecting browser extensions. Abine is a browser add-on that protects an individual's personal information incidentally created during browsing activities.

There are three primary browser add-ons: DoNotTrackMe, DeleteMe, and MaskMe:

- DoNotTrackMe is a browser add-on that was developed to stop many companies (Abine asserts more than 600) from tracking individuals on the Internet. DoNotTrackMe stops these companies by blocking Internet trackers, which are defined by Abine as "a request that a web page tries to make your browser perform that will share information intended to record, profile, or share your online activity." These Internet trackers are placed in individuals' browsers by companies such as Facebook.

- DeleteMe is a browser add-on that deletes an individual's personal information from the Internet. The premise behind this product is that every activity by an individual leaves a record, and then data brokers collect this information to sell public profiles about the individual and his or her behavior. DeleteMe removes:
  - Individual's public profile from leading data sites
  - Contact, personal, and social information
  - Photos of individual, family, and home

- MaskMe is a browser add-on that keeps an individual's e-mail address private. Abine equates the importance and privacy of your e-mail address to that of your Social Security number on the Internet. Once e-mail addresses are solicited by a commercial entity, individuals can send a "Masked Email" instead. These e-mails are then forwarded to their in-box so they can receive all the communication they want, but also have the power to block senders from their in-box in one click. An individual's e-mail address is regularly sold to spammers as well as being collected by companies who can potentially lose, share, and spam the individual themselves.[38]

- **Collusion.** A Mozilla Firefox add-on for viewing third parties tracking your movements, Collusion is a browser add-on that allows an individual to view which third parties are tracking them online. It displays in real time how the data the individual creates is a spiderweb of server calls and links between companies and other trackers. Individuals control whether the tracker is on or off. The full version of Collusion will allow individuals to opt in to sharing their anonymous personal information in a global database of web tracker data.

  Mozilla is also working with the Ford Foundation in an outreach campaign to help individuals understand the benefits and issues of online data tracking. This aids the individual in weighting the pluses and minuses of allowing or not allowing online tracking—that is, the trade-off of volunteering personal information for utility/rewards of higher content relevance and enhanced online experience. Currently, most online tracking occurs without the individual's consent or knowledge.

Confluence gives the individual knowledge and control to decide when, how, and if the individual agrees to be tracked.[39]

- **Disconnect.me.** Browser extensions to stop unwanted tracking and to control data sharing enable individuals to visualize and block websites that track web behavior. Disconnect was founded in 2011 by Brian Kennish, a former Google and DoubleClick engineer, and Casey Oppenheim, a consumer- and privacy-rights advocate and attorney. This browser extension is used by a million people every week and is rated 4.6 out of five stars.

  Features include:
  - Total number of tracking requests on every page:
    - Green indicates all the requests on a page are blocked.
    - Gray indicates some are unblocked.
  - Number of tracking requests on a page by company:
    - Green or checked means the requests are blocked.
    - Gray or unchecked means they're unblocked.
  - Common tracking sites such as Facebook, Google, and Twitter are shown separately to facilitate blocking or unblocking.
  - Sites are tracked by category—advertising, analytics, social networking, content (also by company).
  - Whitelist site or Blacklist site button lets individuals unblock or block all requests on the site they visit.
  - Secure Wi-Fi check box enables an individual to prevent wireless eavesdropping by forcing sites to encrypt the individual's data.[40]
- **Ghostery.** A browser extension for tracking the trackers, Ghostery gives the individual visibility into certain tracking web components (e.g., tags, web bugs, pixels, and beacons). Ghostery also tracks over 1,400 trackers and gives the individual a listing of the ad networks, behavioral data providers, web publishers, and other companies that show interest in the individual's online behavior. This browser extension also gives the individual control to determine how much browser personal information is exposed. This includes giving the individual the ability to block a company's web scripts, delete local shared objects, and block images and iframes.[41]
- **PrivacyFix.** Providing browser extensions and services to individuals and site builders for keeping track of trackers, PrivacyFix estimates an individual's privacy risk of using a website based on how the site handles individuals' personal and tracking data. PrivacyFix's browser extension scans for privacy issues based on the individual's Facebook and Google privacy settings, as well as other sites the individual visits and the companies that track the sites. PrivacyFix then takes the individual to the settings that need to be changed or fixed. PrivacyFix also warns the individual of new or changed privacy issues or policies—for

example, if Facebook changes its privacy policies, or there is news of privacy breaches.

PrivacyFix is based on two dimensions:

1. How the site's policy protects the individual's personal data
2. Privacy qualifications of trackers on the site

PrivacyFix is calculated on four areas:

1. Sharing = 30 points
   ■ Degree to which individual's personal information is shared (e.g., name, e-mail address, and phone)
2. Notice = 5 points
   ■ Notification of government requests for personal information
3. Deletion = 10 points
   ■ Promptness of personal data deletion when relationship or account is terminated
4. Vendors = 5 points
   ■ Confidentiality required from service providers with data access[42]

Databases

■ **InfoGrid.** Graph database for personal networking applications.[43]
■ **ProjectDanube.** Open-source software for identity and personal data services. ProjectDanube is an open code and advocacy project in the field of identity and personal data services for individuals on the Internet. ProjectDanube is focused on solving the deeper political and social issues of an individual's anonymity versus so-called veronymity (individual revealing their true identity), centralization versus decentralization of personal data, and the appropriate handling of personal data online.[44]

ProjectDanube supports two major projects—XDI2 and Freedom-Box:

■ **XDI2.** This is an open-source project designed to support personal clouds, personal channels, and the Respect Network (provides personal cloud network). It functions as a personal cloud desktop web interface that uses XRI Data Interchange (XDI) messaging to store and access personal data in an XDI-based personal cloud. The code behind this demo is open source and part of the XDI2 project. This interface's connectors can also access data in Facebook, Personal. com, and Allfiled through XDI.

   ■ XDI (XRI Data Interchange) is a semantic data interchange format and protocol under development by the OASIS XDI Technical Committee. The name comes from the addressable graph model XDI uses: Every node in the XDI graph is its own RDF that is uniquely addressable with an extensible resource identifier (XRI).

- RDF (Resource Description Framework) is a family of World Wide Web Consortium (W3C) specifications originally designed as a metadata data model. It has come to be used as a general method for conceptual description or modeling of information that is implemented in web resources, using a variety of syntax notations and data serialization formats.
- XRI (Extensible Resource Identifier) is a scheme and resolution protocol for abstract identifiers compatible with uniform resource identifiers and internationalized resource identifiers, developed by the XRI Technical Committee at OASIS. The goal of XRI is a standard syntax and discovery format for abstract, structured identifiers that are domain-, location-, application-, and transport-independent, so they can be shared across any number of domains, directories, and interaction protocols.
- XDI graph model is the XDI data interchange model that builds upon the RDF graph model as defined by the W3C Semantic Web activity.[45]
- **FreedomBox Project.** This is a community project to develop, design, and promote personal servers running free, open-source software for distributed social networking, e-mail, and audio/video communications. One of the key aspects of this project is a small and inexpensive physical device that operates similarly to an Internet gateway or Wi-Fi router but has added functionality to operate as a personal server running an open-source operating system and applications designed to create and preserve personal privacy. The primary assumption is that individuals can better manage their privacy through a decentralized approach to networks. FreedomBox uses a quasi BitTorrent principle, which is the most common protocol for peer-to-peer file sharing over the Internet (i.e., 43 to 70 percent of all Internet traffic).[46]

Messaging Services and Brokers

- **Gliph.** Providing private, secure identity management and messaging for smartphones, Gliph is the easiest way to get started with bitcoin payments. Sign-up comes with one free "cloaked" e-mail address for e-mail privacy on Craigslist and other websites. Gliph's features include private messaging, four-digit PIN security, options for either person to delete messages permanently on both sides of conversation, option to delay delivery of message with expiration date, and cloaked e-mail.[47]

Bitcoin is a cryptocurrency where the creation and transfer of bitcoins is based on an open-source cryptographic protocol independent of any central financial authority. Bitcoins can be transferred through a computer or smartphone without an intermediate financial institution (i.e., peer-to-peer electronic cash system).

- **Directly.** A customer service Q&A site connecting to experts who have worked in big companies and are willing to help when the company can't or won't, Directly functions as a community of experts who work independently on their own free time. These experts include current or former employees, partners, or other people who know the company and products well enough to be considered experts. To become an expert, the person has to demonstrate that he or she knows the company well enough via a LinkedIn profile or public expertise profile. The validation process is adequate in most cases. The expert's own reward is an expanded and enhanced reputation. The experts can "cash out" their rewards or donate them to one of the nonprofit causes that Directly supports. Directly's services are free with optional paid services for better and/or faster help. Directly is not sponsored by big companies but the companies have informally encouraged team members to sign up and help customers.

  Directly's process is that an individual asks a question on the site, the site does a general analysis of the question, and then it matches the question to the expert with the right expertise via the expert's mobile phone. The experts use mobile apps to answer the questions. Most questions get answered within a few hours. Once your question is answered, you can follow up with the respective expert. Directly is testing a mortgage site with the mission to help home buyers and homeowners get fast, personal attention directly from mortgage experts who know specific mortgage companies. Directly launched publicly in December 2012 with a network that reaches 3.2 million individuals monthly and has helped 35,000 airline, bank, cable, and wireless customers with a 97 percent response rate and an average response time of less than 10 minutes.[48]

- **Pingup (Getabl Inc.).** A text utility to engage merchants instantly,[49] Pingup provides a search, discover, and connect interface to enable individuals to find a business and then connect to the business as they would by texting a personal friend. The basic Pingup service is free to both individuals and businesses and is accessible through a web-based interface as well as through mobile apps. For example, if individuals want to know the dress code and wait time of a particular restaurant, they would text the message to the restaurant and receive a response from one of the restaurant managers. Another example would be hailing a taxi in Boston. Pingup has a relationship with more than 500 taxis in Boston. All of these Pingup-enabled taxis can be hailed via a text message. Another example would be if an individual would like to cancel or add a cable subscription service, the person could simply text HBO "Cancel HBO" or "Add Showtime." Pingup has signed up over

550 businesses in the Boston area, and plans to expand to other markets, including New York and San Francisco.[50]

■ **TrustFabric.** This service for managing relationships between individuals and businesses allows individuals to keep their personal information up-to-date in one place and then selectively and securely share that information with businesses they have relationships with. TrustFabric gives individuals control over how businesses contact them via e-mail, phone, text message, and snail mail. TrustFabric also provides businesses with up-to-date contact information for their customers.[51]

Personal Data and Relationship Management

■ **ComplainApp**—an iOS/Android app to "submit complaints to businesses instantly—and find people with similar complaints"

■ **CozyCloud**—personal cloud storage and service

■ **DataBanker**—lets individual consumers aggregate and understand their personal behavioral data, and sell that data to product designers, marketers, and social researchers

■ **Geddup.com**—personal data and relationship management

■ **Mydex**—personal data stores and other services

■ **OneCub**—*le compte unique pour vos inscriptions en ligne* (single account for online registration)

■ **Paoga**—personal data, personal agent

■ **Personal.com**—personal data storage, personal agent

■ **Personal Clouds**—personal cloud wiki

■ **Privowny**—privacy company for protecting personal identities and for tracking use and abuse of those identities, and for building relationships

■ **QIY**—independent infrastructure for managing personal data and relationships

■ **Singly**—personal data storage and platform for development with an API

Transaction Management

■ **Dashlane**—simplified login and checkout

Trust-Based or Trust-Providing Systems and Services

■ **Respect Network**—VRM personal cloud network based on OAuth, XDI, KRL, unhosted, and other open-standards, open-source, and open-data initiatives. Respect Network is the parent of Connect.Me.

■ **Trust.cc**—personal social graph–based fraud prevention, affiliated with Social Islands

■ **TrustCloud**—empowers individuals to claim their trustworthy online data and use it anywhere on the web

The following is a list of innovators that provide services for the new personal data industry as well as specific projects that support the individual as the personal information shareholder.

Service Providers or Projects Built on VRM Principles

- **The Banyan Project**—community news co-ops owned by readers/members
- **belmewel-register.nl**—the "Dutch YouMayCallMe registry," "reverses the customer paradigm"
- **Cloudstore**—personal clouds
- **dotui.com**—intelligent media solutions for retail and hospitality customers
- **easyDNS**—customer-driven managed DNS hosting, domain tools, and registration with no lock-in
- **Edentiti**—customer-driven verification of identity
- **First Retail Inc.**—commodity infrastructure for bidirectional marketplaces to enable the personal RFP
- **Flamingo**—Service company working toward leveling the playing field between service providers and customers
- **Hover.com**—customer-driven domain management
- **Hypothes.is**—open source, peer review
- **MyInfo.cl**—transitioning from VRM.cl
- **MyWave**—"MyWave CMR puts the customer in charge of their data and the experience."
- **Neustar**—"cooperation through trusted connections"
- **NewGov.us**—government relationship management (GRM)
- **OwnYourInfo**—personal information storing and sharing application
- **Real Estate Café**—money-saving services for do-it-yourself (DIY) home buyers and for-sale-by-owner (FSBO) home sellers
- **Reputation.com**—service for controlling one's reputation online
- **Spotflux**—malware, tracking, unwanted ad filtration through an encrypted tunnel
- **SwitchBook**—personal search
- **Tangled Web**—mobile, person2person (P2P), and Personal Data Store (PDS)
- **TiddlyWiki**—reusable nonlinear personal web notebook
- **Ting**—customer-driven mobile virtual network operator (MVNO—a cell phone company)
- **Tucows**—parent of Ting and Hover
- **VirtualZero**—open food platform, supply chain transparency
- **Vū**—user-driven personalized content delivery

The following is a list of innovators that provide infrastructure services that support the new personal data industry dedicated to the individual as the stakeholder in one's personal information.

Concepts
- **EmanciPay**—development project for customer-driven payment choices
- **GRM**—government relationship management, a subcategory of vendor relationship management (VRM)
- **ListenLog**—personal data logging
- **Personal RFP**—crowdsourcing, standards
- **R-button**—user interface (UI) elements for relationship members

Hardware
- **Freedom Box**—personal server on free software and hardware
- **Indie Box**—run open-source web applications on personal server in your home
- **Precipitat, WebBox**—new architecture for decentralizing the web, little server
- **Scanadu**—scanner packed with sensors designed to read your vital signs and send them wirelessly to your smartphone

Standards, Frameworks, Code Bases, and Protocols
- **Datownia**—builds APIs from Excel spreadsheets held in Dropbox
- **Digital Asset Grid**—S prototype for secure and accountable intentcasting infrastructure, funded by SWIFT Innotribe
- **Evented APIs**—new standard for live web interactivity
- **Kinetic Rules Language (KRL)**—personal event networks, personal rule sets, programming live web interactions
- **Kynetx**—personal event networks, personal rule sets
- **The Mine! Project**—personal data, personal agent
- **Mozilla Persona** (www.mozilla.org/en-US/persona/)—a privacy-protecting one-click e-mail-based way to do single sign-on at websites
- **Oneswarm**—privacy protecting peer-to-peer data sharing
- **TAS3.eu**—trusted architecture for securely shared services—R&D toward a trusted architecture and set of adaptive security services for individuals
- **Telehash**—standards, personal data protocols
- **Tent**—open decentralized protocol for personal autonomy and social networking
- **UMA**—standards
- **webfinger**—personal web discovery, finger over HTTP
- **XDI**—OASIS semantic data interchange standard

The following is a list of individual analysts and consultants who provide insight and consulting to support the new personal data industry with the individual as the centerpiece of personal information.

People (Analysts and Consultants)
- Ctrl-SHIFT—analysts
- HealthURL—medical
- Synergetics—VRM for job markets
- VRM Labs—research

The following is a list of consortia and work groups that work to evolve the thinking and practices around supporting the new personal data industry with the individual as the primary beneficiary.

Consortia, Work Groups, Communities
- Fing.org—VRM fostering organization
- Information Sharing Workgroup at Kantara—legal agreements, trust frameworks
- Pegasus—eID smart cards
- **Personal Cloud (wiki)**—This is an online community/wiki intended to be the place where the personal cloud community can collect relevant links and other relevant knowledge. Feel free to constructively contribute.
- **Personal Data Ecosystem Consortium (PDEC)** (www.pde.cc)—This community connects with companies building personal control over personal data into their products.
- **ProjectVRM**—ProjectVRM is a development and research community of the Berkman Center for Internet & Society at Harvard University. It has two purposes: (1) to encourage development of tools by which individuals can take control of their relationships with organizations, especially in commercial marketplaces, and (2) to encourage and conduct research on VRM-related theories, usage of VRM tools, and effects as adoption of VRM tools takes place.

The following events occur on a regular basis to give the industry an opportunity to commune on the latest challenges facing the personal data ecosystem industry.

Meetups, Conferences, and Events
- **Internet Identity Workshop (IIW)** held twice a year (fall and spring)—unconference in Mountain View, California
- VRM Hub—meeting[52]

Contrasting the Approaches

Many of the examples in this book can be placed along a spectrum between business-oriented customer centricity and customer empowerment centricity. On one end of the spectrum, the approach for leveraging the new voice of the customer is more oriented toward the business as the stakeholder (business-oriented customer centricity), whereas on the other end of the spectrum the approach for leveraging the new voice of the customer is more oriented toward the customer as the stakeholder (customer-empowerment centricity). Both have the potential of being effective at leveraging the customer's new voice and reaching the goal of extreme product and service relevancy and customer experience. As always, the probability of success lies in the culture change supported by operational execution excellence.

BUSINESS-ORIENTED CUSTOMER CENTRICITY[53] In practice, leveraging the customer's new voice by business is fundamentally restructuring the traditional supply chain. The current supply chain mechanics are serial in nature and cannot engage customers at extreme levels of relevancy and experience without placing the consumer squarely in the center.

Supplier ↔ Manufacturer ↔ Integrator ↔ Distributor ↔ Retailer ↔ Consumer

The new supply chain enabled by the customer's new voice is no longer serial in nature but operates in a synchronous fashion based on mutual value.

Start-up MyWave represents a good illustrative example of how the win-win of the customer's new voice is executed in the real world in the following financial services use case. MyWave's approach reveals the inner workings of how its direct-to-customer next-generation customer relationship management (CRM) platform functions with the customer's new voice.

MyWave describes itself as a customer-managed relationship (CMR) technology platform. CMR turns CRM on its head by putting the customer in control of getting personalized experiences anytime, anywhere, on any device. Their user interface is a mobile or web-based personal digital assistant powered by a personal cloud in conjunction with an events-, rules-, and conversation-based commerce engine. Users own, control, and update their own data based on their own preferences and buying intentions, and share their real-time preferences and needs, enabling a business to tailor products and services in a far more targeted and relevant way.

MyWave Commercial Model for a Bank or Financial Services Customer The commercial model is co-designed with each bank or financial services customer. The bank is charged for services in design, co-creation, and customization according to a master services agreement. A software as a service (SaaS) fee per customer per annum is paid by the bank, or a micro transaction fee, as agreed with the bank. The bank's customers receive the personal cloud "personal assistant" interface free of charge up to an agreed personal cloud data storage amount. Merchants aggregated by the bank into the bank's customers' personal clouds may be charged either micro transaction fees or any other appropriate fee structure agreed between bank and merchant.

Figure 7.1 illustrates how MyWave enables a new type of banking value network that enables a broader and potentially "disruptive" digital banking model. The traditional bank is transformed into a facilitator or orchestrator of "wishes and wants" from the bank's customers on the left, for example, I want: insights, money management, payments; MyWishes: home, holiday, transport, car, food and the business commercial ecosystem on the right, for example, airlines, retailers, hotels, realtors, motor dealers, and SMEs.

Financial Services Value Proposition   The MyWave proposition from a bank's perspective is around the opportunity to grow business from existing customers as well as attract new customers, while reducing costs, lessening churn, and growing overall revenue. For example, in the context of the levers of risk, cost, revenue, and loyalty the bank can:

- **Reduce risk** by having up-to-the-minute accurate data about customers' intents, assets, preferences—and their satisfaction with the services offered.
- **Improve the cost/income ratio** by empowering customers to control and maintain their own data. This enables customers to communicate their preferences and share more about themselves—in return for mutual value received from better experiences, products, and services.
- **Increase revenue** through a mix of co-creating with customers' fresh next-generation products and services, and mobilizing the bank's customers to become the bank's best sales force.
- **Move up the value chain** where working with money can be looked at in the context of the customer's life—potentially linking willing buyers with willing sellers facilitated by the bank leveraging the MyWave CMR platform. By customers, we mean both consumers and business customers, enabling the bank to add value to both sides of the relationship. As mobile wallets are deployed, new monetized services differentiating the bank could be provided or enabled by the CRM platform.
- **Improve customer experience, loyalty, and advocacy** by empowering customers and building relationships that are based on mutual value.

These four levers, pulled in the right way with the CMR platform, increase return on equity (ROE) by a bank to its stakeholders. This also demonstrates to regulators that products and services are designed and co-created with customers in mind. The bank is leveraging the power of its own network of consumers and businesses for the benefit of its customers and the bank—mutual value.

Bank customers don't want a loan so they can sit on the pile of cash at home. They want the loan for something else. Helping with that something else is what they want. MyWave makes this possible. Providing real service

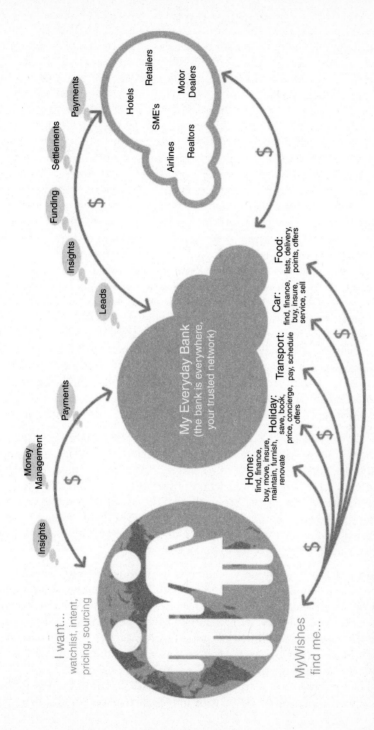

FIGURE 7.1 New Banking Value Network

203

builds loyalty above and beyond price alone. This need for service can be satisfied today by getting a human personal assistant to do the legwork for you, but is cost prohibitive for all but a few.

Further, a consumer revolution has already taken place. Through the mobile device there is more power in the hands of the consumer than at any previous time in the history of the planet. Youths or Millennials are social digital natives who are looking for fresh ways to be engaged by businesses. Generation Connected or Gen C is comprised of people of any age who adopt great technology and experiences, which are often created initially with and by Millennials. Facebook is a good recent example of this. Banks are being digitally disrupted and are facing increasing competition, generational shift, increasing customer expectations, increasing regulation, and low margins. Many banks are responding with various initiatives, including delayering, simplification, new core systems, increasing risk oversight, better customer experience, and an arms race around apps wars.

These are important moves, but on their own won't be enough. Apps are ephemeral, offering temporary technical advantage until the next app. Too many apps lead to app fatigue where customers cease to engage. Successful banks will seek to leverage their strengths and co-create with their business and consumer customers. They will become a positive disruptive force in their market. They will develop an ongoing capability to innovate with the customer at the center, empowering customers and enabling them to signal and obtain the experiences they want and need. This approach will see banks leveraging their own financial value chains and monetizing new value networks. The MyWave platform enables and facilitates this process.

Customer Proposition and Experience   Customers get real service via a personal assistant that helps them get what they want, when they want it, relevant to them and their needs—a true end-to-end service. It makes their lives easier and more fun and removes the friction of getting things done. They control their own data with the bank. They share more about themselves in return for getting a better experience or more value. The bank builds a closer direct relationship with every customer in a cost-effective way, delivering fresh, relevant, sticky customer experiences.

The Customer Journey   Customers can enter through whichever door they are most comfortable entering. For example, existing bank customers could be signed up to MyWave by the bank, have their personal cloud populated, and then be notified by the bank that they have a new and exciting offering. Similarly, a customer could be onboarded by MyWave. The role of MyWave as a customer entry point grows over time as a wide array of companies and brands join the MyWave platform.

Either entrance needs to be as simple and pain-free as possible for the customer and provide them with immediate utility. Seeing their bank statements in their personal cloud or how much they are spending on their pet dog with money management services might be just such a utility. The CRM platform would define what experiences are desired with the bank as part of the customer experience design. The personal cloud interface can bring the bank's brand to the fore or can use the MyWave brand as a "fourth party" in the fore or background. Either model works.

Some customers may sign up directly with the CRM platform personal assistant and then link to the bank, but early financial services customers are more likely to opt for a highly customized personal cloud-based personal assistant with new, fresh experiences and offerings. This gives customers the ability to opt in, owning their data with the bank.

The narrative would be: "Here is what we know about you; in order for us to be able to serve you better in these areas, we would like to know a little more about. ..." The relationship becomes a conversation between the customer and the bank, and, like all good relationships, grows over time.

The Search for Goods and Services—Intentcasting Customers are not searching, but finding or pulling to them what they want based on signaling their intents and preferences—for example, "I want a bike," "I want to go on a holiday," "I want to buy a new car," "I want to buy a new house," "I want to get a new refrigerator," or "I want to build a new deck." This would be the CRM platform technology facilitated by the bank or the CRM platform. It's the bank's customer network, and MyWave would work with the bank to define new moments of mutual value across that network—which the bank may monetize and with which it may create strong and sticky competitive advantage over other banks.

MyWave Platform Compared to Search/Product Platforms The MyWave CMR platform is not a search platform (Google) or a product platform (eBay or Amazon). MyWave is an assistance and relationship platform.

Further, with Google, eBay, or TradeMe, the customer is not in control of the experience. Customers don't own their own data around their preferences, their intents, and what they want to do next. This means they can't signal and pull to them what they need and want, when they want it.

Google tries to personalize, but attempts to do this via tracking. It sucks up customer data in order to serve the customer Google Ads. Google is trying to infer what the customer wants, but the customer has no control.

There has been a consumer backlash in recent times over privacy and "who has my data" articles on the so-called stalker economy where beacons and big data attempt to track and follow the customer around. The problem is that much of this data is inaccurate, nonliving data, creating a broken consumer experience with a sometimes creepy factor.

Marketing ROI is also declining. ComScore and other agencies have recently published data showing a 97.5 percent decline in click-through rates of online ads. Click rates of 0.1 percent are the norm, resulting in wasted advertising dollars.

The MyWave CMR platform can permit consumer and customer engagement around ads—but only if they are opted in, entertaining, and relevant. This means promotions and offers relevant to what customers have signaled as their needs and preferences. Such offers generate a 36 percent return versus the 0.1 percent rate.

Social sharing, crowdsourcing, and peer sourcing can also be integrated. A bank can take a percentage of its marketing spend and use it directly with an individual customer. This may serve to reward referrals of new customers, increase advocacy, or directly reward loyalty in authentic, positively surprising, relevant, and meaningful ways—for example, putting $50 toward that bike a person is saving for.

Small and medium-sized enterprises (SMEs) struggle to reach customers and to generate leads. MyWave gives banks the ability to link willing buyers with willing sellers and monetize that linkage along the value chain—for example, by introducing a qualified lead to an SME versus spending thousands of dollars every month on Google click ads with modest returns.

Data Ownership, Location, and Privacy   MyWave makes no use of the customer data. It is held securely in the customer's personal cloud shared through opt in with the bank. MyWave regards customer sovereignty and empowerment as being central to its platform business model. Customer data is not analyzed to serve up ads. It is the end customer who controls which parts of the information is shared with whom, through opt in. The customer is in control of opting in or not.

The personal clouds are secure and federated, enabling relationships to be built up between personal clouds. For example, a customer may have a personal cloud and the car they are insuring and purchasing with the bank may also have a personal cloud. That data is shared with the insurer affiliated with the bank and the vehicle dealer for service history. When the car is sold and financed again, all the history with the vehicle's personal cloud goes to the next customer. The MyWave platform enables the Internet of Things.[54]

CUSTOMER-EMPOWERMENT CENTRICITY   In this approach of customer-empowerment centricity, the restructuring of the supply chain is driven primarily from the demand side of the equation. As with the business-oriented customer centricity approach, the "serial" supply chain is transformed yet becomes more radical in its reincarnation and potentially disruptive relative to the business-oriented customer centricity approach and traditional supply side business strategy and culture.

Omie/Customer Commons[55] The second example of these contrasting approaches is Omie. Omie is under the Customer Commons umbrella and is powered running on the Respect Network, which is weighted more toward the customer empowerment approach.

The strategy of Customer Commons (a California-based nonprofit) is to restore the balance of power, respect, and trust between individuals and organizations that serve them. The organization stands with the individual and therefore does not take contributions from commercial entities. While Customer Commons is a member of Respect Network, Omie will exist in both a "blank sheet" version *and* a Respect Network version, as not all individuals may opt to join the Respect Network. Those who do join the Respect Network will have access to specific features on their Omie devices.

The Respect Network is a global private network of personal and business clouds. Its purpose is to enable members anywhere in the world to share sensitive private data over trusted private connections just as easily as they can share data publicly on social networks like Facebook, Twitter, LinkedIn, and Google Plus today.

The Respect Network differentiates itself by the following three tenets:

1. **Decentralized.** Major social networks are centralized databases run by a single company that has access to all the data and sets all the terms. On the Respect Network, all private data resides in the members' own personal and business clouds hosted by their choice of cloud service provider (CSP) anywhere in the world. All sharing is over direct peer-to-peer connections—there is no middleman.
2. **Mutual trust framework.** Centralized social networks ask that all members must agree to terms of service from a single company that can change at any time. On the Respect Network it is the exact opposite: All members agree to the Respect Trust Framework, the groundbreaking legal contract for mutual privacy assurance that won the Privacy Award at the 2011 European Identity Conference.
3. **Member-supported business model.** Centralized social networks monetize by advertising and data brokering, so they need to learn as much about you as possible. There is no unauthorized advertising or data brokering on the Respect Network because it's all private. So the Respect Network is supported directly by members through membership fees and usage fees just like any other global trusted exchange network (e.g., banking, credit cards, and ATMs).

Omie itself is a category of devices that puts the device owners in charge of their own data, the tools they use to manage relationships with their suppliers, and the products and services they get from them.

Omie equates to a tablet PC with a specific set of configurations, operating system tweaks, a personal data cloud, and early applications. As the Omie project evolves, additional form factors will emerge, as will the range of sensors and other devices that Omie will talk to. Omie is being developed by Customer Commons.

In yesterday's model, each app is a silo. At best, individuals get a copy of their data, leaving behind a trail for the silo to leverage under obscure terms and conditions.

How Yesterday's Model Scores

Low   Efficient use of an individual's time

Low   Quality of data

Low   Depth of data

Low   Quality of metadata generated

Low   Privacy of personal data

In today's model, Omie acts as a hub, coordinating and improving information flows and the usefulness of the data generated while data sharing is minimized without compromising outcomes.

How the Omie Model Scores

High   Efficient use of an individual's time

High   Quality of data

High   Depth of data

High   Quality of metadata generated

High   Privacy of your data by design

Your Data over Time with Patterns for Decision Making   Omie creates a three-part virtuous cycle of snowballing value.

1. Omie helps store information.
   ■ Your actions as input.
2. Omie tracks all your information.
   ■ Your information in context.
3. Omie helps you decide.
   ■ Your choices become high-value information.

In Omie's model as it runs on the Respect Network, individuals pay a membership fee of $25. Free social networks, search engines, and other online services make money through advertising and brokering the individual's personal data. There is no unauthorized advertising or data brokering on the Respect Network because all personal and business cloud data is private—Respect Network Corporation does not have any access to it.

Both of these approaches are valid and sound in achieving the win-win enabled by the customer's new voice, and both will continue to evolve as this new industry progresses.

The Customer's Voice

The Customer's Voice is another example of the customer-empowerment centricity approach. The Customer's Voice is an entrepreneurial UK-based company, creating online and mobile services that place the individual's specific needs and intentions for products and services at the heart of the online buying process. With other like-minded companies and individuals, they are working toward a new approach in which buyer and supplier power is more evenly balanced than in the current supplier dominated relationship. There alpha service is a first step along this road.

Their aim is to help individuals buy online more effectively by providing tools that help individuals gather, manage, and set out their buying requirements, and then share them with the market in strict accordance with the individual's preferences. The alpha service began in June 2014, which allows their closed user group also to become members of Respect Network.

The Customer's Voice is based on I-Buy, which is a personal shopping application for the individual. It allows individuals to find the products they want safely and simply, without being targeted by advertising, by pop-ups, or by unwanted encouragements to register, and without the responses to the individual's searches being skewed toward those paying the most to Google. The service doesn't obey Google's rules, or Amazon's rules, but works for the individual, to their rules and preferences, and will always be on the individual's side.

Whether the individual is considering buying a specific product or service now or just starting to research options and prices, fill in one of I-Buy buying requests or carry out a "Quick Find" of what's available on the market from their panel of over 25 well-known UK online retailers. The individual will get back a stream of product descriptions with clear information and helpful images that best match your requirements. These will come to the individual in a simple sequence, starting with items that have had a price drop today, followed by other items from lowest to highest in price. There will be no advertisements or unprompted details of other products to clutter up this simple clear information.

The individual can choose which of the retailers the individual wishes to respond to in their buying requests, and the individual can work on a number of buying requests in parallel. Working with the Snaptaps service from their partner Ensygnia, the initial retailers include UK household names, such as John Lewis, Debenhams, My M&S, Uniqlo, Curry's/PCWorld, and Carphone Warehouse, and also more specialist online brands such as Ebuyer.com, Very.co.uk, Lastminute.com, and Groupon.

The individual can also build up a small but powerful buying information bank of their favorite brands and suppliers, of products and services that the individual buys regularly, and of transactions whose details the individual wishes to store as a record or for further analysis. The individual retains total control over their own data and none of it will ever be shared without the individual's specific permission and then only to support a further buying request.[56]

Notes

1. Rachel Botsman and Roo Rogers, *What's Mine Is Yours: The Rise of Collaborative Consumption* (New York: HarperBusiness, 2010).
2. Kathryn Hough, "A Short History of Collaborative Consumption Start-ups," Techli, techli.com, February 26, 2012.
3. Rip Empson, "Meet Helpouts, Google's Secret Project That Turns Hangouts into a Commerce Platform," July 24, 2013. www.networkedblogs.com/NudcY.
4. Quantified Self Labs, "Quantified Self-Guide to Self-Tracking Tools." http://quantifiedself.com/guide/.
5. http://techcrunch.com/tag/quantified-self/.
6. http://mashable.com/category/wearable-tech/.
7. U.S. Food and Drug Administration, "Mobile Medical Applications," Protecting and Promoting Your Health, June 4, 2014. www.fda.gov/MedicalDevices/ProductsandMedicalProcedures/ConnectedHealth/MobileMedicalApplications/ucm255978.htm.
8. U.S. Food and Drug Administration, "Protecting and Promoting Your Health, Examples of Mobile Apps for Which the FDA Will Exercise Enforcement Discretion," Protecting and Promoting Your Health, June 11, 2014. www.fda.gov/MedicalDevices/ProductsandMedicalProcedures/ConnectedHealth/MobileMedicalApplications/ucm368744.htm.
9. Cisco, "The IoT Opportunity." Trends. www.cisco.com/web/solutions/trends/iot/indepth.html.
10. Postscapes.com. http://postscapes.com/internet-of-things-examples/.
11. Ibid.
12. "How Will the Internet of Things Affect Your Business?" Solar Communications. www.solar.co.uk/internet-of-things-business/.
13. Elyse Betters, "Internet of Things Explained: What Is It, and Can It Really Change the World?" Pocket-lint.com, January 15, 2014. www.pocket-lint.com/news/126559-internet-of-things-explained-what-is-it-and-can-it-really-change-the-world.

14. Sensor wiki: http://en.wikipedia.org/wiki/List_of_sensors, www.sen sorsmag.com/, http://developer.android.com/guide/topics/sensors/ sensors_overview.html, www.sensorsportal.com/HTML/.
15. Ibid.
16. Lance Whitney, "Facebook Gets Thumbs-Up from Feds to Buy Virtual-Reality Firm Oculus," CNET, April 23, 2014. The Federal Trade Commission gives its stamp of approval to the $2 billion deal, according to Reuters, as Facebook readies for "the platforms of tomorrow."
17. Vamien McKalin, "Augmented Reality vs Virtual Reality What Are the Differences and Similarities? Tech Times, April 6, 2014. www.techtimes .com/articles/5078/20140406/augmented-reality-vs-virtual-reality-what-are-the-differences-and-similarities.htm.
18. Forrester Research, "Understanding Online Shopper Behaviors, US 2011," May 17, 2011. www.pwc.com/en_us/us/retail-consumer/publications/ assets/pwc-us-multichannel-shopping-survey.pdf.
19. Research IBM, "Augmented Reality Makes Shopping More Personal, New Mobile Application from IBM Research Helps Both Consumers and Retailers." www.research.ibm.com/articles/augmented-reality.shtml.
20. Creative Guerrilla Marketing, "10 Examples of Augmented Reality in Retail, Clare Evans—Green Room," March 17, 2014. www.creativeguer rillamarketing.com/augmented-reality/10-examples-augmented-reality-retail/.
21. A partial VRM FAQ, July 23, 2014. http://blogs.law.harvard.edu/vrm/.
22. Ibid; Berkman Center for Internet and Society at Harvard University. http://cyber.law.harvard.edu/research/projectvrm?page=1.
23. https://www.taskrabbit.com/.
24. https://www.liveninja.com/.
25. www.care.com/.
26. www.askforit.com/.
27. https://bodyshopbids.com/.
28. http://intently.co/.
29. Neil Harris, Intently.
30. http://offersby.me/, Adam Goldberg—OffersByMe; longweekendmobile .com.
31. http://prizzm.com/.
32. www.thumbtack.com/.
33. http://trovi.co/.
34. www.esnipe.com/.
35. https://www.ubokia.com/intro.
36. https://www.zaarly.com/.
37. https://www.airbnb.com/.
38. https://www.abine.com/index.html.
39. https://www.mozilla.org/en-US/lightbeam/.

40. https://disconnect.me/.
41. https://www.ghostery.com/en/.
42. https://www.privacyfix.com/start/install.
43. http://infogrid.org/trac/.
44. http://projectdanube.org/.
45. Drummond Reed, XDI/XRI/RDF wikis; Markus Sabadello, Markus's XDI Personal Cloud Demo.
46. https://freedombox.elevate.at/.
47. https://gli.ph/.
48. https://www.directly.com/.
49. http://pingup.com/.
50. Nibletz.com.
51. https://www.trustfabric.com/.
52. ProjectVRM, VRM Development Work Harvard Law. http://cyber.law.harvard.edu/projectvrm/VRM_Development_Work
53. This text is reproduced from MyWave. Sources: MyWave CEO Geraldine McBride; MyWave CTO James Ladd; and MyWave CXO Amy Johnson.
54. Ibid.
55. Iain Henderson, Information Answers, www.informationanswers.com; and Customer Commons.
56. The Customer's Voice, "Our Alpha Service," I-Buy. www.thecustomers voice.com/?page_id=853.

CHAPTER 8

Practical Guide: How to Leverage the Customer's New Voice Today

With Dr. David Schrader

Previous chapters have outlined various trends and provided examples that significant boosts in relevancy through directly volunteered personal information not only are possible but are being executed today by leading innovators. Most industries will be significantly impacted by this trend over the next 10 years. In this chapter, the focus is on how a business can interpret these trends so that the business is, at minimum, ready to react, and, it is hoped, is proactive about exploiting the business opportunities that shared consumer information enables.

Two scenarios will set the stage for the discussion in this chapter.

Scenario 1: Jeff's Shopping Trip

It's Wednesday morning. A consumer named Jeff is on his mobile device, before coffee, planning his Saturday morning shopping trip. He needs three items:

1. Some new jeans, because he's been dieting and working out.
2. A new cell phone and cell phone plan, because he's coming up to the end-of-contract date, and he is not happy with the number of dropped calls and billing errors by his current provider.
3. A new refrigerator, because he can hear the motor constantly running on his 22-year-old model, plus the electric bill has been going up.

In his case, he has his personal data store in the cloud, and while at the kitchen table puts out some personal requests for information (RFIs) for these three purchases. For each, he fills out a form (or uses a prepopulated form from previous purchases, built by his personal buying assistant). This includes brand preferences and sizes for the jeans, a link to his historical call detail record data as well as phone and plan preferences, and size and color specs for the refrigerator. Within the RFI, Jeff can explicitly identify vendors that are not allowed to participate in the RFI—for example, the current cell phone provider providing unsatisfactory service. All respondents to the RFIs need to be local (within 10 miles of where he lives), because on Saturday morning he wants—within two hours—to try on the jeans, play around with various cell phone models, and double-check the features of the refrigerator. And finally, of course, any respondent needs to ensure that the items are in stock.

By Friday noon, Jeff's personal assistant presents the various offers that have come back from vendors in these reverse auctions (buyer and seller reverse places—sellers compete against each other). Jeff can see the options and selects the top few that he likes, and can see on a map exactly how to optimize his Saturday morning shopping experience.

Scenario 2: Jill's Grocery Shopping

It's Thursday, and Jill has had a very busy week. She had her results meeting for her annual physical with the doctor, who pointed out that her cholesterol level has gone up. As usual, she's been told to exercise more and eat better, with a suggestion that if her numbers don't improve by the next checkup, she'll need to start taking statins. This time, she's resolved to follow the doctor's directions.

The good news is that all her health records are now accessible via her personal digital assistant (PDA), including the doctor's new recommendations on calorie, salt, and fat content. She's happy with her doctor so she's unlikely to change—but it's convenient to know that all her health records are easily accessible and portable. Because she's got a loyalty card for the supermarket located near her, she fires up some new apps it has advertised that are aimed at healthier eating. She can easily link the store's menu planning system to her health recommendations, and let the app drive suggestions and substitutions for products she traditionally buys. The store provides new recipe ideas for meals that will help her maintain and improve her health numbers. She notices that it's also easy to link to the data from her wearable devices when she goes walking or jogging, as well as the exercise systems at her local gym. With all this data and personal apps that span medical, food, and exercise areas, Jill can easily achieve her new health goals—if she takes the recommendations to heart and avoids her favorite Oreo.

In order to accomplish all of these goals, specific preferences and personal information need to be present in her personal data store.

- Jill's personal data store:
  - Multiprovider integrated information: my health records
  - Analyze exercise history versus
    - Lab tests
    - People like me
  - Analyze known conditions across providers
    - Best doctors
    - Dentists
    - Optometrist
    - Therapist

Overview

If a business wanted to participate in these direct personal information scenarios, and in other future data scenarios where consumers have much more information and thus power, what would a business need to do?

The goal of this chapter is to provide practical advice for evolving a business's strategy, marketing operations, customer service groups, and information technology (IT) organizations, with checklists for taking action. In each of the four sections, specific instructions are given as to what a business will need to *start* doing, *stop* doing, and *continue* doing on its current path. Obviously, each business is different, so each suggestion will need to be adapted to a particular environment and situation.

These scenarios represent a different worldview, one in which consumers have rights to data, and much more power over the timing of their transactions and interactions. While push-based marketing might still be used, companies will need to change their marketing processes and IT systems to accommodate such interactions as reverse auctions, in which consumers initiate the buying process at a time and location that suits them. Companies will also need to incrementally build direct consumer information exchanges while respecting consumers' rights to access and leveraging their data in mutual ways for their incremental benefit and utility.

Possible future scenarios could be:

- Merchant-provided stores for personal information
- Third-party intermediaries that provide them
- Cloud stores directly under consumer control
- Mobile phone storefronts under consumer control

Strategy

The most efficient and effective starting point is educating the business's leadership. How this is accomplished and its timing depend on the rigor of a business's planning processes and whether an organization does top-down or bottom-up planning. The following are suggested questions a change agent will need to explore:

- Is there a forum for explaining new trends and brainstorming on the ramifications to your organization?
- Who are the forward-looking executives who have the time, interest, and power to explore future scenarios?
- Who will need to sponsor the strategy work that needs to be done?
- What "reason to believe" materials will be needed to conduct a one-hour or half-day workshop?
- How can examples outside your industry be adopted to create likely scenarios happening within your industry?
- Can your company identify what current and future legislation may create risks to your current business processes from not being proactive?
- Can your company identify competitors that are likely to drive or lead your industry in these changes?

One potential starting place for these types of initiatives in large organizations is a dedicated strategic planning group that operates year-round. Other options would be an ad hoc approach that depends on business opportunities in addition to an annual plan. In either case, an organization will need a forum to address the evolving directly volunteered consumer information opportunities.

Identifying the list of executives who attend these forums is critical. In particular, who among them will be the likely sponsor of a direct consumer personal data initiative within the organization? This person will need to have the ability to drive the initiative through the organization. In similar situations where big data initiatives have needed a champion to drive strategic initiatives within organizations, the following change agents have been successful:

- At a large international bank, the sponsor works in business development, without the normal day-to-day pressures of running the business. His job is to look further into the future and champion projects that test the waters of what customers might want, run trials on new product offers, and monitor both legal and societal drivers of change.

- At a large retailer, the chief marketing officer (CMO) has the luxury of several associates who can work on special projects. Their focus is to investigate new trends and translate the impacts into opportunities for her organization.
- At an international telecommunications provider, the head of corporate business intelligence (BI) is the champion for new projects that span various business groups around the world.
- At another international phone communication provider, which operates with more bottom-up change, multiple operating groups within selected country organizations are known for their ability to innovate faster than others. As a result, they end up leading change for the other parts of the organization.

Typically, smaller organizations have an advantage over larger ones because there are fewer organizational layers. It's also more obvious who are the risk takers, who are the forward-looking executives, and who are the change agents who directly influence the organization.

Next, it's important to understand which business units will be most likely impacted and build likely scenarios that will engage the senior leadership in those groups. Clearly, the directly volunteered personal data trend will impact mostly organizations that are consumer-driven. In these cases, the consumer marketing and sales leaders will need to be involved (see the next section, "Marketing and Sales").

It's important to take a look at the entire personal data ecosystem, including existing and potential partners. There are also plenty of opportunities for organizations that are intermediaries in the personal data supply chain to study this trend—organizations that aggregate and resell data, as well as organizations that are personal data matchmakers. Two examples of middlemen data businesses that span multiple consumer-oriented companies and help customers find the best deal or the best match are travel agencies and mortgage loan companies. The most complete scenarios show the impact to both business to consumer (B2C) and business to business (B2B) companies, and those in the middle, like the B2B2B2C data supply chains. Ultimately, the business's operating premise will be that of a consumer to world/world to consumer (C2W/W2C) environment where consumers are interacting with the world and the business's operating model functions in that context. To some extent, leading personal data innovators will be those organizations that become the preferred and trusted advisers for the entire span of services needed, hence the need to potentially focus on or think like a personal data aggregator. This focus is with a win-win data scenario to both the organization and the consumer even if personal data aggregation is not the organization's current area of focus.

Another area of opportunity is for organizations to move into the "white space" niches, in which new apps that span multiple formerly siloed consumer spaces come together. The first example with Jeff highlighted the need for apps that help put bids out and collect them, and organize the results geospatially. The second example describing Jill showed how a B2C grocery retailer might need to work with a health care provider as well as sports and fitness chains and vendors of wearable sensor devices. These illustrate the expanded scope of strategy with directly volunteered personal data. Once management and line of business managers are educated on these expanded strategies, it will be clear whom to engage as potential partners.

In addition to these efforts to proactively educate the organization's leadership and identify new market opportunities, there are also benefits to investing in opportunities to avoid risk. This may involve legal or risk management groups if they have relevant competencies. Many forward-looking organizations have chief privacy officers (CPOs) in place, which can be helpful. Creating a chief privacy officer position could possibly be another outcome from the suggested new strategy work. A task force can be formed to monitor legislation that might impact your organization's ability to collect data about customers or to develop answers to expected challenges, as highlighted by the following questions:

Will you be ready to proactively address these likely future threats and challenges?
- Will you be ready when consumers ask:
  - What data did you collect about me?
    - When?
    - Where?
  - Was the data direct or indirect?
    - If indirect, where did you get it?
    - How much did you pay?
    - How did you know it was accurate?
  - How did you use my data?
    - What apps?
    - How many times?
    - When?
  - Did you sell that data?
    - To whom?
    - How did they use it?
  - Can you retract erroneous data?
    - Insights?
    - Provably recall bad data?

Part I and Part II of this book are good starting points to proactively monitor these ever-evolving threats and challenges. A good starting place to identify these likely future threats is in Part III of this book:

- Government/advocacy personal data initiatives
- New personal information industry (consumer as stakeholder)

There is also a myriad of articles related to monitoring, collecting, and learning about not only privacy but data breaches (e.g., Target).[1] The backlash from awkward marketing efforts and poor customer service can be particularity instructive. It can help your organization measure the rate of consumer awareness and response to inappropriate information collection efforts, or perceived misuses of not just personally identifiable information but simply personal consumer information.

The next step will be reviewing an organization's key performance indicators (KPIs) and then conducting a brainstorming session on how the personal data sharing trend will impact your organization's top line; that is, examine marketing spend dollars and how they are spent. Look for clues. Are opt-out rates increasing for e-mail campaigns? Are customers increasingly putting your organization on the Do Not Call list? Which communication channels effectiveness numbers are dropping? These metrics are fairly easy to collect, which can help construct and instrument the trends of the organization.

Another task is to check for competitor initiatives:

- Are competitors launching efforts (e.g., cloud offers) to get ahead of the game in terms of capturing, monitoring, monetizing, and using customer information?
- Are there new market entrants that are aggregators jockeying to interpose themselves between you and your customers?
- Are there upstream vendors that are bypassing your organization to collect customer information, cutting your organization out of the loop?

Once this type of situational analysis is completed, then your organization can shift to brainstorming sessions on what new offers might be possible. Participants in these sessions are best populated across the organization. The best results will be obtained when there is a diverse demographic (e.g., younger associates) who have a broad appreciation of how consumers want to be treated and how much personal information can be collected, rewarded, and ultimately tolerated.

Successful strategies build trust and often need to be coupled with corporate culture change, as well as operational changes in various groups.

The bottom line: Directly volunteered personal data initiatives can be treated like any other strategic opportunity or threat. If the organization has forums for conducting strengths, weaknesses, opportunities, and threats (SWOT) assessments, these forums are likely the best environments to fold in these new personal data initiatives as part of the process to obtain funding of new strategic analysis and new pilot projects.

Using the start/continue/stop construct, the following tasks are recommended:

Activity	Tasks
Start	Adding personal data education and investigations to your strategy planning (SWOT) efforts; monitoring regulatory and competitor activities in this space.
Continue	Identifying and launching exploratory projects to increase your company's expertise.
Stop	Believing that your traditional customer processes just need a little fine-tuning.

Marketing and Sales

Many of the opportunities of the directly volunteered personal information evolution impact an organization's sales and marketing function. These not only impact an organization's current products and services but the development of new products and services.

Businesses engaging in direct consumer information exchanges create a new level of consumer relevancy. In parallel, consumers have a significantly improved ability to determine competitive relevancy by utilizing the Internet to gather more information earlier in the buying cycle. As a consequence they are smarter consumers when the business first has the opportunity to engage them. Not only do they view local businesses and their competitors, but now they also view a global marketplace with higher competitive value propositions. Being better informed raises the bar of competitiveness that must be achieved by the business. In addition, consumers enter the buying process much later in the sales cycle, which inherently limits the business's time to educate them. This forces the competition into more of the price arena and thus puts additional pressure on margins.

Another dimension is the impact of social media and, in particular, word of mouth (both positive and negative), coupled with opinions that impact all stages of the buying/service cycle. Many studies have shown that buyers believe the opinions of other consumers far more than they believe a company's advertising; 84 percent of consumers trust recommendations from people (friends and family) whereas only 48 percent trust search engine ads, and only 42 percent trust online banner ads.[2] This has important ramifications for the marketing mix of spending on channels for customer acquisition, growth, and retention.

Traditional loyalty programs become less effective as a more educated consumer will be more transient and fleeting. The consumer will be more apt to respond to businesses with the highest relevancy in value. In other words, traditional loyalty programs will be replaced with consistent relevancy programs based on directly volunteered customer knowledge. This competency of relevance will be a sustainable new loyalty dimension of tomorrow's direct consumer.

These programs will be the key to truly understanding what consumers really want and value. Other traditional dimensions of marketing campaigns will evolve, often radically. The following is a list of marketing campaign elements that businesses will need to evolve to catch the new direct consumer:

- **Targeting and segmentation.** Segment of one becomes the norm, not the exception. Each customer is unique, and will provide varying amounts of information that can help your business decide whether to react to an initiated request to engage (e.g., personal RFIs/RFPs). Instead of targeting your customers, the customer will increasingly target the business based on an almost completely transparent reputation record.
- **Messaging and offers.** One-size-fits-all messaging won't work anymore, except for commodity products and branding campaigns. Most customers will expect that your company will customize products or services specifically for them and their articulated needs. While much of this focus may be based on price, expect to spend more time and effort articulating the competitive differentiation of your company's feature functionality or service capabilities. In addition, if your business earns the reputation of delivering incremental value for direct information exchanges with the consumers (while keeping their data safe), the opportunities to overtly monetize their data into additional product offers and services will significantly increase.
- **Timing.** Push campaigns will be replaced with an increasing number of just-in-time responses to consumer-initiated requests for information or requests for proposals. This completely inverts the usual approach to broad-based push marketing and advertising. It also requires better listeners with "listening posts" to identify real-time opportunities, and then very quickly apply insights to decide whether to respond.

- **Channels.** Internet use and mobile will continue to grow for all industries for consumer awareness and product/service education, and will also increase for fulfillment. Consumers are increasingly impatient not only about push marketing but also pure responsiveness and product availability. If your business doesn't have a product in stock, they are a mouse click away from your competitors that stock the product. Businesses with great listening abilities and nimble supply chains will be the winners.
- **Metrics.** KPIs for acquisition, growth, and retention will continue but there will be an increasing focus on consistent relevancy (the new loyalty) and respectful treatment of personal information (the new trust). Social network KPIs on influencers or kingpins and on corporate and competitor reputation management and monitoring will also be added and fortified.

One of the most important aspects of marketing is the addition of context surrounding buying intent. The only entity that will have a complete and robust view of context is the consumers themselves. If businesses can develop a reputation for providing added utility or financial value exchange for a more complete picture of consumer buying context, the relevancy and value for that customer can create a platform during the stream of high-quality customer experiences.

Reflecting on our scenarios, in Jeff's case, the clue that he needs jeans in a smaller size may mean that he has dieted successfully, or simply is getting older (perhaps the business knows his age from previous interactions, or acquired this information from a third-party data provider).

If it's the diet situation, then chances are that Jeff needs more than just jeans, which can lead to more differentiated add-on marketing. Businesses can couple a service message ("Did the jeans arrive on time?" "Did they fit?" with add-on offers for other merchandise that might be relevant). Asking "Why did you order these jeans?" as a follow-on in a trial might elicit all the various reasons that could be turned into pull-down menus for full production marketing. Asking "How often do you buy jeans?" might give rise to a triggered campaign at a later point in time. If consumers see value in answering the questions, they will respond. If they perceive no value and regarded the queries as selling, they will likely not respond.

In contrasting the purchase of jeans versus the purchase of a refrigerator, the context is always the key to understanding the purchase behavior (i.e., the "why" of what they are buying). If Jeff were buying a refrigerator instead of a pair of jeans, the critical component is still the "why" or purchase context. Perhaps Jeff is remodeling (in which case there may be opportunities for selling stoves, dishwashers, sinks, and trash compactors). Jeff may be buying a second refrigerator for a downstairs recreation room or the garage, in which case a freezer might be a next-best offer. If Jeff does not directly reveal the buying context, the business's marketing algorithms typically produce on average a 2 to 5 percent campaign success rate. In situations where the consumer reveals purchase context, that success rate can range from 20 percent to 50 percent.[3]

In Jill's case, the grocery example can be augmented from selling food items to selling experiences—but again, only if she's willing to reveal buying context to the business based on some perceived utility or personal gain. For example, if Jill bought a large number of packages of pancake mix and syrup (larger than her usual purchase), knowing that she was running an event may be insightful to the business (i.e., "Are you in charge of something?"). She may communicate that she is planning a pancake fundraiser at her child's school, and would welcome some event-planning services. Grocery operations could then decide to expand into fundraising contexts. A sudden surge of the purchase of candy might indicate she's relapsing on her diet and healthier-eating goals—or it may be the case that's she's buying candy for a school function where she's in charge of this month's party. Either assumption by the business may produce an awkward marketing offer based on traditional marketing campaign algorithms. If she believes that the grocery business can provide her utility in either scenario, the business is better off to have a track record of providing her utility in similar situations. Or if the business notices the purchase of high-end meats or fish, Jill might reveal to the business that she is inviting friends over for a special dinner and might even consider hiring a chef the business could provide, either for the event or to teach her how to cook gourmet dinners regularly for her friends. Consumers will reveal a tremendous amount of personal information if they perceive the relative benefit (i.e., making their lives easier or financially better).

Granted, not all of these, or perhaps not any of them, will apply to many types of businesses. The central point is to expand the thinking beyond more covert data collection to proactive, overt discovery of what consumers need or want beyond specific products to the overall goals that consumers have, and how your company can help them to achieve those goals while exchanging incremental content knowledge that often only they can provide.

It's likely that competitors and others in the consumer information supply chain will start heading in this direction, so your business will need to monitor these activities as well as new market entrances. Many small start-ups (as noted in Chapter 7) are attacking the new niche opportunities, so it would be advantageous to research and monitor their progression. Chapter 7 lists an array of services that will continue to evolve and expand.

So what kinds of plans and changes are required for the CMO and the marketing department?

Activity	Tasks
Start	Thinking about how your company needs to be more transparent with customers about their data.
	Thinking about reverse auctions and what impact they would make on your marketing processes.
	Trying out the ideas in this book as some marketing experiments, to turn data collection into a positive advantage for your customers—new or better offers, or new or better service.
	Figuring out the context around product or service purchases, and ways of obtaining context from consumers so your company has the wider view of their goals.
	Monitoring what competitors are doing to proactively reach out to customers with marketing programs that encourage customer data sharing.
Continue	Evolving your company's marketing processes, infrastructure, and tool base to be ready for event-based marketing triggered by consumer activities. Treat every customer interaction as an opportunity to collect data and grow customer insights.
	Launching social media listening campaigns.
	Monitoring traditional KPIs, but address the fact that the future of campaigns will be based more on pull versus push marketing techniques. Add KPIs for those efforts.
	Planning on how existing or new KPIs could help your company monitor consumer behavior, especially when it comes to consumers turning off information collection. Focus on areas like number of opt outs, number of bailouts in response to information collection, number of complaints about information collection, and measures of consumer engagement and dissatisfaction.
Stop	Counting on traditional push-based marketing campaigns to carry your company's future performance.

Customer Service

Many of the same principles and recommendations for marketing apply to the customer service function. Customer service has become increasingly automated and moved to the web for cost-reduction reasons. But there are still many roles for care centers, which have expanded their functions from just answering phones to web chat and e-mails. Smart customer service groups have evolved to build knowledge repositories that can be shared across the company (e.g., customer complaints about product features flow back to engineering groups working on next product versions). Information gleaned from numerous customer service interactions can be standardized for training purposes, and answers to common questions can be accessed by consumers on the web.

The latest holistic approaches to customer service analyze customer flows across touch points. For example, if someone calls the care center, were they on the website right before calling, and what sequence of web pages did they look at? What caused the call to customer care, and how could your company's systems be changed to increase customer self-service? This analysis can even include the interactive voice response (IVR) button push sequences, and result in optimization of these to speed people through the system if reasons for calling can be predicted, either by real-time analysis of what they were doing on the web ("spent 2 minutes on the bill pay page") or knowledge of their account information ("customer is now 2 weeks late paying a bill). The first button on the IVR could be "If you are calling about your overdue bill, press 1."

With the advent of consumers managing more of their personal information as well as ultimately having their own persistent and consistent personal data stores, customer service will become even more important. The reason is that with a customer's personal data store, much richer context can be provided during a customer service interaction. Your business will be able to see the customer's view of what happened around a service event, not just the limited amount of information that your business's information systems collect.

For example, suppose your business is telecommunications. Think about the case of a telecom customer experiencing multiple dropped calls while transiting an area with spotty coverage by multiple vendors, including some that are your partners. Chances are that your business can get the complete customer view—from your systems' perspectives, plus those of your partners—but often those data points on dropped calls don't come in real time. However, on a consumer device, all the activity can be captured across multiple vendors, and when the customer calls customer care and gives you access to their personal data store, your company can do a better job of fault isolation and causative factors, using the consumer's data as opposed to (or more likely in conjunction with) your company's customer information and switching system information.

In the case of the travel industry, perhaps your airline will have access to your customer's personal data store with location-based information. Your company knows that your customer is booked on the 5 P.M. flight to Los Angeles from Chicago but also notices from geo-spatial information that the person is two hours away from Chicago's O'Hare Airport. Current weather and road reports indicate that it will impossible for him to get to O'Hare in time for the flight, so your airline can automatically rebook him on the 7 P.M. flight and send him a notice to that effect. Making the customer's life better is tomorrow's new loyalty metric.

Being proactive in customer service is possible only if your company has the complete context of the plan or goal, the current conditions, and options. Traditionally, all your company would have had is a piece of the overall travel plan and little relative context (i.e., a transactional view only, not what the customer really plans on doing). But if your company can get the customer to convey more complete context, then your company can do a better job of servicing.

Most current travel and reservations systems take a minimalist approach to allowing the consumer to convey what's actually happening. For example, it's typical that a traveler might want to combine a work trip with some personal travel. The work part of the trip probably has hard deadlines for when and where someone needs to be, but there is flexibility on the personal side. For example, the consumer might say, "I need to fly from Washington, D.C., to Dallas for a work meeting on Wednesday from 8 A.M. to 5 P.M. but would like to see my sister in Houston either before or after for a day, if it doesn't cost too much more." That's the true context. The systems need to take into account hard constraints but also soft ones, perhaps offering a trip that starts on Monday to Houston, Tuesday afternoon to Dallas, and Wednesday night back home, or one that starts Tuesday afternoon to Dallas, with options on how long to stay in Houston after the business meeting. This kind of flexibility in customer service could be further augmented with suggestions based on sharing friend information from the personal data store (e.g., "Do you also want to see your former college roommate, who lives just outside Houston?"). Again, more consumer-side context makes for a better personalized experience.

Some travel companies like Travelocity already infer what travelers want, either explicitly or implicitly. For example, a traveler can sign up for deals between selected groups of destination cities that the traveler enters into the system. But Travelocity also monitors (even if the traveler is anonymous and it knows the traveler only as a cookie) what browsing behaviors the traveler makes. If the traveler has looked three times at Baltimore-to-Jamaica trips in the past two weeks, but not bought, the travel company remembers those web clicks and watches each night as new fares are loaded for 30 percent drops in the prices of airfare, hotels, and/or cruises. Once it discovers those deals, it dynamically creates a personalized part of the website so the next time you come back (recognizing you from the cookie), or if you are known to the company, it will send a personalized e-mail with the deal and a link driving you back to the Travelocity website. So customer needs can be explicit ("Here's what I want") or implicit (by watching behavior). Some psychologists think that what you do is more important than what you say, which has ramifications for both marketing and customer service.

Social media is an increasingly popular area for capturing consumer sentiment. By building a customer listening post, companies can automatically monitor for tweets that mention your company's name, your competitors' names, your product names, your competitors' product names, and scores about the positive or negative tone of the comments. It's not always possible to do identity management to go back to individuals to correct their problems, but your company can make good-faith efforts to resolve issues and communicate that. And sometimes your company can turn complaints into opportunities for sales:

> *A European-based airline monitored tweets to discover dissatisfaction that there were no direct flights from their hub to a U.S. city hosting a music concert. In response, the marketing team issued a challenge—they would add a special flight if they could fill it within a few weeks. To their surprise, they sold out 341 seats within 5 hours.*[4]

The delineation between marketing and customer service is decreasing. Both require deep insights about customers. Both require data from multiple channels, and increasingly those channels are bidirectional, fostering the need for personalized dialogues.

An Australian bank was already doing good marketing and customer service by using event-triggered marketing. The bank often saw response rates of up to 40 percent on targeted offers based on nightly runs of 400 "event detectives" that surfaced opportunities for add-on sales or service. The only problem was that those outbound calls weren't always timed right, so the bank shifted to making the offers add-ons to conversations when customers called their customer service centers. After resolving whatever problem motivated a call, then the rep could make the add-on offer. So is that customer service or marketing, or both? Is there really much of a distinction if your business is customer centric?

In summary, just as in marketing, there are opportunities to use direct consumer knowledge to glean greater insights about the context for providing customer service, thereby increasing customer satisfaction and loyalty by anticipating and correctly resolving consumer problems.

Activity	Tasks
Start	Reworking your business's customer service portion of the website to incrementally capture customer data (with customers' permission).
	Reworking your contact center scripts to incrementally capture customer data via dialogues.
Continue	Creating customer support dialogues that are event-driven.
	Building and using social media listening posts to discover customer issues earlier.
	Evolving your business's customer service processes, infrastructure, tools, and training to incorporate best practices for event-driven and data-driven customer service.
Stop	Thinking of customer service as a silo. Instead, think holistically about the entire life cycle of customer needs, including a much tighter linkage with the marketing group.

Information Technology

Once your company has a good strategy and has selected some key projects to test the waters for increasing the amount of directly volunteered consumer information, it's up to the information technology (IT) organization to determine how to translate project goals into realities. There are numerous new technical requirements, which range from new policy decisions about data capture, retention, and use, to new applications, to new infrastructure and architectures. In addition, the game plan will need to involve multiple IT groups, ranging from data warehouse and cloud groups to the tech teams for building and supporting new or revised marketing and customer service applications. This section touches on many of these requirements.

Referencing the two scenarios at the beginning of this chapter, the technical requirements are described next.

Step-by-Step Processing Requirements.

In Scenario 1, Jeff filled out three RFIs for the jeans, cell phone plan, and refrigerator. Generally, consumers will need forms-based templates for expressing their RFIs. If your company is the leader, you may be able to set the standard with downloadable apps and templates for all the products and services your company offers. For some period of time, expect there to be multiple competitors. Ultimately, standards committees will get involved (and your company will need to have your technical people participate), or a handful of predominant demand aggregators will set requirements for your company. Expect this area to evolve rapidly.

In Scenario 2, Jill linked information across various traditionally siloed areas of health care, groceries, and wearable sensors. Here again, standards will evolve and stay in flux. Early leaders will help set the standards with proprietary forms and data exchanges (probably XML-tagged).

In both cases, the RFIs are then launched. This requires consumer-side software to push the RFIs out to all possible bidders, and that each of those bidders have software in place to "listen for" the bids, then process them. Your company will need to build "listening posts" or software to plug into common bid aggregator platforms if customers do not come to your company directly. In the former case, these are likely to be much like current social media Twitter capture platforms. In the latter case, your company will need to comply with the bid exchange protocols of the aggregator.

Processing each personal RFI means deciding whether to bid (assuming you are allowed to bid—recall that Scenario 1 gave Jeff the option of screening out some vendors with whom he had a bad experience). Bidding can depend on numerous factors, and most of the decision processes and scoring can use information already in your data warehouse, such as:

- **Consumer trustworthiness.** Have we dealt with this customer before? Is he trustworthy? Does he pay on time and is he creditworthy?
- **Consumer experience.** If we know the past history, have we had problems with the customer? Excessive complaints? Excessive product returns?
- **Consumer value.** Do we have lifetime value and profitability projections for this customer? Do we know the customer's life stage and the value of building an ongoing relationship with this customer?
- **Product match.** If we bid, is it a good match to the customer's specifications? Do we have a high likelihood of acceptance? Can we meet the terms and conditions?
- **Product availability.** Do we have the product in the store near this customer, or can we ship it in the required time frames? If provisioning requires others in the supply chain (e.g., shippers or even custom manufacturing), can they meet the requirements in time?
- **Service availability.** Can we service this customer given current resources and geography?
- **Bid history.** Have we responded to this customer's asks before? Can we compute the likelihood of bid acceptance?
- **Pricing.** At what price should we bid? How badly do we need this business to meet both short- and long-term goals? Are we willing to price-discount to acquire a new possibly high-value customer? If an existing customer, do we give a discount for loyalty? If a troublesome existing customer, is it time to "fire the customer" by not bidding at all, or at a high rate? In Scenario 1, a telecom bidding on Jeff's cell phone business will need to access his previous calling patterns and do a scenario simulation to see (assuming Jeff's calling patterns don't change) what the costs, revenues, and profits might be by bidding at selected price points. Awareness of competitor pricing and special offers in that geography may also be factors.

Note that many of these analytics may already exist but may need to be marshaled in real time in order to provide a timely bid response. In addition, since there will be a time lag between bidding and acceptance or rejection, the business may need a new process to put a tentative hold on products to ensure availability.

Assuming that a vendor responds to the bid, then intermediary software on the consumer side will aggregate the responses, perhaps rank-order them, and present them for the consumer to choose. This may involve immediate decisions (e.g., making an immediate order over the Internet, Jill buying a substitute product while in the store) or deferred decisions (Jeff thinking about which cell phone and plan to pick).

After this point, then the usual fulfillment and replenishment processes apply.

Architecture Changes

The advent of big data has driven most vendors to augment traditional data warehouse architectures to incorporate more types of data sources, arriving at greater speed, with new processing requirements. Figure 8.1 shows a typical vendor's architecture, in this case the Teradata Unified Data Architecture. The traditional flow of data in this picture goes from left to right. A wide variety of traditional and new data sources feed information into a Data Platform. Periodically, a Discovery Platform is used to analyze the data, looking for insights, trends, and patterns. The ones that pan out are added to the traditional data warehouse, which drives operational systems like marketing campaigns. Ultimately, the consumer receives a marketing

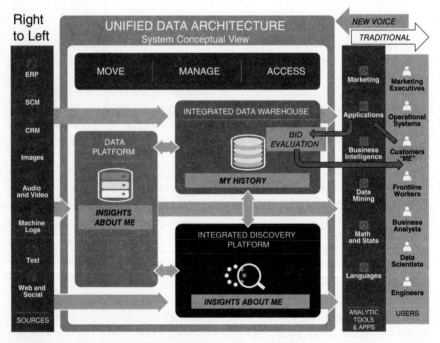

FIGURE 8.1 Unified Data Architecture
Source: Teradata Unified Data Architecture.

message and responds. This represents probably 85 percent of all uses of data for marketing. Big data has been added to the number of sources on the left and for growing the number and type of insights in the Discovery Platform, but after that the rest of the picture remains the same.

With these new scenarios, the information based on consumer-driven information from consumer-initiated interactions and transactions flows backward, from right to left as shown in Figure 8.1. The activity is initiated by consumers on the right side of the diagram. The consumer initiates the purchasing (e.g., personal RFIs), and corporate listening platforms monitor for consumer activity. Once the listening process finds an opportunity to bid, it kicks off the process for evaluating whether to respond, which may require accessing other platforms to determine insights, history, and previous bid results. The insights may be created on the Data Platform or in the Discovery Platform, or reside in the Integrated Data Warehouse. Over time, new factors from big data might be taken into account (e.g., "Do we have scores from this customer's angry calls to customer service?"). Ultimately a bid decision is made, coupled with terms and conditions that flow back to the consumer. Then your company awaits a response.

In addition to architectural changes, there are also some critical policy decisions that will impact IT. Going back to the defensive strategy discussion, IT will need to plan for new data life stage and tagging requirements (metadata) about every piece of consumer information collected. For each piece of data collected directly or purchased/exchanged with other firms, controls will need to be put in place and monitored.

Expect consumer challenges. For each piece of consumer data, can your company respond with source, date, and all uses? Do you keep track of data lineage, and, if challenged, can your company prove all uses were legitimate? This extends to the data supply chain. Your company will need to know where you acquired data (especially from third parties, including use restrictions), and to whom you gave data (especially if you are an intermediary). In addition, it's likely that your company will need to open up your company's website to answering these kinds of consumer questions. Metadata about these types of data as well as the entire data life stage is required, from consumer-generated information on the website, to up-front consumer privacy information on your website, to the use and verifiable ultimate disposal of data.

Finally, your company will need to plan to revise its marketing and customer service systems to support pull-based marketing and real-time customer service. Listening bid platforms will likely be new but are similar to social media listening platforms, but with greater needs for standards as opposed to free-form inputs. Customer service systems will need to have much more customer information on the screens, perhaps personalizing for each inbound call based on situational awareness that's real-time (e.g., predicting why a customer is calling, and having all context on the screen so the agent is smarter and knows the options for problem resolution for that particular customer).

Activity	Tasks
Start	Gathering requirements for the scenarios your company plans to pilot.
	Thinking about reverse auction ramifications to your current systems, and identifying what real-time web services will be needed for responding to bids.
	Investigating listening platforms.
	Looking for standards in your industry or adjacent industries that will impact your IT.
Continue	Evolving your IT architecture to accommodate new sources of data.
	Working across all organizations that use data to make decisions, including marketing and customer service. Continue to make investments in analytics and predictive modeling tools.
	Building out metadata information systems to capture data lineage and use.
	Investigating the ramifications of privacy legislation on IT.
Stop	Assuming that usage of your IT platforms will remain the same.

If your company can build a safe haven for consumers to volunteer high-value personal information, if you can build convenience and utility, and if you can provide novel value fulfillment and financial benefits, then consumers will directly share their purchase intentions with context. This will be your company's vehicle to then be an active information exchange agent with future personal data stores. This opens up new opportunities for customer insight and service that go far beyond what's possible today.

The vaunted 360-degree view of the customer now becomes truly obtainable. Today, even with the very best customer management systems, companies have maybe a 30-degree (or less) view of the customer, because in our example Jill engages in many other interactions with other vendors, and your company likely will have no idea what the total, composite picture really is. Guessing from a meager set of clues represents the state of the art. When the customer trusts you enough to provide wider access so your company can serve her better, this opens up new vistas for better marketing, better product development, better customer service, and better customer relationships.

Getting there won't happen overnight. It begins with recognition of the trends highlighted through this book. It starts with recognizing that your company's strategy has a hole, one that needs to be investigated and plugged. It starts with pushing the reset button for marketing, and rethinking customer service. It may require significant changes to your IT architecture and data practices.

Notes

1. Maggie McGrath, "Target Data Breach Spilled Info on as Many as 70-Million Customers," Forbes.com, January 10, 2014. www.forbes .com/sites/maggiemcgrath/2014/01/10/target-data-breach-spilled-info-on-as-many-as-70-million-customers/.
2. Nielsen "Under the Influence: Consumer Trust in Advertising," Nielsen global survey, September 17, March 8, 2013. www.nielsen.com/us/en/insights/news/2013/under-the-influence-consumer-trust-in-advertising.html. 29,000 consumers in 58 countries throughout Asia-Pacifi c, Europe, Latin America, the Middle East, Africa, and North America were polled.
3. Center for Information-Based Competition 2014 Direct Consumer Research Study.
4. Travelweekly.com, "KLM Does Charter Deal on Twitter," January 5, 2011. www.travelweekly.com/Travel-News/Online-Travel/KLM-does-charter-deal-on-Twitter/.

PART III

Engaging Tomorrow's New Voice

Tomorrow's consumers will bear little resemblance to yesterday's consumers in how they buy products and services to fulfill their wants and needs. The information consumers generate both intentionally and incidentally will continue to increase exponentially with the continued rapid evolution of technology interconnected by the Internet. To put this in perspective, present-day consumers already hold in their hands not only tremendous computing power but also a gateway to the world's information.

Tomorrow's consumer will not only have direct access to virtually any type of information but also experience continued rapid escalation of personal computing power with the proliferation of low-cost embedded sensors in everything from clothing to wristwatches. The resulting consumer data exhaust and direct information-sharing potential will eclipse today's consumer information environment.

Their information will reside in a personal cloud of which they will have full and transparent control and ownership. Data from their smart objects, sensors, wearable technology, commercial transactions and interactions, health, and a myriad of other digital information will reside there. Their digital life will be there as an information "onion" that they will use to peel back layers of purchase intentions and context to a select group of suppliers as needed. To a large extent, these will be real-time, locally expressed buying intentions that will be shared passively. Organizations will have evolved from a defensive mind-set about consumer-initiated interactions and information to a true partnership where information and data flow freely between themselves and the consumers in a modern, reusable format through automated processes. During every interaction and transaction, the resulting data will populate the consumer's personal cloud, creating a persistent and consistent lifetime record of that consumer's personal and commercial activities.[1]

As a result, the attributes of tomorrow's consumer will have more of the following:

- Professionalized buying: Similar to the automation of corporate buying requests for information (RFIs) and requests for proposals (RFPs).
- Independence: Buy how, what, when, where, and at the price consumers want.
- Personal telemetry: Embedded sensors quantify any aspect of their lives.
- Computing power: $400 iPhone has same performance as $5 million supercomputer in 1975.
- Information: Creation, access, and sharing as Internet, computing, and sensors evolve.
- Information competency: A 10-year-old's information technology competency matches that of a data professional 30 years ago.
- Transparency: Synchronous transparency—consumers view business transparently, and allow business discretionary views of themselves and their information.
- Advocacy groups for privacy: Continued expansion of industry and other privacy advocates.
- Government privacy legislation: Privacy legislation has doubled over the past decade.
- Expectations: Ultrahigh service levels and experience online get transferred to offline.
- Information ownership: Zero monetization of the past transforms into monetizing personal asset of the future.
- Sharing: Sharing personal information has doubled every two years; it is more passively shared yet managed.
- Disruptive opportunities: Market transparency to consumer coupled with connectivity radically fuels industry disruptions.
- Intolerance/control of irrelevant selling: Enabling buying is the new selling.
- Digitization: More automation of everyday consumer objects.

Information, technology, connectivity, and mobility will continue to define the future consumer. One of the innovation areas that is spawning great innovation for consumers is the smartphone revolution. Innovations enable a wide range of low-cost microelectromechanical systems (MEMS), which includes accelerometers (measuring consumer's or object's motion and/or acceleration), gyroscopes (measuring consumer's or object's orientation to things), and magnetometers (location acquisition [compass] of consumer or object in mobile phones or tablet computers). These three technologies continue to become very inexpensive, which enables embedding of these capabilities in almost any physical product. This will explode the digital footprint/digital exhaust of tomorrow's consumer. MEMS technology will exist in everyday items such as clothing or a can of beans, enabling the consumer to make their lives easier (e.g., finding that lost sock or automatic replenishment of their favorite brand of beans). These two examples are simple applications of MEMS.

Far more sophisticated uses of MEMS will help make the consumer's life better in more profound ways. Relative to the can of beans example, sensors will also be able to detect the nutritional value and coordinate that with the selected preferences of the consumer. The "lost sock" example extends to MEMS sensors in a sock that detect and monitor temperature, heart rate, speed, and acceleration of the consumer or an object. The same smart sock will also simultaneously transmit geolocation data at the consumer's discretion. Starting in 2008, Cityzen Sciences began specializing in smart textiles conception and development. Other sensor technology ranging from Kolibree's sensor-embedded toothbrush that sends data directly to the consumer's smartphone is just a glimpse of what tomorrow's consumer's environment will hold. Mobility is key to the consumer's information future, with wearable technology in its infancy. Accenture's Digital Consumer Tech Survey 2014 indicated that more than half of consumers are interested in buying wearables (e.g., fitness products, smart watches, and connected eyeglasses). Today's list goes on for harbingers of the future consumer. Fitbit and Jawbone collect and store information on steps taken, calories burned, and sleeping habits. Consumer wellness of the future will rely on products like iHealth and Withings, which include sensor-based technologies measuring pulse, blood pressure, sleep, weight, and glucose levels. Products like the JUNE bracelet from Netatmo will monitor sun exposure and what level of sunscreen consumer requires.[2]

Over the next decade, as more personal data becomes natively created, consumers will increasingly have:

- Practical and legal sovereignty over its discretionary sharing
- Consistent and persistent personal data stores
- The information culture, competency, and expectations of digital natives
- Real-time data streams from smart objects
- Professional and advocacy assistance for managing buying preferences and sharing parameters
- Professionalized buying on their terms and conditions (i.e., personal incarnation of RFIs/RFPs)
- Limited sharing of the most valuable personal data except when receiving personal utility or financial reward (versus one-sided $500 billion of commercial monetization and capitalization of personal data by, e.g., Google, Facebook, Yahoo!, and LinkedIn)

- Privacy agenda replaced by compensated and controlled intentional personal data sharing

Businesses will be evolving from the indirect consumer data model to the direct-from-consumer buying models as the accepted industry norm with inference-based models playing a supportive data role. Businesses will have also completely integrated into the consumer to consumer (C2C) sharing economy. Business analytics will migrate toward a focus on consumer-initiated buying activities as well as the consumer's personal data stores. Government legislation and advocacy groups will continue to evolve the rights of consumers over their personal data sovereignty as a legally enforceable personal asset. Far greater controls will be in place for consumers to easily select from a range of sharing options, from "share everything" to "share nothing" (e.g., from full data streams from all online and offline behavior and transactions, coupled with data streams from all personal smart possessions, to the "right to be digitally forgotten"). The personal data industry will continue to evolve, with a full array of services supporting consumers managing and monetizing their personal data. This industry will involve a support infrastructure for the full range of consumers, from do-it-yourselfers (i.e., several generations managing a smartphone's data or an individual's Facebook profile) to an infrastructure of professionals similar to today's range of accountant services.

Notes

1. Iain Henderson, "Omie Update," Customer Commons. http://customer commons.org/?s=omie+project.
2. Paul Nunes and Larry Downes, "The Five Most Disruptive Innovations at CES 2014," Forbes, January 10, 2014. www.forbes.com/sites/bigbangdisruption/2014/01/10/the-five-most-disruptive-innovations-at-ces-2014/.

CHAPTER 9

How Consumers Will Buy Tomorrow

The recent decade of evolution has seen tremendous growth in tools to help consumers buy rather than one-way selling and marketing techniques that have previously dominated the consumer's world. The best-known example of this evolution from one-way selling and marketing techniques to more of a buying enablement utility is Amazon's buying utilities for consumers. Amazon doesn't explicitly sell or advertise but instead provides buyers with useful information that is largely independent of a one-sided business agenda (i.e., buy our product because we want to sell it).

To assist a consumer's buying, Amazon has provided support of buying tools that are not based on a business bias (except when there is financial benefit to the consumer) but more real information about other consumer buying behavior (i.e., straightforward transparency):

- Special Offers and Product Promotions
- Frequently Bought Together
- What Other Items Do Customers Buy After Viewing This Item?
- Customer Reviews and ranked "Most Helpful Customer Reviews"
- Product Details
- Customers Who Bought This Item Also Bought
- Customers viewing this page may be interested in these sponsored links
- Customer Questions and Answers
- Your Recently Viewed Items and Featured Recommendations

The next decade will see an evolution of these types of tools for the consumer with a migration of similar tools that are independent of a particular business platform such as Amazon. The focus will be on business-independent advocacy of the consumer's buying initiatives and will incorporate the analytical tools of companies like Amazon. Ultimately, selling will be reincarnated as buying with such tools.

Selling Reincarnated as Buying: New Buy/Sell Process

The reincarnation of selling as buying will usher in a new buy/sell process when interacting and transacting with the consumer. For several decades prior, real selling or marketing innovation has been curtailed by the fact that consumers don't like to be sold or marketed to and are therefore far less willing to engage with businesses. Consumers have far greater power now to ignore a large portion of sales and marketing initiatives. This negates many of the tried-and-true marketing processes, as they are no longer relevant to the buying environment that the consumer currently operates in. As consumers' buying became more competent and powerful, the next logical step was to have it professionalized, much as corporate buying had been professionalized many decades ago.

Figure 9.1 depicts the consumer's actions on the left, and the organization's actions on the right. The consumer initiates the interaction with the activity of search and the buying context of that search. This search will be either the consumer's request for information (CRFI) or the consumer's request for proposal (CRFP). The tools and processes to initiate CRFIs and I-RFPs have emerged from the new personal data ecosystem industry that has evolved over the past decade as well as the evolution of business processes and innovation. The organization deploys segmentation based on the consumer search and context. With the consumer's act of finding the desired product or service, engagement begins. The organization then goes into inquiry management with the consumer. The consumer then enters into a negotiation phase with the organization. If this negotiation results in a mutually acceptable agreement, a transaction takes place.

The consumer and the business then enter into a series of steps following the actual transaction. Each party welcomes the other into that party's world. The business then goes through a series of relationship servicing and development with problem management if necessary. If the relationship between the consumer and the business is unsatisfactory, then both manage the termination of the relationship with the resulting new personal and commercial data being managed based on the terms and conditions of the consumer and the business. At this point, there is an opportunity for the business and/or the consumer to reengage if doing so is mutually acceptable. The following are more detailed dimensions of each new step in the process.

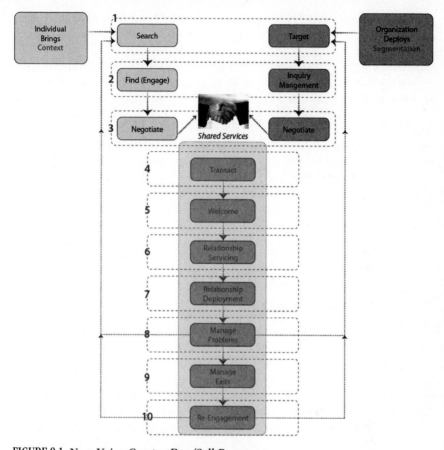

FIGURE 9.1 New Voice Creates Buy/Sell Process
Source: Iain Henderson, Information Answers, www.informationanswers.com.

Search/Target*

This step in the process in previous decades was traditional search, and it is now transformed into a personal request for information (PRFI). The major change from previous marketing processes is that the consumer brings context to the initial interaction. The added dimension of context will enable the targeting to be more precise by the business. With the addition of buying context, this will better enable the business to find consumers closely matched to

---

*The following text (up to the heading Advertising Inversion) was written in conjunction with Iain Henderson and Joe Andrieu. Used with permission.

its unique selling proposition. The business will be interacting with the new tools the consumer has deployed in the search process. As consumers search for their desired products with specific options, this will prequalify them for businesses segmentation and targeting. At this point in the interaction, the consumer will be engaging anonymously with a pseudonym ID, as there is no need to share personal data at this point in the process. Intermediaries or "infomediaries" from the new personal data ecosystem industry may or may not be involved at this point in the process to assist the consumer. They will be acting as the consumer's buying agent (i.e., fourth-party-driven services). Fourth parties (infomediaries) have a fiduciary responsibility to first parties (consumers). Third parties (e.g., Amazon) may or may not have a fiduciary responsibility to anyone (independent entities). Second parties (either re-tailer or consumer) have a fiduciary responsibility to themselves, as do first parties (e.g., consumer or retailer). First and second parties are symmetrical and determined by whose perspective is taken; consumers are the retailer's second party and the retailer is their first party.[1]

Find (Engage)/Inquiry Management

At this point in the process, personal request for proposals (PRFPs) are initiated to a prequalified set of businesses or suppliers. Both parties make available qualifying data to be used for the step; that is, both parties have enough information to qualify each other in order to proceed to the next step in the process. This qualifying data also enables a more refined and de-tailed discussion about the needs and requirements of the consumer and the relevancy of the business's offers. This enables both parties to migrate up the solution axis with only the amount of personal data required for this step in the process. As the step continues, both parties can request more detail. This is also the step where data from the search/target step is verified. Another distinction of the step from previous marketing campaign incarnations is that the step is engaged in equally by both parties. As in the previous step, intermediaries and infomediaries are likely to be involved in the step.

Negotiation

At this point in the process, the consumer is talking to one referred solu-tion provider. This is where the actual proposed deal is on the table. Unlike in previous decades, terms and conditions are negotiated and exchanged by both the business and the consumer. Another distinction from previous decades is that the terms and conditions are far more easily understood and transparent. They are also distinguished by not only to what the consumer desires but also how he or she wants it. These terms and conditions also cover the current and future use of the newly created transaction data. The consumer also has professionalized tools to compare the solutions offered in a standardized format. Reputation tools are also a new aspect of this new tool set (i.e., managing the consumer as the demand side of a commercial entity).

Transact

The transact step of this process will involve a new form of payment process and party—payment intermediaries. This is another aspect of the consumer's buying professionalization. This will have an added benefit to business's credit card fraud and related identity theft issues. Individually managed identity will be a key aspect of every transaction and will likely have a significant impact on identity theft.

Welcome

The welcome step is the relationship setup phase where each party becomes more acquainted with the other. The products and services that were purchased are set up and configured accordingly. Ongoing account management and billing are coordinated. If this business is a new supplier to the supply network, the consumer welcomes the newly acquired business to the personal supply network or federation. The distinction of this welcome phase from previous generations is that the consumer is far more engaged in the process with the new supplier or business.

Relationship Servicing

The relationship servicing step is focused on fixing the operational or service delivery issues. It is the customer service aspect of the relationship. This step also has the purpose of dealing with ad hoc issues (e.g., change of address, contact details, and payment details). An important distinction in this new version of customer service is that the consumer doesn't follow the businesses processes but instead the business follows the consumer's information and processes—for example, consumers communicating to all the siloed businesses they deal with that their addresses have changed versus all businesses obtaining the records from a single, direct, updated information source.

Relationship Development

This relationship development step has replaced the previous customer relationship management (CRM) cross-sell/up-sell activity. This step will also be in the context of the solution set in the previous customer service step.

The distinction of this step is that the business will be far more informed with the consumer's active engagement rather than just having a momentary snapshot of the supplier observed during the transaction. With expectations in terms and conditions well defined, consumers will be more welcoming (versus avoidance) toward cross-sell and up-sell activities by the business. These cross-sell/up-sell activities will be laser-focused and highly relevant because of the open data-sharing environment between each consumer and the business.

Manage Problems

This step is initiated only if there are significant problems. The step would constitute tier 1 customer service of frustrated, angry, or upset customers. The distinction of this iteration of significant problem solving is that it will likely be far less painful if and when it occurs because of a far more engaged and educated consumer.

Manage Exits

This step occurs when the consumer and business decide to detach themselves from each other either permanently or for a period of time. It will be caused by either significant problems between the two entities or a change in the consumer's needs or buying context. From a business's perspective, this can occur when a business decides to leave a particular marketplace or terminate a specific directory service. This step is also far more proactive in that there is more information about impending market exits and rationales. Managed exits rather than silent and unexplained exits also increase customer retention, as attrition is less of a surprise and more of a planned event with both parties far more engaged.

Re-Engagement

This step replaces the previous generation's win-back campaign relative to typical CRM processes. Lost customers can be targeted with offers to return based on the well-documented reason or circumstance for attrition. The consumer's return will also be based on a time-driven change of context (e.g., "I will receive a big promotion in three months, so I can now take that big vacation in January of next year"). This will enable the business to create a laser-targeted win-back offer that is perfectly synchronized with the consumer's change in situation. The distinction from the previous generation of win-back efforts is that the consumer has now retained all of the shared knowledge of the previous relationship and will be more informed.

Advertising Inversion

Reincarnating selling as buying also necessitates the reincarnation or inversion of advertising. Push or supply-side advertising will follow the same conversion to pull or demand-side initiatives from the customer. Future advertising will be driven by the customer's direct wants and needs rather than the business's initiatives to conduct advertising campaigns for products and services based solely on internal performance edicts.

Evolution (and Inversion) of Today's Interactive Advertising Infrastructure

Today's interactive advertising technical infrastructure and processes of how incidentally (unintentionally) volunteered personal information is gathered and leveraged for interactive advertising to individuals has most of the elements that will be required in tomorrow's individual-driven advertising model. Because of the nature of the indirect information, the advertising infrastructure (including the client business) only knows that someone may be interested but does not know the actual identity of the individual.

In today's world, the retailer typically operates at arm's length with the individual, as the true identity and explicit buying intentions are masked and at best inferred. For example, when an individual visits a retailer's website via a browser, the retailer must first try to determine if the individual is anonymous or a new potential customer. If the retailer determines that this visitor is a current customer, the retailer refers to its own data set to determine how best to interact with this individual. Reference data for known customers would be such data as past purchase history, interactions with the retailer's customer care agents, and enriched data about known visitors from third-party data providers (Experian, Axiom for address, householding). In the case where the visitor appears anonymous, the retailer will typically leverage data such as browsing history, including what products have been viewed and/or placed in the visitor's shopping cart, blogging or forums activity on the retailer's site, and social media related activity. In either the "known" or the "anonymous" scenario, the retailer would attempt to personalize the visitor's browsing experience.

The more the retailer knows about the visitor, the better the experience the retailer can provide (e.g., relevant product recommendations, tailored web-page content to potential areas of the visitor's interest, germane offers and promotions). Today's retailers typically extend their data insights by using additional third-party data platform providers when the visitor is determined to be anonymous (e.g., demand-side platform, supply-side platform, demand management platform). Data platform providers such as BlueKai, nPario, Magnetic, M-spatial, Database Marketing Solutions, and Lookery provide additional insights into anonymous visitors by building online interest profiles of those visitors.

Even with the data sophistication of these data platform providers, retailers still have a myopic view of visitor behavior because they are not sourcing the data directly from the individual. For example, if an individual has shown an interest in sports equipment on the site (e.g., a baseball glove), the fact that the visitor has also been looking for camping equipment from an unaffiliated site will likely be obscured from the first retailer's view. As a partial data workaround, the retailer will also engage third-party online data aggregators, such as Acxiom, Datalogix, Epsilon, and ChoicePoint to get a broader perspective on the visitor's online activity. These data aggregators will collect browsing behavior anonymously across a wide set of websites within their network. In this example, the visitor may have visited several camping supply websites and the data aggregator may have access to that data. The retailer works with the data aggregator to serve up camping supply offerings recommendations the next time that anonymous visitor visits that retailer's website. Figure 9.2 is a very simple representation of the basic data flow for anonymous visitors.

Despite the highly sophisticated data collection and analytics of today's approaches, the retailer is still relegated to guessing or inferring an individual's purchasing or browsing behavior from a relatively small set of secondary and historical buying indicators. As a result, these secondary and historical buying indicators only result in roughly a 10 percent relevancy factor with the retailer's online offer to the individual visitor.

In this new model, individuals will fundamentally invert the current advertising model by directing what advertising (request-specific information or personal request for information [PRFI]) they desire by intentionally volunteering personal information and ultimately their identity (if and when

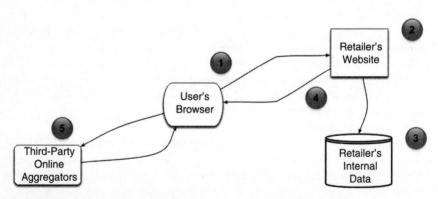

FIGURE 9.2 **Current Advertising Model (Business Driven)**
Source: James Semenak.

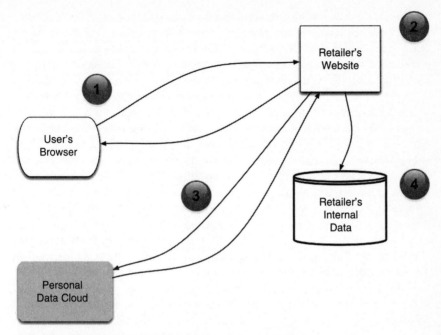

FIGURE 9.3 Inverted Advertising Model (Consumer Driven)
Source: James Semenak.

appropriate and necessary) directly to businesses; that is, individuals segment, direct, and determine the advertising that businesses serve to them.
The reality of today is that advertising would likely have a relative relevancy
score of less than 1 out of 10 because the advertising is based on indirect
information with limited context in the inference model. Tomorrow's advertising will take the form of a business's response to a PRFI, which will likely
have a relative relevancy score of greater than 9 out of 10 because the business is responding to direct information from the individual with complete
context and intent. Individuals will initially communicate anonymously and
then incrementally reveal additional pertinent information that only the individual is privy to. They will reveal their identity once they are engaged
sufficiently with the business prior to the transaction.

Figure 9.3 illustrates the basic data flow changes when evolving to this
direct-from-individual explicit buying intent model (i.e., intentionally volunteered personal information).

The individual visits the retailer site using the web browser in search
mode. As in the current information ecosystem, the retailer will attempt to
determine whether it knows this visitor. If the individual is willing to engage

with the retailer, the visitor's personal data store will be open for the retailer, and based on their reviews they set up privacy and authentication rules. Once the retailer determines this visitor's personal data store, the retailer will send a request to access, authenticate, and extract the information the individual has allowed based on the person's privacy settings. As the engagement and/or negotiation progresses, the individual will incrementally reveal more personal information as needed to the retailer via the retailer's access to the individual's personal data store. This incremental revealing of personal data will be partially automated and partially driven by the individual's input and engagement preferences. Once the retailer has queried the individual's personal data store regarding the set of preferences and specific purchase intentions (e.g., the individual desires outdoor clothing of a particular brand, color, size, and price range), the retailer combines the individual's personal data store information with any historical data it may have on the individual. The retailer then uses its internal recommendation algorithms and decisioning engines to determine how best to respond to the individual's explicit buying intentions on outdoor clothing.

The professionalization of an individual's buying (i.e., personal RFIs and requests for quotations [RFQs]) transforms the concepts of inbound and outbound communications. When the individual browses the retailer's site, the retailer is then prompted to go to the individual's personal data cloud—that is, an individual's inbound data flow. When an individual creates an explicit personal request for information (PRFI) or personal request for proposal (PRFP) for retailers or other businesses, the retailer or business will need to respond to the individual's initiated outbound request. This will require the business to create new server environments to serve such requests by individuals or their buying agents. Traditional inbound and outbound communications will transform from primarily asynchronous communications (i.e., one-way shotgun approach of advertising) to more synchronous communications (i.e., more iterative, targeted, and cooperative communication) between the individual and the business.[2]

Notes

1. Joe Andrieu, Tom Wilson.
2. James Semenak.

CHAPTER 10

New Privacy

Privacy as we know it today will take a significantly different form over the next 10 years. Privacy itself is a complex concept with many varying definitions in an ever-changing context. Its metamorphosis will evolve along the following dimensions:

Controllability by Consumer
- Do not track; right to be forgotten; global unsubscribe.

New Cultural Norms of Individual's Digital Pragmatism
- I'm on the grid; that's my life. I don't care about most things you can scrape off the web about me, but if you want the really valuable information, you're going to have to give me a compelling reason and control over what is shared with whom and why.
- It's binary. Either you're on or you're off the grid.[1]
- The web is a big copy machine.[2]

New Cultural Norms of Businesses
- Realization that most vital information is at the sharing discretion of the individual.
- Covert noncompensated information acquisition becomes overt rewarded sharing.

Government Regulation Relevancy
- Governments playing catch-up to the digital world.

Professional Support from New Personal Data Industry
- Personal data would become tomorrow's currency.
- The new personal data industry will support the management and monetization of personal data, with the consumer as the primary shareholder.

Businesses Replace Exploitive Privacy with Value Exchange Privacy
- We will monetize your personal information for our agenda and benefit versus...
- We will monetize your personal information for an agreed-upon value to you:
  - Product/service relevancy
  - Better experience
  - Making your life easier
  - Financial reward

When the future Personal Information Masters are given sufficient motivation from businesses coupled with personal information protection similar to the protective framework of Privacy by Design, they will likely volunteer far more personal informational proactively with businesses. Privacy by Design is an internationally recognized framework, which encourages people and organizations to be proactive regarding privacy across all aspects of their operations. This framework was developed by the Information and Privacy Commissioner of Ontario, Canada. Privacy by Design advances the view that the future of privacy cannot rely solely on compliance with legislation and regulatory frameworks. Privacy by Design helps organizations create a win-win scenario for both businesses and consumers, promoting trust and confidence.

The objectives of Privacy by Design are to ensure privacy and personal control over one's information and for organizations to gain sustainable competitive advantage for supporting these practices. In October 2010, Privacy by Design was recognized as the global privacy standard in a landmark resolution by the International Conference of Data Protection and Privacy Commissioners in Jerusalem. The following 7 Foundational Principles of Privacy by Design have been translated into 30-plus languages.

1. **Proactive, not reactive.** Privacy by Design "does not wait for privacy risks to materialize, nor does it offer remedies for resolving privacy infractions once they have occurred—it aims to prevent them from occurring."
2. **Privacy as the default setting.** "Seeks to deliver the maximum degree of privacy by ensuring that personal data are automatically protected in any given IT system or business practice."
3. **Privacy embedded into the design and architecture of IT systems and business practices.** "The result is that it becomes an essential component of the core functionality being delivered."
4. **Full functionality.** Privacy by Design "seeks to accommodate all legitimate interests and objectives" so that all parties can achieve gains. It "avoids the pretense of false dichotomies, such as privacy versus security, demonstrating that it is possible to have both."
5. **End-to-end security.** Privacy by Design "extends throughout the entire life cycle of the data involved, from start to finish. This ensures

that at the end of the process, all data are securely destroyed, in a timely fashion."

6. **Visibility and transparency.** It supports "operating according to the stated promises and objectives" in the privacy policies, subject to independent verification.

7. **Respect for user privacy.** Maintaining user-centric privacy practices—for example, strong privacy defaults, appropriate notice of privacy changes, and "empowering user-friendly options" for products and services.[3]

The proliferation of mobile and web apps as well as smart objects signifies a historical transformation from one-way communication relying on static information to an in-the-moment, highly interactive exchange between the individual and business. The opportunity to engage the individual based on in-session behavior with automated discovery tools coupled with opt-in retargeting is transforming both the business's revenue opportunities and the individual's shopping experiences and product relevancy.[4]

Government/Advocacy Personal Data Initiatives

The significantly increasing level of personal data protection by governments and advocacy groups is directly proportional to the increasing past, current, and potential personal data infractions. As data grows exponentially, so does the probability for exploitation, meaning a growing environment of control over personal data.

Personal data exploitation historically has been collection and use that is:

- Not limited
- Potentially unlawful
- Unfair to the individual
- Without consent or knowledge
- Without a specified purpose at time of collection
- Without a notice of purpose
- Without granting rights to the individual at time of collection
- Without uses and disclosures that are limited to the specified purposes
- Not sufficiently secure with effective safeguards
- Not open regarding personal data practices
- Not accessible to individuals after the fact (rights to access)
- Not correctable by individuals (right to correct)
- Not accountable

It will be the growing realization that businesses can access far more valuable information from consumers in an information partnership that is direct, overt, and mutually beneficial than in the historically indirect, covert, and financially one-sided monetization of personal data.

To create a reasonable projection of the level of regulation for the protection of personal information from consumers, it is helpful to look at the trajectory of legislation over the past decade. Governments began the first half of this decade with significant legislative activity that indicates the balance of power and control over an individual's personal information will continue to shift from businesses to the individual. While governments are clearly attempting to strike a balance between the individuals' increasing need for their personal data to be protected and the businesses' need to monetize their personal data, the nature of information on the web and its potential risks and abuses has driven legislators to provide increasing protection and control to individuals rather than the businesses that serve them (e.g., United States' Do Not Track and Consumer Privacy Bill of Rights, and the European Parliament's personal data protection, midata, Right to Be Forgotten, and ban on profiling).

The rate of expansion of new privacy legislation globally has averaged 2.5 laws per year for 40 years, with this number increasing significantly each decade. The number of new data privacy laws globally, viewed by decade, is as follows:

- 9 (1970s)
- +12 (1980s)
- +20 (1990s)
- +39 (2000s)
- +19 (2000–2013)[5]

Governments in different regions around the world have been increasingly active in attempting to address the increasing challenge of managing privacy and balancing corporate interests. The pages that follow list some of the major personal information legislation that is in progress for this decade to date. As indicated, advances are being made in giving the individual more control and rights over both incidentally and intentionally volunteered personal information.

The last point will be the evolution of governments to mature their legislation to protect citizens and their personal data sovereignty, which will likely result in nearly complete control and ownership over an individual's personally generated information as well as his or her identity management. Just the first three years of the current decade yielded legislation that functioned as a harbinger for the next iteration of personal data protection and ownership.

This legislation focuses on one or more of the following 10 privacy principles:

1. Data quality—relevant, accurate, and up-to-date
2. Collection—imited, lawful, and fair; with consent or knowledge

3. Purpose specification at time of collection
4. Notice of purpose and rights at time of collection (implied)
5. Uses and disclosures limited to purposes specified or compatible
6. Security through reasonable safeguards
7. Openness regarding personal data practices
8. Access—individual right of access
9. Correction—individual right of correction
10. Accountable—data controller with task of compliance[6]

These are the dimensions that drive personal data protection. They are also dimensions in which ultimately consumers need to feel comfortable sharing their most valuable information with businesses. To create a winning value proposition in the future for customers, businesses will need to deliver incremental value toward creating a better life for consumers as well as providing a safe environment in which to collect the information that businesses need to understand what products, services, and utility create that better life.

Government/Advocacy Personal Data Protection

As of early 2014, there were 99 countries with data privacy laws; 21 additional countries are known to have official bills before their legislatures or under government consideration.[7] The reality is that global privacy regulations will never keep up with the pace of the emergence of new technologies, although they are closing the significant gap that existed over the past 10 years. Governments and advocacy groups will ultimately create a far more empowered consumer relative to the value of control of personal information.

Businesses can proactively start now to forge direct, voluntary consumer information sharing that elegantly navigates the inevitable rising gauntlet of personal data control and protection and, most important, achieve direct access to the mind of the consumer.

Pending U.S. Bills

At the beginning of 2014, everything from the Edward Snowden leaks to the new issues of drones is driving the legislative agendas in the U.S. Congress.

The following is a summary list of 20 pending personal data–related bills that will be the focus of the 113th U.S. Congress.

Senate

- **Personal Data Privacy and Security Act of 2014 (S. 1897, Leahy).** Expands civil/criminal penalties for data breaches and the misuse of personal information.

- **FISA Accountability and Privacy Protection Act of 2013 (S. 1215, Leahy).** Amends numerous provisions of the Foreign Intelligence Surveillance Act.
- **Electronic Communications Privacy Act Amendments Act of 2013 (S. 607, Leahy).** Makes numerous amendments to ECPA, including eliminating the different warrant requirements that depend on whether communications were stored for fewer or more than 180 days.
- **Restore Our Privacy Act (S. 1168, Sanders).** Makes numerous changes to the Foreign Intelligence Surveillance Act, including requiring the director of the Federal Bureau of Investigation (FBI) to apply for an order requiring the production of any tangible things (e.g., obtain foreign intelligence information not concerning a U.S. person, investigation concerning international terrorism).
- **Do Not Track Online Act of 2013 (S. 418, Rockefeller).** Requires the Federal Trade Commission to create rules for implementation of a mechanism that would enable an individual to "simply and easily indicate whether individual prefers to have personal information collected by providers of online services" (i.e., "Do Not Track").
- **Healthcare Privacy and Anti-Fraud Act (S. 1666, Rubio).** Amends the Affordable Care Act to require privacy protections and training for safeguarding patient data.
- **Drone Aircraft Privacy and Transparency Act of 2013 (S. 1639, Markey).** Amends FAA Modernization and Reform Act of 2012 to provide guidance and limitations regarding integration of drones into U.S. airspace.
- **Password Protection Act of 2013 (S. 1426, Blumenthal).** Fines employers for requiring employees to provide their personal e-mail or social media passwords.

House
- **Cyber Intelligence Sharing and Protection Act (H.R. 624, Rogers).** Directs federal government to conduct cyber security activities to provide shared situational awareness enabling integrated operational actions to protect, prevent, mitigate, respond to, and recover from cyber incidents.
- **Aaron's Law Act of 2013 (H.R. 2454, Lofgren).** Amends Computer Fraud and Abuse Act (CFAA) prohibiting computer fraud to replace the phrase "exceeds authorized access" with "access without authorization," which is defined as obtaining information on a protected computer that the accesser lacks authorization to obtain by knowingly circumventing measures that are designed to exclude or prevent unauthorized individuals.
- **Email Privacy Act (H.R. 1852, Yoder).** Amends ECPA to prohibit a provider of remote computing service to the public from knowingly

divulging to any governmental entity the contents of any communication.

- **We Are Watching You Act of 2013 (H.R. 2356, Capuano).** Prohibits an operator of a video service from collecting visual or auditory information from the vicinity of the video programming device unless the operator displays a message that reads "We are watching you."
- **APPS Act of 2013 (H.R. 1913, Johnson).** Requires mobile apps to display privacy notices and obtain user consent before collecting personal data.
- **Protecting the Privacy of Social Security Numbers Act of 2013 (H.R. 2104, Frelinghuysen).** Amends the federal criminal code to prohibit the display, sale, or purchase of Social Security numbers without the affirmatively expressed consent of the individual.
- **Do Not Track Kids Act of 2013 (H.R. 3481, Barton).** Amends the Children's Online Privacy Protection Act of 1998 to apply the prohibitions against collecting personal information from children to online applications and mobile applications directed to children. Adds protections against the collection of personal or geolocation information from children and minors.
- **Privacy Advocate General Act of 2013 (H.R. 2849, Lynch).** Amends the Foreign Intelligence Surveillance Act of 1978 to establish as an independent office in the executive branch the Office of the Privacy Advocate General, to be headed by the Privacy Advocate General.
- **Cyber Privacy Fortification Act of 2013 (H.R. 1221, Conyers).** Establishes criminal penalties for intentional failures to provide required notices of a security breach involving sensitive personally identifiable information.
- **FACE Act of 2013 (H.R. 2645, Duncan).** Prohibits social media providers from intentionally or knowingly using a self-image uploaded by a minor.
- **GPS Act (H.R. 1312, Chaffetz).** Establishes criminal penalties for the intentional interception of geolocation information.
- **Mobile Device Tracking Bill (H.R. 210, Serrano).** Requires a retailer that uses mobile device tracking technology to display in a prominent location a notice that such technology is in use and that individuals can avoid being tracked by turning off their mobile devices.[8]

Most or all of these proposed bills point to increasingly empowered consumers where their personal data will be increasingly at their discretion to share or not to share. Businesses will need to make a strategic decision whether to continue down the path of skirting the ever-increasing personal data restrictions or to proactively invest in creating explicit and voluntary information partnerships with consumers.

Data Breaches

Data breaches will always occur. Where there is a gain to breach data, individuals will figure out a way to breach data. A significant advantage that the future personal data ecosystem will have concerning individual personal data stores is that data will be distributed and less of a large target for data theft perpetrators. In other words, compared to a large retailer such as Target, the economics of investing in compromising one individual's personal data store will not be sufficiently motivating to invest the time and money into the data breach.

The following is a list of major data breaches where large commercial entities were targeted because of the economics of scale of the data breach. The frequency and size of data breaches have significantly increased over the past decade.

Data Breaches Time Line

- **2011:** Epsilon has customer lists of major brands compromised (e.g., Kroger, TiVo, U.S. Bank, JPMorgan Chase, Capital One, Citi, Home Shopping Network (HSN), Ameriprise Financial, LL Bean Visa Card, Lacoste, AbeBooks, Hilton Honors Program, Dillons, Fred Meyer, TD Ameritrade, Ethan Allen, TIAA-CREF, Verizon, Marks & Spencer (UK), City Market, Smith Brands, McKinsey & Company, Ritz-Carlton Rewards, Marriott Rewards, New York & Company, Brookstone, Walgreens, The College Board, Disney Destinations, Best Buy, Robert Half, Target, QFC, bebe Stores, Ralphs, Fry's, 1-800-Flowers, Red Roof Inn, King Soopers, Air Miles, Eddie Bauer, Scottrade, Dell Australia, Jay C).[9]
- **2012:** Hacker activist organization breaches FBI computer, gathering 12 million Apple unique device identifiers (UDIDs), and makes one million of them public.
- **2012:** Utah Department of Health—780,000 Medicaid patients' and children's records are stolen.
- **2013:** Edward Snowden leaks top-secret United States and British government mass surveillance programs (e.g., U.S./European telephone metadata, National Security Agency (NSA)'s PRISM, Tempora Internet surveillance programs).
- **2013:** Target's data breach hurts No. 3 U.S. retailer's profits and shakes customer confidence; prompts congressional hearings.
- **April 2014:** AOL—millions of its account holders are exposed to data breach to the system (2 percent of its accounts); AOL urges them to change their usernames and passwords.
- **May 2014:** Hospital for Veterans Affairs—two biomedical computers are stolen from a locked room in the hospital, containing data from tests on approximately 239 VA patients.

- **May 2014:** Humana—Humana associate's vehicle is broken into and an unencrypted USB drive along with the associate's laptop computer are stolen. The information contained on these devices includes medical record information and Social Security numbers.
- **May 2014:** San Diego State University—SDSU reports breach at Pre-College Institute with names, Social Security numbers, dates of birth, addresses, and other personal information misconfigured.
- **May 2014:** EBay—user records were hacked between late February and early March using login credentials obtained from employees; a database was accessed containing user records of approximately 145 million users. The information includes e-mail addresses, encrypted passwords, birth dates, and mailing addresses.
- **May 2014:** Lowe's—current and former drives of Lowe's vehicles was managed by a third-party vendor that stored compliance documentation and information using a computer system "E-DriverFile". This information was unintentionally backed up to an unsecure computer server that was accessible from the Internet. The information that was compromised included names, addresses, dates of birth, Social Security numbers, driver's license numbers, sales IDs, and other driving record information.

Pivotal Personal Data Protection Initiatives

There are many personal data protection initiatives that will be driving privacy in protecting personal information over the next decade. Several have been around for many years and will continue to evolve whereas others will be continually introduced as government and advocacy groups attempt to catch up to the rapidly advancing personal data ecosystem.

2010 Federal Trade Commission Privacy Report

The U.S. Federal Trade Commission (FTC) published its preliminary version of its report on online consumer privacy. The report, entitled "Protecting Consumer Privacy in an Era of Rapid Change," was a set of recommendations, including a call for a do-not-track tool enabling individuals to opt out of data collection and targeted marketing programs on the web. The FTC recommends that the Internet and advertising communities develop meaningful codes of conduct that provide individuals with more awareness into how their personal information is being collected as well as how it is being used. The FTC also supports tools that limit the access to personal data (e.g., do-not-track option browsers). The report addresses three dimensions that businesses should observe while collecting personal data on the Internet:

1. Privacy should be proactively incorporated into new products and services.
2. Businesses should simplify how individuals control their personal information.
3. Business data collection practices should be transparent to individuals.

Other areas addressed in the final report are personal data privacy with mobile devices. The report also addresses the need for data brokers to be more transparent in how they collect and use individuals' personal data. The report also addresses increasing privacy concerns regarding large platform providers (e.g., Internet service providers, operating systems, browsers, and social media companies) that seek to comprehensively track consumers' online activities. The report also supports having self-regulatory codes of conduct that can be monitored and enforced.

2010 Do Not Track

Origins (1995) of the United States' privacy guidelines come from the FTC Fair Information Practice Principles (FIPPs), which address the practice principles of notice, choice, access, security, and enforcement to protect online privacy. The decade opens with some significant activity around "Do Not Track" (DNT). The Do Not Track header is the proposed HTTP header field DNT that requests that a web application disable either its tracking or cross-site individual tracking (this ambiguity is still to be clarified) of an individual user. DNT gives the individual the power to turn off the flow of incidentally volunteered personal information when using the browser.

In December 2010, Microsoft announced support for the DNT mechanism in its Internet Explorer 9 web browser while Mozilla's Firefox became the first browser to implement the feature, and Internet Explorer, Apple's Safari, Opera, and Google Chrome have or will follow suit. The DNT header will accept three values: (1) Individual does not want to be tracked (opt out); (0) individual consents to be tracked (opt in); or (null)—no header sent, if the individual has not chosen a preference. The default behavior is null, which is no preference. The Do Not Track system is voluntary by both the companies building the browsers as well as the individual, and there are no legal or technological requirements for its implementation. Mozilla is currently in testing mode, while

Apple's Safari browser allows cookies from websites the individual has already visited, but blocks cookies from sites the individual has not visited yet. Comprehensive DNT capabilities will likely be the ultimate control by which individuals control their personal information in the following decade.

2011 Commercial Privacy Bill of Rights Act

This privacy bill is intended to address the growing issues of an individual's privacy in a single, unified package. The bill states that any personal information, unique identifiers, geographic location, e-mail addresses, phone numbers, bank and credit account numbers, nonwork phone numbers, biometric data, and the like are all covered as information that should be protected, and individuals should be able to access that information anytime in order change it or opt out. If individuals switch services or companies, they can demand that any collected information be purged. The bill also requires that businesses make available easy opt outs and provide a complaint mechanism for individuals. "If there was no law to stop a person from collecting or selling that personal information collected, you'd feel beyond violated," Kerry said during a press conference on Tuesday. "It goes on unregulated every day in the digital world. . . . Right now, there is no law protecting the information that we share."

The 2011 Groupe Speciale Mobile Association (GSMA) Privacy Principles address the privacy needs of individuals regarding how their personal information generated from their mobile devices should be respected and protected. The key to GSMA's principles is that it is attempting to promote "transparency and notice" as key dimensions of the privacy principles. Openness and honesty are the key characteristics that GSMA promotes to its association.

Their "high-level privacy" principles are:

- Openness, Transparency, and Notice
  - Responsible persons shall be open and honest with users and will ensure users are provided with clear, prominent, and timely information regarding their identity and data privacy practices. Users shall be provided with information about persons collecting personal information about them, the purposes of an application or service, and about the access, collection, sharing, and further use of users' personal information, including to whom their personal information may be disclosed, enabling users to make informed decisions about whether to use a mobile application or service.

- Purpose and Use
  - The access, collection, sharing, disclosure, and further use of users' personal information shall be limited to meeting legitimate business purposes, such as providing applications or services as requested by users, or to otherwise meet legal obligations.
- User Choice and Control
  - Users shall be given opportunities to exercise meaningful choice, and control over their personal information.
- Data Normalization and Retention
  - Only the minimum personal information necessary to meet legitimate business purposes and to deliver, provision, maintain, or develop applications and services should be collected and otherwise accessed and used. Personal information must not be kept for longer than is necessary for those legitimate business purposes or to meet legal obligations and should subsequently be deleted or rendered anonymous.
- Respect User Rights
  - Users should be provided with information about, and an easy means to exercise, their rights over the use of their personal information.
- Security
  - Personal information must be protected, using reasonable safeguards appropriate to the sensitivity of the information.
- Education
  - Users should be provided with information about privacy and security issues and ways to manage and protect their privacy.
- Children and Adolescents
  - An application or service that is directed at children and adolescents should ensure that the collection, access, and use of personal information is appropriate in all given circumstances and compatible with national law.
- Accountability Enforcement
  - All responsible persons are accountable for ensuring these principles are met.

2012 EU Strictly Enforcing Cookie Directive

All businesses that market to EU citizens using cookies (and other tracking technologies) must:

- Inform individuals their data is being analyzed and processed.
- Get individual's consent prior to storing or accessing information on the individual's device.

- Give individuals access to their data to correct or delete it.
- Use individual's data only for the disclosed purpose(s).
- Get informed consent before the cookie/tracking technology is placed on the individual's device.[10]

2012 U.S. Consumer Privacy Bill of Rights

The Obama administration unveiled a Consumer Privacy Bill of Rights as part of a comprehensive blueprint to protect individual privacy rights and give individuals more control over how their personal information is handled. This Bill of Rights is meant to protect all Americans from having their information misused by giving users new legal and technical tools to manage and safeguard their privacy. While this blueprint is not enforceable without an action from Congress, companies could voluntarily agree to abide by it, and the Federal Trade Commission (FTC) could monitor their compliance. One of the mechanisms is that the Commerce Department's National Telecommunications and Information Administration (NTIA) will be convening Internet companies and consumer advocates to develop a set of enforceable codes of conduct that comply with the Consumer Privacy Bill of Rights that the Federal Trade Commission could enforce.

A significant aspect of this movement is that major Internet companies and online advertising networks are committing to using Do Not Track technology from the World Wide Web Consortium in most major web browsers to make it easier for individuals to control online tracking. Companies that deliver 90 percent of online behavioral advertisements (e.g., Google, Yahoo!, Microsoft, and AOL) have made this FTC-enforceable commitment. The Consumer Privacy Bill of Rights applies to personal data (i.e., aggregated data linkable to an individual, and personal data linked to a specific computer/device). The administration supports federal legislation that adopts the principles of the Consumer Privacy Bill of Rights. With or without this legislation, efforts are in place to convene multistakeholder processes that apply these rights as a template for codes of conduct that are enforceable by the Federal Trade Commission. The plan is to also work with the U.S. Congress to enact comprehensive personal information privacy legislation based on the rights outlined next.

- **Individual control.** Individuals have the right to control what personal data companies collect from them and how they use it. Companies should provide consumers with control over the personal data that they share with others, as well as how companies collect, use, or disclose personal data. Companies should enable these choices by providing individuals with easy-to-use and accessible mechanisms. Companies should offer individuals simple choices to enable meaningful decisions about personal data collection, use, and disclosure. Companies should offer individuals the ability to withdraw or limit consent of their personal data as well.

- **Transparency.** Individuals have a right to easily understandable and accessible information about privacy and security practices. Individuals also need to understand the privacy risks and how the privacy controls impact those risks. Companies should provide clear explanations of what personal data they collect, why they need the data, how they will use it, when they will delete the data or detach the data from a specific individual, and whether and why they may share this personal data with third parties.

- **Respect for context.** Individuals have a right to expect companies to collect, use, and disclose personal data in ways that are consistent with the original context in which consumers first provided the data. Companies should limit their use and disclosure of personal data to those purposes that are consistent with both their current relationship and the context in which the individual originally disclosed the data. If companies will use or disclose personal data outside of these contexts, the company will first make the individual aware of this plan and provide added personal control that is easily actionable by the individual. The companies should also offer greater protections for personal data obtained from children and teenagers.

- **Security.** Individuals have a right to have their personal data secure and have it handled responsibly. Companies should also put in place reasonable safeguards to control risks to that security (e.g., loss, unauthorized access, use, destruction, data modification, and improper disclosure).

- **Access and accuracy.** Individuals have the right to access and correct personal data in usable formats. Companies should use reasonable measures to maintain the accuracy of the personal data. Companies also should provide individuals with reasonable access to personal data to allow the individuals to correct inaccurate data, request its deletion, or limit its use. This access should be in context to the degree of financial, physical, or material harm the misuse of their personal data could cause the individual.

- **Focused collection.** Individuals have a right to a limit on the personal data that companies collect and retain. Companies should collect only as much personal data as they need to accomplish purposes specified under the respect for context principle. Companies should securely delete or detach personal data once the company no longer needs it.

- **Accountability.** Companies should be accountable to government authorities and individuals for adhering to these principles. Companies should train their employees to handle personal data with these principles and evaluate their performance with full audits. When companies disclose personal data to third parties, they should ensure that their conduct is contractually enforceable for adhering to these principles.[11]

2012 EU Data Protection Reform

The European Union is undergoing a major personal data protection reform in conjunction with the European Commission and the Council of Ministers. This legislation covers general data protection regulation and a personal data protection directive that updates existing 1995 legislation. This legislation was brought about by the fact that, based on the Eurobarometer survey, 70 percent of Europeans are concerned that their personal data may be misused and 72 percent of Internet users in Europe are concerned that they are asked for too much personal data online.

Key Legislative Points
- Citizens
  - Limits to profiling: Gives individuals the ability to block online web tracking and online targeted advertising. Businesses are allowed to collect data and profile individuals only if individuals give their explicit consent. Profiling is defined as the observing, collecting, and matching of an individual's personal data online to analyze or predict the individual's behavior.
  - Right to be forgotten: The entities that control the personal data (e.g., social networks, online shops, online banking services) will be required to delete and remove personal data on those individuals who so request.
  - Clear, plain language: When communicating privacy policies, the data processors (e.g., web businesses, search engines, social networks) will have to use clear and plain language.
  - Explicit consent: Wherever consent is required for an individual's data to be processed, it will need to be given explicitly.
  - Data portability: The individual should be able to easily transfer personal data from one service provider to another.
- Companies
  - A clear, single set of rules dealing with personal data privacy. Benefits to the companies estimated at €2.3 billion savings a year.
  - Cuts red tape. Estimated savings at €130 million a year.

- Possible fines up to €1 million or up to 2 percent of a company's global annual revenue.
- Companies with more than 250 employees should designate a data protection officer.
- Companies are to notify a single national data protection authority in the EU country where they have their main customer base.
- Currently, the major debates center around the following individual data protection dimensions: limits of the right to be forgotten (e.g., when it conflicts with freedom of expression), the right to informed, explicit consent, and data portability. On the companies' side, the major debates center on the level of sanctions and the obligation to appoint a data protection officer.

Key Focus of EU Directive
- Data protection in the context of criminal act.
- Broadens scope in terms of enforcing cross-border personal data processing.
- Addresses major differences across EU member states.
- The United Kingdom, Ireland, and Denmark are not bound by the directive.

This Bill of Rights is a harbinger for the ultimate conditions of how personal information will be managed and governed in the coming decades.[12]

2013 California Department of Justice Agreement

In 2013 the California Department of Justice forged an agreement with leading operators of mobile application platforms to improve privacy protections for individuals around the world who access the Internet through mobile apps. The agreement involves technology companies that comprise the majority of the mobile apps market: Amazon, Apple, Google, Hewlett-Packard, Microsoft, and BlackBerry (formerly Research In Motion). These companies have agreed to conform to California law requiring mobile apps that collect personal information to have a privacy policy. The majority of mobile apps available today do not contain a mobile privacy policy. "Your personal privacy should not be the cost of using mobile apps, but all too often it is," said Attorney General Kamala D. Harris. The objective of this agreement is to strengthen the privacy protections for California individuals (and globally) when using mobile apps. This agreement is an effort to increase transparency and give individuals more control over their personal information.

The agreement also commits to the ticketing developers about their obligations to respect individual privacy and to disclose to individuals what personal information is being collected, how it will be used, and with whom it is being shared. The businesses also agree to improve compliance with privacy laws by giving individuals tools to report the noncompliance of mobile apps as well as businesses implementing processes to respond to noncompliance reports.

The rapid expansion of the mobile app industry is the impetus behind California's mobile initiatives. There are more than 50,000 individual mobile app developers with over 600,000 mobile apps applications for sale in the Apple App Store and over 400,000 for sale in Google's Android Market. Mobile apps have been downloaded over 35 billion times. Estimates are that 100 billion mobile apps will be downloaded by 2015, and the $7 billion mobile app market is expected to grow to $25 billion within four years. One recent study found that only 5 percent of all mobile apps have a privacy policy. California's constitution directly guarantees an individual's right to privacy, and "we will defend it," states California's Attorney General Harris."[13]

2013 UK's Enterprise and Regulatory Reform Bill with Midata Rights

The UK government amended the Enterprise and Regulatory Reform Bill to implement the government's desire for individuals to have access to transaction details from the purchase of goods and services in an open, standard electronic format (i.e., midata), which they can then use to inform future purchasing decisions. The current Data Protection Act of 1998 gives individuals the right to access their data in "an intelligible form" either a printed copy or in an electronic form. These new provisions will allow the Secretary of State to make secondary legislation causing suppliers of goods and services to provide personal historical transaction and consumption data (i.e., individuals' transaction data) to their customers in an electronic format. These provisions will initially focus on the energy, mobile phones, and financial industries. The bill is currently at the committee stage in the House of Lords. This legislation would significantly advance the transparency of personally volunteered information as well as the public visibility of what personal information is extracted and monetized by businesses.[14]

2013 Network Advertising Initiative (NAI) Code of Conduct

In 2013 the Network Advertising Initiative (NAI) released a draft revised code of conduct for public comment. One of the primary changes would be for advertisers delivering targeted advertising to provide notice regarding data collection and use practices "in and around the targeted ads they serve." The draft code is also asking that an "enhanced notice" of data collection and use practices be given relative to advertising practices as well as the prospective opt-in/opt-out choices to individuals. The new revisions also require that advertisers disclose the technical approaches they use for interest-based advertising (both delivery and reporting).

This new revision is intended to bring a higher level of transparency to the advertising industry. It would also forestall advertisers from using certain "inappropriate" eligibility factors in advertising criteria (e.g., employment eligibility, credit eligibility, health care eligibility, and insurance eligibility). The revised code also promotes a stronger opt-out mechanism relative to the sensitivity intended use of the personal information. NAI specifically cites the use of non-personally identifying information for interest-based advertising. This includes stronger opt-out connections to an individual's geolocation data. NAI has expanded the definition of "sensitive data," adding the new category of sexual orientation that includes sexual behavior.

The NAI requires that advertisers "honor" the individual's opt-out choice only relative to the specific browser or device they opt out with. In other words, if they opt out on their laptop Chrome browser and not on their mobile Android device, the advertiser can still employ behavioral tracking. The advertiser can also still collect data for "internal operations" practices after a user has opted out. In a future information world where individuals control the use of their personal information, these added protections would be inherent in the individual's controls as the individuals would make all decisions on every aspect of their data in terms of what is shared and not shared.[15]

NAI's self-regulatory principles correspond to the U.S. FTC staff revisions of Online Behavioral Advertising Principles in 2009. Nuances of NAI's self-regulatory principles for online advertising will continue to evolve, as will the FTC's advertising privacy tenets over this decade and the next. The fundamentals of NAI's founding principles will likely stay consistent (e.g., education, transparency, control, security, material change, data sensitivity, and accountability). They have been designed in concert with the Federal Trade Commission's principles. All of these principles are set forth to be consumer-friendly and at no charge. The ultimate goal is to balance the individual's privacy rights while maintaining a robust ecosystem for online advertisers.[16]

Here are the fundamentals of NAI's founding principles for online advertisers:

- Education Principle
  - Educate individuals and businesses regarding online behavioral advertising and the principles.

- Transparency Principle
  - Clearer and easily accessible disclosures to individuals about data collection and use.
  - "Enhanced notice" on the page where data is collected through links embedded in or around advertisements, or on the web page.
- Consumer Control Principle
  - Provide individuals with a more comprehensive ability to choose whether data is collected and used for online behavioral advertising purposes.
  - Available through a link from the notice provided on the web page where data is collected.
  - Requires service providers such as Internet access service providers and desktop applications software providers (web browser tool bars) to obtain the individual's consent before engaging in online advertising, and take steps to de-identify the individual's personal information.
- Data Security Principle
  - Ensure appropriate security, and limit data retention, collection, and use for online advertising.
- Material Changes Principle
  - Obtain individual's consent before a material change (i.e., substantive or impactful change) is made to an advertiser's data collection and use policies unless that change will result in less data collection and use.
- Sensitive Data Principle
  - Recognition that data collected from children under 13 requires heightened protection as well as parental consent.
  - Heightened protections to certain health and financial data when attributable to an individual.
- Accountability Principle
  - Continued development of accountability principles.
  - Enhanced monitoring and reporting processes of noncompliance to appropriate government agencies.
  - Collaboration of accountability activities with the Council of Better Business Bureaus (CBBB) and Direct Marketing Association (DMA).[17]

NAI also spearheads a Digital Advertising Alliance (DAA) with three distinct dimensions of its own self-regulatory principles:

1. **Mobile environment.** These implementation guidelines address specific data privacy requirements when both first parties and third parties

operate across multiple channels including mobile, and address the need for consistency across all channels.

2. **Multisite data.** These implementation guidelines address advertisers who collect website data to be used outside of online behavioral advertising.

3. **Cross-industry.** These implementation guidelines address the fact that most online behavioral advertising is cross-industry in nature and needs added clarity as to how to address the unique nature of cross-industry privacy limitation.

NAI's principles are fundamentally balancing an individual's best interests with the advertising community's best interests and therefore represent compromises to both. As the current decade of volunteered personal information evolves, individuals will likely garner more control over their personal information used by advertisers from two dimensions. First, government regulation and advocacy groups will continue to evolve their regulations and principles. The second and more important dimension is that an individual's power over one's personal information will evolve, as has the individual's power as a consumer.[18]

2012 EU Commission Cloud Computing Report

In 2012 the European Commission published its "Cloud Computing" report for Europe, which focused on cutting through the jungle of standards that have proliferated for cloud computing services.

2013 California Department of Justice's "Privacy on the Go"

In 2013 the California Department of Justice published recommendations ("Privacy on the Go") for mobile application app developers and the mobile industry to help safeguard individual privacy. This report provides guidance on creating strong privacy practices with mobile-friendly policies and transparency. "Californians want to know what personal information their apps collect, how it is used, and with whom it is shared," said Attorney General Kamala D. Harris. "To meet this need and keep pace with rapidly changing technology, these recommendations strike a responsible balance between protecting consumers' personal information and fostering the continued growth of the innovative app economy." The report is meant to serve as a template for the mobile industry to develop mobile-friendly privacy policies and practices that will improve individual privacy without stifling mobile app innovation. The report on mobile privacy notes that as much as half of American adult cell phone owners access the Internet from their phones, and more than 1,600 mobile apps are released every day.

To protect consumers' online privacy, Attorney General Harris forged an agreement among the seven leading mobile and social app platforms in 2012. The agreement—with Amazon, Apple, Facebook, Google, Hewlett-Packard, Microsoft, and BlackBerry (formerly Research In Motion)—involved displaying app privacy policies that users could find in a consistent location in the platform store and review before downloading an app.[19]

2013 EU's Article 29 Data Protection Working Party Opinion

In 2013 EU's Article 29 Data Protection Working Party issued a new set of privacy recommendations in an Opinion on mobile apps. The new recommendations were catalyzed from recent EU probes to the privacy practices of high-profile technology organizations, such as Google. (Article 29 is a watchdog group comprised of the EU's top privacy groups.) This is a new set of recommendations aimed at app developers and tech giants that run the mobile application stores in the latest attempt to bring order to how your apps handle your private information.[20]

The new set of more detailed recommendations arrives following the recent EU probe into the privacy practices of Google and other tech firms.

The Opinion provides key recommendations for mobile app compliance with the Data Protection Directive and the e-Privacy Directive, with a focus on ensuring (1) that device users are adequately informed of the ways in which the information on their mobile devices can be accessed and used through apps, (2) that device users are in control of such access and use, and (3) that adequate security measures are put in place to protect data collected and used by apps. Although most of the recommendations are aimed at app developers, other players in the app market may be subject to the same data protection responsibilities. The following are some of the key recommendations from the Opinion:

- App developers should include information directed to users in the EU in mobile app privacy policies.
- App developers should work with operating system and device manufacturers and app stores to determine how best to provide adequate information to mobile device users about issues like data breaches.
- Operating system and device manufacturers should facilitate the implementation of icons to alert users about the different ways in which apps use their data.
- App developers should create tools that enable users to customize retention periods for their personal data.

- Operating system and device manufacturers should enable users to uninstall apps and ensure that all user data is deleted.
- Operating system and device manufacturers should facilitate regular security updates.
- App developers should take into account the relevant guidelines with regard to specific security risks and measures.[21]

2013 UK's Internet Advertising Bureau (IAB)

In 2013 the Internet Advertising Bureau (IAB) launched an ad campaign in the United Kingdom giving individuals greater awareness and control over targeted online ads. This initiative is targeted at driving individual's awareness, providing information, and enabling consumer choice.

Designed by Mediacom Beyond Advertising, the "unzipped" campaign features a zip with statements such as "How do websites know which adverts suit your interests?" and "Find out what goes on behind the ads you see online." The zip opens to reveal the blue triangular "AdChoices" icon that has been appearing on behavioral ads in the UK and EU markets for over a year.

When the ad is clicked, it links to a landing page explaining the role of the online ad.[22]

2013 European Interactive Digital Advertising Alliance Campaign

In 2013 the European Interactive Digital Advertising Alliance (EDAA) launched a pan-European consumer awareness campaign for individuals relative to online behavioral advertising (OBA) and their privacy choices:

> *The European Interactive Digital Advertising Alliance (EDAA) has launched the first phase of its pan-European consumer awareness campaign today in the UK—with the aim of providing information about Online Behavioural Advertising (OBA), or interest based advertising, to empower internet users across Europe. This "Unzipped" campaign, funded and coordinated by EDAA with the support of IAB Europe and its local members, will help raise consumer awareness of the OBA icon, as well as increasing consumer understanding and choice when it comes to OBA. The campaign ads feature a zip that opens to reveal the blue, EDAA licensed, OBA icon. By clicking on the ads, consumers are taken to Youronlinechoices.eu where, in clear, user-friendly language, they can find out about their online ad choices, how online advertising is used to support the sites and services they use, and how they can safeguard their privacy. The TRUSTe*

UK 2012 Consumer Data Privacy Study showed that 79% of UK consumers were aware of Online Behavioural Advertising (OBA) and 53% did not like it. One in three users had felt uncomfortable about targeted advertising. However the research also showed 51% would be more inclined to click on an advertisement that gave them the option to opt out of Online Behavioural Advertising and 42% of consumers were more favourable towards digital advertising if presented with the OBA icon.[23]

Pivotal Business Event Time Line

The following is the time line of the more important events influencing the volunteered personal information phenomena:

- **2010**: Microsoft Exchange Server/Microsoft Outlook—300 million on-premises/hosted mailboxes; expected to grow to a total of 470 million by 2014.
- **2010**: Mobile apps start accelerating and take off through the decade.
- **2010**: MasterCard MarketPlace; searching for offers near you.
- **2010**: FTC issues a privacy report that calls for a "do not track" system.
- **2010**: Do Not Track (DNT) begins with several browsers.
- **2010**: Quantified self—data acquisition on aspects of a person's daily life.
- **2010**: Pinterest.
- **2010**: eBay Garden; plant seeds of new ideas, try out features, and tell us what you think.
- **2010**: Blue Button: patients to view online and download their own personal health records.
- **2010**: Truste launches mobile apps certification.
- **2011**: Motoactv (styled MOTOACTV) is a smartwatch sold by Motorola.
- **2011**: Mozilla Persona: decentralized authentication system for web based on the open BrowserID.
- **2011**: Facebook generates $3.15 billion in ad revenue for the year.
- **2011**: eBay buys Hunch.com (launched in 2009); answers from 10 questions or less.
- **2011**: Groupon IPO is largest IPO since Google.
- **2011**: eBay Acquires Recommendation Engine Hunch.com ("Taste Graph")—Drive More Personalized, Relevant Experiences on eBay.
- **2011**: Google Plus.
- **2011**: Sony's video game online network (PlayStation) has 77 million user accounts' information stolen but is not sure which data was stolen (e.g., credit card data).

- **2011**: *Time* magazine features privacy on cover.
- **2011**: Amazon launches Amazon Local, a daily deal service and deal aggregator.
- **2012**: 2.8 zettabytes—that's 1 sextillion bytes, 24 quintillion tweets—are created.
- **2012**: Facebook acquires Instagram (photo share) for $1 billion.
- **2012**, December: Instagram updates terms and conditions, granting itself right to sell users' photos to third parties without notification or compensation. Criticism makes it withdraw the policy.
- **2012**: At the beginning of 2012, Facebook's mobile ad revenue was literally nonexistent, but by end of year, it was 23 percent of Facebook's total advertising revenue.
- **2012**: 50 percent increase in engagement (e.g., likes, comments, postings; introduction of ads to news feed causes 2 percent reduction in terms of people's activity on Facebook.
- **2012**, December: In United States, comScore: #1 desktop site. People spend 6-plus hours on Facebook. On mobile, average U.S. use 11.5 hours, 2x as mobile user; everything built is mobile first.
- **2012**: Apple moves from unique device identifiers (UDIDs) to identifiers for advertising (IDFAs)—more secure for the individual (device cannot be traced back to individuals), better for advertisers (allows advertisers to track individual surfing and interactions with conversions).
- **2012**: Volt stats: uses OnStar to collect data of Chevy Volts' driving MPG.
- **2012**: Rapleaf begins selling segmented data tied to e-mail addresses.
- **2012**: Facebook focuses on going public.
- **2012**: Facebook hiring ad for "inventing the future of Social CRM."
- **2012**: Nike's Fuelband.
- **2012**: Facebook settles suit for using Facebook users' names and likenesses in sponsored story ads without permission, paying $20 million.
- **2013**: Year of Facebook monetization (e.g., news feed/mobile ads, Facebook Exchange, Facebook Gifts, promoted posts, offers, sponsored results, logout ads, paid messaging, subscription payments, mobile ad network, premium services, collections, Nearby, App Center/PMD Center, news feed modules.
- **2013**: Firefox to begin blocking third-party cookies by default.
- **2013**: First Google Glasses available for testing.
- **2013**: Green Button—access energy usage information.
- **2013**: Apple's iWatch—tells time but will also allow you to monitor yourself and control other devices (e.g., where you are). It will be an intelligent device that would communicate with other devices such as the iPhone, iPad, and Apple TV, and be connected to the Internet. This will

enable you to operate your phone using voice control, be discretely alerted to incoming calls and messages, make credit card payments (contact less and without getting your card out), get weather forecasts, customize the display, download apps, get access to buildings, know how many calories you have burned and how well you have slept, and so forth.

- **2013**: eBay acquires Decide. Decide.com "specializes in helping consumers find the best times to buy products based on billions of data points across the web." The service advises consumers when to buy—by which it means that the product's price won't get any better in the next two weeks, or no new model is expected for the next five months; eBay will utilize Decide to offer repricing services to sellers.
- **2013**: U.S. FBI shuts down Silk Road online black market and seizes 144,000 bitcoins worth US$28.5 million. The United States is considered bitcoin-friendly compared to other governments.
- **2013**: Apple buys Topsy, which has full access to Twitter firehose.
- **2014**: AT&T to buy DirecTV for $48.5 billion as cellular growth eases.
- **2014**: Comcast buys Time Warner Cable for $45 billion.
- **2014**: Yahoo! acquires self-destructing messaging App Blink.
- **2014**: Google acquires enterprise-friendly device manager Divide. Divide allows smartphone users to keep personal data apart from work data on their mobile devices.
- **2014**: Google looking to buy Twitch, a popular online service for live-streaming video game footage among Sony PlayStation and Microsoft Xbox users. The service allows gamers to share game play tricks and tips. Twitch has over 45 million monthly unique users.
- **2014**: Apple purchases Beats Electronics for $3 billion, shifting its emphasis from music downloads to online streaming.
- **2014**: Microsoft acquires Nokia's phone business.
- **2014**: Tesco's Dunnhumby buys ad tech firm Sociomantic Labs—engage with customers in real time while they shop, whether that be online or in-store.
- **2014**: Twitter buys UK social TV firm SecondSync, where people simultaneously watch TV while commenting upon it, and has the advantage of being able to distribute posts in real time.
- **2014**: Twitter buys Gnip, which resells data to a variety of established clients across industry sectors and is one of only four companies with direct access to Twitter's complete stream of tweets (firehose).
- **2014**: Capita buys AMT-Sybex—supplies mobile technology software and smart data management to transport and utility businesses. Allows data to be captured from smart meters, which informs customers how much energy they are using.

- **2014**: Google buying Nest—Nest gives Google its next big data play: energy.
- **2014**: iControl Networks acquires Blacksumac—home automation and monitoring space.
- **2014**: Facebook buys Oculus Rift ($2 billion)—virtual reality headsets not just for gaming but for communications, training across a range of industries, entertainment, and the medical sphere.
- **2014**: Priceline buys Qlika—allows advertisers to adapt their marketing style according to the location of where the ad will be placed to allow for market, cultural, keyword, and demographic differences.
- **2014**: Intel buys Basis Science—smart watch maker that holds approximately 7 percent of the wearable fitness tracker market.
- **2014**: Facebook buys WhatsApp ($19 billion), most popular mobile chat app, which has more than 450 million regular users, increasing at the rate of 1 million a day. Eroding SMS market and revenue for traditional telecoms. User figures are expected to reach 1 billion during the next few years.
- **2014**: Alibaba buys AutoNavi ($1.6 billion). AutoNavi is China's most successful map app; it provides over 20 million specific location points and allows customers to search for cinemas, restaurants, and accommodations.
- **2014**: Rakuten buys Viber ($900 million)—an instant messaging service with 100 million monthly users and a total of 280 million registered users across 200 countries. Users can send messages and make calls for free to both mobile devices and desktops. Besides WhatsApp, Viber is the only other messaging app service with a global presence.
- **2014**: LinkedIn buys Bright—improve relevance of suggestions to 277 million users to make the recruitment and search process more efficient. LinkedIn has an ambitious plan to reach out to the entire global workforce.
- **2014**: Google buys DeepMind ($400 million), which develops technology to allow computers to copy the human thought process. DeepMind has already incorporated its technology into games, e-commerce, and simulations.[24]
- **2014**: Facebook proactively sends e-mails to members enabling them to opt out of ad targeting in their web browser using the industry-standard Digital Advertising Alliance opt out, and on the mobile devices using the controls that iOS and Android provide.

What is significant in this time line is the vast array of acquisitions that signal how consumers are embracing new technology and new information and communication enablers.

Notes

1. Verna Allee, Value Networks.
2. Doc Searls.
3. Office of the Information & Privacy Commissioner, Ontario, Canada, *Privacy by Design: The 7 Foundational Principles,* http://www.ipc.on .ca/images/Resources/7foundationalprinciples.pdf.
4. "How to Stop Advertising Companies from Tracking Your Online Activity for Targeted Web Ads," Huffingtonpost.com, May 25, 2011. www .huffingtonpost.com/2011/02/25/stop-online-tracking_n_828289 .html.
5. Graham Greenleaf, Professor of Law and Information Systems, University of New South Wales, "Sheherezade and the 101 Data Privacy Laws: Origins, Significance and Global," Journal of Law, Information & Science, April 14, 2014. www.jlisjournal.org/abstracts/ greenleaf.23.1.html.
6. Ibid.; summarized: OECD Privacy Guidelines of 1981 and the Council of Europe (CoE) Data Protection Convention 108 of 1981.
7. Graham Greenleaf, "Global Tables of Data Privacy Laws and Bills." http://papers.ssrn.com/sol3/papers.cfm?abstract_id=2280875
8. Jeff Kosseff, "Twenty Privacy Bills to Watch in 2014," InsidePrivacy, Covington & Burling LLP, January 15, 2014. www.insideprivacy.com/ united-states/congress/twenty-privacy-bills-to-watch-in-2014/.
9. Mike Lennon, "Massive Breach at Epsilon Compromises Customer Lists of Major Brands," securityweek.com, April 02, 2011. www.securityweek .com/massive-breach-epsilon-compromises-customerlists-major-brands.
10. Truste, "4-Step Internet Privacy Policy Process," May 3, 2012. www.truste .com/wiki/index/4-Step_Internet_Privacy_Policy_Process.
11. The White House, Office of the Press Secretary, "We Can't Wait: Obama Administration Unveils Blueprint for a 'Privacy Bill of Rights' to Protect Consumers Online," whitehouse.gov, February 23, 2012. www .whitehouse.gov/the-press-office/2012/02/23/we-can-t-wait-obama- administration-unveils-blueprint-privacy-bill-rights.
12. European Commission, "Progress on EU Data Protection Reform Now Irreversible Following European Parliament Vote, memo, March 12, 2014. http://europa.eu/rapid/press-release_MEMO-14-186_en.htm.
13. State of California Department of Justice, Office of the Attorney General, Attorney General Kamala D. Harris.
14. www.europarl.europa.eu.
15. Richard Newman, "NAI Announces Release of Draft Revised Data Collection Code of Conduct," Hinch Newman LLP (blog), March 7, 2013. www.hinchnewman.com/internet-law-blog/2013/03/nai-announces- release-of-draft-revised-data-collection-code-of-conduct/.

16. Meredith Halama, "NAI Seeking Public Comment on Revised Code of Conduct," Meredith Halama (blog), March 1, 2013. www.networkad vertising.org/blog/nai-seeking-public-comment-revised-code-of-conduct.

17. Network Advertising Initiative (NAI), "About the NAI." http://www .networkadvertising.org/about-nai/about-nai.

18. Network Advertising Initiative, "2013 NAI Code of Conduct." www .networkadvertising.org/2013_Principles.pdf.

19. Office of the Attorney General, State of California Department of Justice, "Attorney General Kamala D. Harris Issues Guidance on How Mobile Apps Can Better Protect Consumer Privacy," press release, January 10, 2013. http://oag.ca.gov/news/pressreleases/attorney-general-kamala-d-harris-issues-guidance-how-mobile-apps-can-better.

20. Christian Zibreg, "EU Watchdog Tightens Privacy Rules Governing Mobile Apps," www.idownloadblog.com, March 14, 2013. www .idownloadblog.com/2013/03/14/eu-guidelines-mobile-apps.

21. Hunton & Williams LLP, "Article 29 Working Party Opines on Mobile Apps," *Privacy and Information Security Law Blog*, March 18, 2013. https://www.huntonprivacyblog.com/2013/03/articles/article-29-workingparty-opines-on-mobile-apps/.

22. Internet Advertising Bureau UK, "Consumers Gain Greater Control over Targeted Online Ads," www.iabuk.net, June 13, 2013. www.iabuk .net/about/press/archive/consumers-gain-greater-control-overtargeted-online-ads.

23. European Interactive Digital Advertising Alliance, "EDAA Rolls out Pan-European Consumer Education Campaign on OBA," press release, June 13, 2013. www.edaa.eu/edaa-news/edaa-rolls-out-education-campaign/.

24. www.out-law.com, "Tech acquisitions in 2014." http://www.out-law .com/articles/2014/february/tech-acquisitions-in-2014/.

CHAPTER 11

Future Consumer Data Ecosystem

Personal data is being transformed from personal exhaust to personal asset and as a result is garnering more respect from its source—the individual. The realization that an individual's personal information has value and utility to the individual will catalyze a redefinition of how it is managed and monetized, and the very nature of its sovereignty. It will remap the underlying structure of how business is conducted with customers, and consumers being the direct source of enterprise and business intelligence.

Consumer as Information Stakeholder

The new personal data industry with the individual as the stakeholder and epicenter is an active, fledgling industry in this decade. This industry's premise is that individuals are the initiators of commercial interactions powered by their irreplaceable knowledge of actual buying intent. This industry's approach is much closer to what individuals actually want and need than its traditional industry counterparts. This is due to the fact that it does not carry the baggage of the legacy approaches that the current industry carries. The opportunities and the challenges are significant. The new personal data industry is addressing the full gamut of top challenges: technical (interoperability, device, server, cloud data), legal, social, usability, and business model transformation.

One of the central technological issues is implementing open standards for the new personal data industry. Another key challenge is addressing the interoperability when businesses function on one technology platform and individuals function on another technology platform, as well as managing the credentialing that will likely reside at the individual's level. Central legal challenges center on addressing the individual as data owner and how the trust is maintained between the individual and the business relative to the individual's rights. There are a myriad of social, usability, and business model standards, opportunities, and challenges that will be addressed as both the monetization and control shift from the business data ecosystem to the individual data ecosystem.

The personal data ecosystem can be divided into three main groups:

1. Software and services
2. Infrastructure
3. People

Software and services include intentcasting, browser extensions, databases, messaging services and brokers, personal data and relationship management, transaction management, trust-based or providing systems and services. Infrastructure includes concepts, hardware, standards, frameworks, code bases, and protocols. People include analysts and consultants, consortiums, workshops, meetups, conferences, and events.

Intentcasting, one of the central initiatives around individuals volunteering their personal information to purchase products or services, is based on services used by individuals to broadcast their buying intentions.

Mature Consumer/Business Information Sharing Models

The matured consumer/business information sharing model is meant to look at the future of where businesses and consumers collaborate in an information partnership that is user centric. This model contains evolved roles from traditional "information" parties as well as the entrance of new information parties to the personal data landscape.

The Collaborative Data Landscape*

The emerging personal data ecosystem models will maximize an individual's utility and value while optimizing profits for businesses and markets in a collaborative information economy.

In the current decade, businesses have been primarily aggregating and extracting value from personal information in their activities with minimal consent and collaboration. Businesses now realize that maximizing consent and collaboration is the path to optimize revenue and profit. This includes individuals increasing their role in validating and editing their personal data.

---

*This section was co-authored by Kaliya "Identity Woman" Hamlin, who created all of the graphics, the definitions in the final diagram, and the model of the ecosystem in this section.

These mature affirmation-sharing models are based on rights-based personal information in an individual-centric approach that distributes benefits and responsibilities from primarily the business to all parties that are involved in the collection, analyzing, interpreting, and acting on the personal information that is generated by the individual. Individual-centric personal data flows through personal clouds to trusted parties, including businesses and markets. This ecosystem is moderated through technology/contractual frameworks and governance services.

Personal Data Flows in an Ecosystem

Innovations in rights-based personal information place individuals at the center of the model. The individuals' personal control over their information extends into the development of unique services and new economic value, as individuals have a stake in its quality and annuity for shared use.

We drew a map of the collaboratively managed data ecosystem. This landscape model briefly explains:

- Roles in the mature ecosystem
- How players interact
- Personal data ecosystem governance

Walking through the Model

The following represent the future personal data landscape with the four critical components of the individual: (1) roles, persona, shared and personal devices, the frameworks; (2) personal cloud with personal data analytics, trusted organizations; (3) product producer, infomediary, data aggregation services, public services, and the marketplace; (4) retailer, vendor agent, service provide.

Personal Zone

A personal data landscape is based on the individual as the stakeholder (see Figure 11.1). Individuals generate personal information as they conduct their normal lives. The individual's personal digitized world (e.g., wearable technology, sensored products, homes, vehicles) holds, captures, and shares behavioral, use, and mechanical information. The individual's multiple roles (e.g., father, daughter, brother, club member, professional, sports fan, brand advocate) affect how an individual shares this personal information and determines which persona the data is presented through

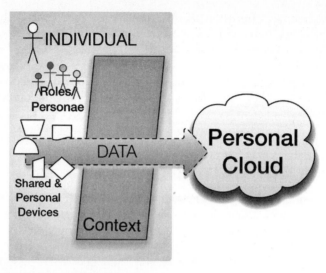

FIGURE 11.1 The Personal Zone
Copyright © 2012 Kaliya "Identity Woman" Hamlin, www.identitywoman.net,
@identitywoman, while Executive Director of the Personal Data Ecosystem
Consortium, www.pde.cc. Used with permission.

relative to personal and professional goals with an ever-changing situational context.

There will be a whole industry of personal data analytic apps that will
allow individuals to better understand their environment (e.g. spending behavior, financial health, physical well-being, and relationships).

Personal Zone Connects Individual to Organizations

An individual's personal cloud is the vehicle by which the person iteratively
shares personal information via personas with organizations they seek interactions and transactions with or currently have a history of interactions and
transactions (i.e., trust-appropriate organizations) (see Figure 11.2).

These can be organizations such as commercial enterprises (manufacturer direct or retailer), nonprofits, groups (churches, clubs, sports organizations) or public/governmental entities. Individuals establish the parameters
for engagement via their personal cloud with the appropriate personas with
each entity. The individual's personal cloud is set up with specific policies
and terms of information servicing and sharing relative to each persona.
The personal cloud then responds appropriately based on the entity and

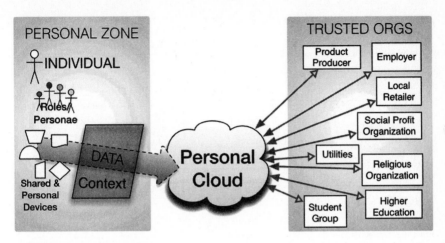

FIGURE 11.2 The Connection
Copyright © 2012 Kaliya "Identity Woman" Hamlin, www.identitywoman.net, @identitywoman, while Executive Director of the Personal Data Ecosystem Consortium, www.pde.cc. Used with permission.

the specified persona. Each entity commits to these terms of its information use and engagement, which then can iterate two different levels of personal information sharing depending on the progression of the interaction. The entity's performance relative to its commitment will determine consuming levels of personal information sharing or the lack thereof.

Infomediaries Work on the Individual's Behalf for Businesses/Markets

Infomediaries will evolve naturally as the personal data industry and eco-system evolve. Intermediaries will facilitate personal information shar-ing in a more responsible, open, effective, and profitable leveraging of personal information as an asset to the individual as well as a vehicle for far greater relevancy and efficiency for organizations. Infomediaries will act as a service to assist individuals in establishing and maintaining their informed consent and preferences relative to their personal information as an asset and vehicle by which commercial activity is executed (see Figure 11.3).

Infomediaries will act as an information filter for advertisers and other commercial entities. Infomediaries will also initiate demand-side requests (personal requests for information [PRFIs] and requests for proposals [RFPs])

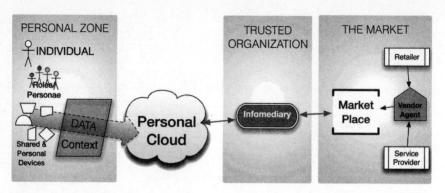

FIGURE 11.3 Infomediaries Facilitate
Copyright © 2012 Kaliya "Identity Woman" Hamlin, www.identitywoman.net,
@identitywoman, while Executive Director of the Personal Data Ecosystem
Consortium, www.pde.cc. Used with permission.

for products and services that meet the individual's specific needs. When an individual's product or service request is not compelling enough to motivate an individual commercial entity to respond, the intermediary can aggregate similar offers from multiple individuals to approach the request as a market request.

Data Aggregators in the Personal Data Ecosystem

Individuals will likely share personal data with a new breed of data aggregation services in order to professionalize and optimize their buying relative to their actual life habits and behavioral patterns, such as driving patterns with a city's traffic services. This new breed of data aggregation services may also transform an individual's personal data through cleansing and normalization data sets to particular markets. Individuals' personal data will be compared to other data sets in comparable markets. Aggregators will combine behavioral insights with buying opportunity alerts either to take advantage of or to avoid risks. The predecessor to this new model has its roots in media-rating firms such as Arbitron and Nielsen. Individuals trust that these organizations will respect an individual's personal information when it is volunteered. If these organizations didn't respect the use of their acquired personal information, individuals would no longer participate in volunteering this type of personal information and the organization would no longer have a business (see Figure 11.4).

FIGURE 11.4 New Breed of Data Aggregators
Copyright © 2012 Kaliya "Identity Woman" Hamlin, www.identitywoman.net,
@identitywoman, while Executive Director of the Personal Data Ecosystem
Consortium, www.pde.cc. Used with permission.

Three Key Components Enabling the Personal Data Ecosystem

Figure 11.5 illustrates the interworkings of the three key components of a
personal data ecosystem:

1. **Infomediary.** An infomediary is the service trusted to have professional insight into an individual's personal information, and it functions
   solely on the individual's behalf. The infomediary manages the individual's personally identifiable information (PII) and other personal
   data assets. Their primary role is to protect individual's personal data
   as a leverageable and monetized personal asset as well as put it to use
   on the individual's behalf.
2. **Data aggregation services.** Data aggregators assemble data sets from
   individuals to support such things as market research, and form synchronous recommendation engines. The benefits to individuals sharing their personal data with data aggregators will likely be that the aggregators will compensate them for their personal data while adhering
   to the individuals' terms and conditions.
3. **Vendor relationship management.** This is a strategy for balancing
   the relationship between consumers and vendors such that consumers have control over their data and vendors have both incentives and
   capabilities to succeed as a business that uses customer data. It depends on vendors respectfully and transparently accessing data about
   individuals in accordance with individual consumers' preferences and
   rules as expressed in their personal cloud.

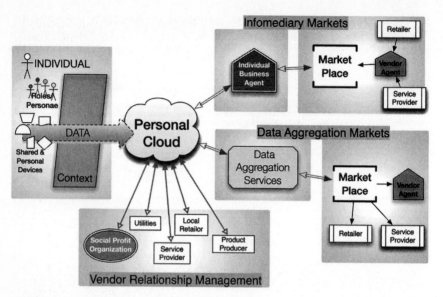

FIGURE 11.5 **Personal Data Ecosystem Enablers**
Copyright © 2012 Kaliya "Identity Woman" Hamlin, www.identitywoman.net,
@identitywoman, while Executive Director of the Personal Data Ecosystem
Consortium, www.pde.cc. Used with permission.

Frameworks: The Major Ecosystem Governance Mechanism

Figure 11.6 illustrates how frameworks use contracts between the parties to
keep value flowing. We need ways to make all transactions and all the selec-
tive uses of shared data safe and reliable. Guidelines need to be developed
and implemented in ways that work across industries and regions. One
strategy for this is the framework. A framework provides standard technical
and legal agreements along with shared business process and policies that
make it easy for everything to work together. Different frameworks have
different assumptions about what's needed and what works, so their terms
and conditions differ, too. A healthy framework protects the individual and
supports thriving markets.

You may hear people talk about "trust frameworks" or "accountability
frameworks." This is what they mean.

Frameworks usually emerge from a framework provider that is responsible for setting the rules of a framework and driving adoption. A different
entity may actually drive the auditing, enforcement, and interoperability
testing needed for the framework to function.

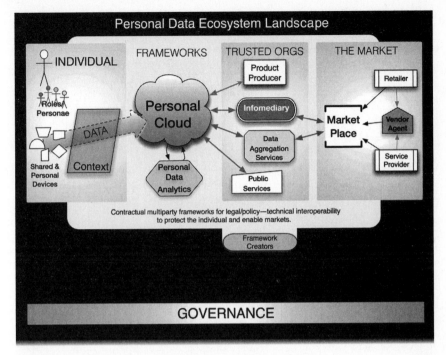

FIGURE 11.6 **Personal Data Ecosystem Landscape**
Copyright © 2012 Kaliya "Identity Woman" Hamlin, www.identitywoman.net,
@identitywoman, while Executive Director of the Personal Data Ecosystem
Consortium, www.pde.cc. Used with permission.

Governance Manages Risk

All real-world situations involve risks, and not all are equal: not all data is equally
valuable. For example, your tweets are presumably less valuable and certainly
less sensitive than your prescription data. Not all data is equally vulnerable or
equally disruptive. Not all parties are equally secure, stable, or trustworthy. So
some framework operators work to discover risk using ratings and tests, and
to share risk through agreements such as mutual insurance pools. Framework
operators design incentives that encourage good-neighbor practices and dis-
courage risky behavior. These feedback loops keep everything in balance.

Frameworks fit within the different governance modalities of today's
information and communication technology (ICT) systems.

LEGAL Frameworks use the court system provided by governments to enforce their contracts. They inherit some assumptions about behavior from

national governments and international agreements, like data protection laws and recourse to courts.

CODE Frameworks incorporate other standards from technical communities and organizations, like what information should be on your driver's license.

IDENTIFIERS Frameworks operate within different names spaces. The choice of which frameworks are recognized changes the system.

PEER Many frameworks provide information that helps entities in a system make decisions about trustworthiness. This information can include peer assessments and testimonials such as ratings, certifications, and accreditations.

Every named polygon in Figure 11.7 has a definition in the list of terms in the recap section that follows.

Where next?

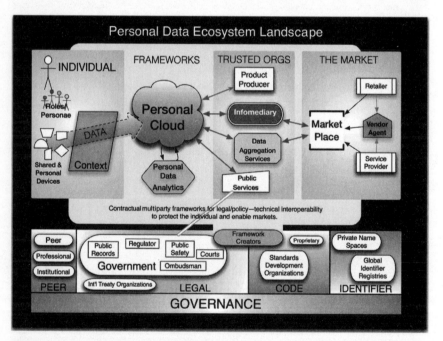

FIGURE 11.7 Personal Data Ecosystem Landscape
Copyright © 2012 Kaliya "Identity Woman" Hamlin, www.identitywoman.net, @identitywoman, while Executive Director of the Personal Data Ecosystem Consortium, www.pde.cc. Used with permission.

Recap

We have described how individuals share their data through their personal clouds, talk to trusted organizations and partners, and put data to work, sometimes in data markets, all held together through accountability frameworks illustrated in Figure 11.7.

Alfred Korzybski said that "the map is not the territory." Reality is always more complex and more nuanced than a simple diagram. The roles are more elaborate, and some come in many flavors. We left out many variations to keep this description accessible. We hope you take this simplification in the spirit it's offered: a map to find your way.

Experience is changing our model.

Variations on this map have been written since 2010. We're going to analyze the trends to find new components in the ecosystem, extract new attributes dimensions, and identify changes in how value flows through those relationships.

Terms Used in Our Personal Space

Individual: A person.

Devices: Mobile phones, computers, self-tracking devices, medical monitoring devices, e-readers.

Context: Where a person is (home, school, work). The role the person is playing (parent, coach, spouse, employee, supervisor, athletic team member). The persona the individual is presenting (video game player, professional, goofy hobby identity).

Data: The bits generated explicitly, such as photos, tweets, or status updates.

Frameworks: Contractual multiparty frameworks connect legal/policy agreements to technical interoperability to protect the individual and enable markets. The personal cloud service provider is at the heart of these frameworks. Chosen by the end user, the personal cloud service works on the user's behalf managing the data and its participation in the framework.

Personal data analytics: Services that help people gain insight into their own personal data. Examples include a daily health status or a personal annual report.

Trusted Organizations

Product producer: This is an example of a vendor relationship management (VRM) connection where a consumer who bought a product from a producer manages an open channel with the maker of the product the person bought and willingly shares information under mutually beneficial terms they set.

Infomediary: A service trusted to have insight into a person's data and working on that person's behalf. The infomediary has an individual's personally identifiable information (PII), protects that data, and puts it to use.

Data aggregation services: Services create aggregate data sets from personal data, like music listening habits. Aggregators may compensate people for their data, people may share altruistically, or people may unknowingly share.

Public services: Governments delivering services to their constituents can enable use of personal data stores for better access and data quality.

The Market

Marketplace: This is where an individual's business agents with PII meet vendor agents without PII.

Retailers: Companies that sell goods to customers.

Service providers: Companies that provide services to people.

Vendor agents: Companies that help retailers and service providers find good potential leads. They do not have personally identifiable information.

Governance: Governance starts with laws and regulations but also includes cultural practices, business norms, and, in digital systems, how identifiers are allocated and the code that connects them.

Legal

Government: Government plays many roles in the systems.

Regulator: Governments set baseline rules for how markets work. They provide the court system where contract law is adjudicated.

Public records: Governments record births, marriages, divorces, and deaths, along with licensing and property title registries.

Public safety: Policing and law enforcement.

Ombudsman: Many states have a data protection commissioner who protects constituents.

International treaty organizations: They support the coordination of international treaties and provide meta-international laws that hold governments accountable to each other.

Code: Computer code and how it runs determines what is possible in computer systems. The phrase "Code is law" was popularized by Lawrence Lessig.

Standards development organizations: Bruce Sterling said, "If code is law, then standards are like the Senate." Standards bodies agree on how code works regardless of the particular language it is written in or system it is running on. For example, the World Wide Web

Consortium (W3C) standardizes the HTML specification for presenting web pages.

Identifier: Networks run on identifiers for each end point. How these are allocated, and the terms and conditions of use in a network, govern the network.

Global identifier registries: Examples include the phone system, domain names, ISBN numbers, radio-frequency identification (RFID).

Private name spaces: Examples include Twitter, Skype, Google, Facebook, and others.

Peer governance: This kind of governance is the most powerful in many ways and helps social systems operate.

Peer-to-peer: People have opinions about each other and also about businesses and services they interact with—like Yelp for small businesses.

Professional: Doctors, lawyers, engineers, geologists, and architects are professions that peer regulate.

Institutional: Institutions figure out what other peer institutions are, such as banks worldwide in SWIFT.

Framework creators: Organizations that create contractual legal policy/ technology frameworks that govern complex multiparty networks.

Volunteered Customer Information Service Characteristics

The characteristics of the new volunteered customer intelligence can be characterized as eight fundamentals of personal data stores. These eight characteristics define the uniqueness of an environment where individuals own, manage, and initiate personal data movement in exchange:

1. **Impulse from the individual.** A key aspect of this new dynamic is that individuals are the primary initiators of interactions and transactions.
2. **Control.** The individual initiates the interaction but also leads the interaction during it and afterward as well as the use and propagation of all the data associated with the interaction.
3. **Transparency.** The key here is simple, obvious, and understandable access to created information. The businesses must create understandable policies in layman's terms. The individual also has access to any and all data retained by the service provider relative to the individual.
4. **Data portability.** Once the interaction or transaction is complete, the individuals can take their data wherever they choose. This is possible by an open architecture that allows data to be easily moved in and out of their system.

5. **Service end point portability.** The individual can easily move from one service provider to another without switching costs or information-movement barriers.
6. **User generativity.** Individuals are free to create their own data environments compatible with personal data store standards.
7. **Self-managed identity.** This environment allows individuals to have their own identity online. This will help exposure risks to identity theft, and unwanted correlation of online activity. This enables maximum control over information before different types of identities are used online (e.g., authentication, presentation, reference, and internal). Not only does this enable individuals to have transparent, participatory, and collaborative ID management, but it also allows them to control how much personal information they share. OpenID is one of the technologies that will help enable this capability. This ability also runs parallel to the United States' Open Government initiative.
8. **Duty of care.** These types of user-driven services watch over the user's well-being. If a service acting in their best interests, the service will take measures to protect users from harm. Duty of care services ideally will consistently work to minimize the user's exposure to liability and risk.[1]

All of these capabilities require certain inalienable information rights and principles for individuals. Doc Searls has done important pioneering work in capturing these fundamentals with his work at Harvard University's Berkman Center for Internet & Society through ProjectVRM. Harvard's Berkman Center focuses on the study of cyberspace. ProjectVRM was a follow-on to the *Cluetrain Manifesto* book he coauthored with Christopher Locke, Rick Levine, and David Weinberger (Perseus Books, 2000). Vendor relationship management (VRM) principles and enabling tools are that individuals are independent from businesses. VRM inverts the idea that customer relationship management (CRM) operates under (that the business captures, controls, locks in, and manages individuals). Five VRM principles are:

1. Individuals enter relationships as individual agents.
2. Individuals are the integration point of their own data.
3. Individuals control the data they generate or gather, and share this data selectively and voluntarily.
4. Individuals assert their own terms of engagement.
5. Individuals are free to express their demands and intentions outside of an organization's control.[2]

Personal Information as a Sovereign/Monetized Asset

Individuals now have an unheard-of personal information competency and supporting infrastructure, unprecedented commercial power, governmental/legislative protection, and legal ownership/sovereignty of their personal information, and as the new norm, consistently and intentionally volunteer large portions of their personal information (under the individual's terms and conditions) to businesses for commensurate utility and reward. This personal information maturity of competency and capability is primarily enabled by the ubiquitous, transparent, and mobile information infrastructure of the Internet and mobile devices. Individuals will have persistent and consistent personal data stores on a local personal device integrated with the cloud. This personal data cloud will be supported by a matured personal data industry with the individual as the primary stakeholder, not the business as in the previous decades.

Individuals will have controlling rights over their personal data as defined by a matured personal data governmental legislation as well as managing their own identity. Consequently, they will be the primary beneficiaries and stakeholders of how their personal information is monetized by themselves and others. Generationally, individuals will be that much more information engaged as digital natives and information natives who have grown up with personal technology. Individuals will have a personal data quality rating that is far more important than their credit rating. This personal data quality rating will be monitored and/or validated by external parties similar to today's Experian and in the Consumer Reports Union. It will also be self-rated, similar to eBay's buyer/seller ratings. Individual buying will be professionalized as was business several decades ago. This will take the form of personal RFIs and RFPs, which will be made available to individuals' trusted information networks. The individual's demand-side innovation from the professionalization of an individual's buying will now release a wave of innovation on the previously stagnated supply side for businesses.

Businesses will have completed a customer behavioral model inversion, where behavioral models will be primarily fueled by personal information directly and intentionally volunteered from individuals as opposed to legacy in-house or third-party proxy-based inference behavioral models. This new direct-from-individual model has far less of a signal-to-noise ratio relative to the mathematically impossible trajectory of the previous decade where unstructured data was outpacing the analytical ability to predict an individual's buying behavior. For example, the previous decade's best analytics were yielding less than 10 percent marketing effectiveness (average campaign conversion rates) with a 90 percent failure rate using nondirect customer models (i.e., irrelevance message/offer to individual). The 90 percent irrelevancy communicated to individuals that "We don't know you," "We don't respect you," "You can't trust us," and "You're not important."

This decade will also bring a migration back from primarily unstructured data volumes to more leverageable structured data sets with the advent of directly volunteered information from personal data stores (i.e., more data overall but far less unstructured complexity). This was primarily due to the fact that individuals' lives and the resulting volume and complexity of digital data they and their smart objects produced grew exponentially in the previous decade. Just in terms of the number of relationships (digital or terrestrial) through commercial and other entities, individuals previously had far fewer relationships than in current and future decades (e.g., 1980s—20 relationships, 1990s—30, 2000s—100, 2020s—200 [750 if counting entities that held personal data], 2020s—2000 relationships). Strictly from a database perspective, the complexity is far greater than what an organization previously was managing and analyzing as it was only a fraction of an individual's life. For example, if an organization's database had 20,000 attributes (including metadata) regarding the individual, 400 to 600 of those data attributes would be critical from an analytical perspective; that is, they needed to make decisions regarding an individual based on the logical data model. In a best-case scenario, an organization's view of an individual would be less than 50 percent of the individual's 360-degree view of themselves. In an individual's personal data store in the future, the individual would have the real, built-in, 360-degree view with likely 100,000 attributes, with 3,500 of those data attributes being highly actionable by an organization (i.e., 8 to 1 ratio). This large number of data attributes that would be encompassed in an individual's personal data store will be supported and managed by professionals from the new personal data industry with the individual as the stakeholder.

The next decade will also bring fundamental infrastructure cost redistribution as 70 percent of a business's previous cost infrastructure is in place to compensate for not knowing what individuals already know about their current and future buying behavior. As individuals supply personal information direct to businesses, businesses will have an opportunity to invert their relevancy and therefore efficiency levels. For what the businesses previously spent on "cost of quality" issues from attempting to use a data sources other than "direct from individual," businesses had to include costs both in efficiency and effectiveness (e.g., low campaign relevancy, excessive inventory levels, low product relevancy).

The transformation from indirect to direct-from-individual data sourcing is not just a technological or informational transformation but impacts every facet of the business. To still achieve the fundamentals of effective and profitable selling, the business must transform itself along the following seven areas:

1. People (associate)—require new information/technical skills/insights/ new thinking.
2. Process—reengineering information flow, processes, and monetization from in-house to direct.
3. Technology—open standards, enterprise data warehouse (EDW), cloud, personal device interoperability, bring your own device (BYOD).
4. Information—individual managed identity, data quality, new sovereignty, big/little data, bring your own information (BYOI).
5. Organizational—structure to support demand-side initiation, consumer to business (C2B), new value proposition delivery.
6. Leadership—individual advocacy, individual utility visionary, privacy and monetization innovation.
7. Cultural—information transparency, respect for individual, incrementally building trust.

At the conclusion of this transformation, over half of the business's customer data models will be sourced with information directly from the individuals' personal data clouds along with their constant and passive data streams from their personal devices and intelligent objects. Push (CRM) marketing will be replaced by individuals initiating explicit personal RFIs and RFPs. To respond to this fundamental change, it will be a shift from in-house analytics to analytics being performed against the vast amount of personal data stores. While this revolution will be tumultuous, it will unleash significant opportunities for business innovation on the supply side, which will reverse the declining innovation trend of the past decade. Historically, business innovation on the sales and marketing side had experienced significant innovation with the advent of analytical customer business models and technology architecture, such as enterprise data warehouse (EDW); massively parallel processing (MPP) architectures; business intelligence (BI) tools to extract, transform, and load; metadata tools; and Hadoop, MapReduce, and YARN (open-source distributed data applications). After years of high innovation with these new technological developments, the current decade has shown that real innovation has slowed to relatively small incremental innovations and improvements. Business relevancy to individuals in real terms has been anemic—3 to 4 percent campaign conversion rates. It will not be until business enables innovation on the demand side with individuals that businesses can then begin to open up significant innovation again on the supply side (i.e., sales and marketing).

Businesses will navigate this transformation because of the opportunity it presents but also out of necessity in order to catch up with an individual's new buying processes and information sophistication. Business's historical customer relationship management (CRM) approaches where businesses could or had to manage the consumer or customer relationship will invert to a world where individuals have the power, control, or competency to manage their commercial relationships with businesses. The following are the major power factors for the individual relative to business:

- Negotiating power from transparent knowledge
- Crowdsourcing negotiating power from communities
- Independence from and intolerance to push-type sales and marketing
- New convenience to consider purchases on their time and terms
- Ability to engage businesses later in the buying process (i.e., real-time)
- More pointed questions during a moment of truth
- Ultimately, government legislation for near-complete opt-in/opt-out power to ignore business

Personal Data Ecosystem

The new personal data ecosystem comprises the new information environment for individuals including the traditional "information" players and long-standing information flows with the addition of newly created information flows with new information ownership characteristics and agendas.

PDE Data Elements

The personal data ecosystem (PDE; see Figure 11.8) encompasses a vast amount of an individual's personal and commercial data. Everything from individuals' governmental records to their posts on Facebook have been recorded digitally for many decades and exists as a record in governmental and commercial forms. Figure 11.8 illustrates the types of personal data that exist in the personal data ecosystem relative to their commercial and governmental counterparts.

PDE Roles and Flows

In contrast, Figure 11.9 illustrates the parallel data ecosystem of business and its intricacies. It illustrates the roles (e.g., retailer, individual, marketer, data analytics provider, aggregated data set broker) in the personal data ecosystem and respective data flows (e.g., order, request attribution verification, network address, proof of attribution). From the marketer, analytics providers, aggregators, network providers, and payment processors, all surround the flow of data to and from the individual. The typical

Personal Data Covers All Aspects of Our Lives

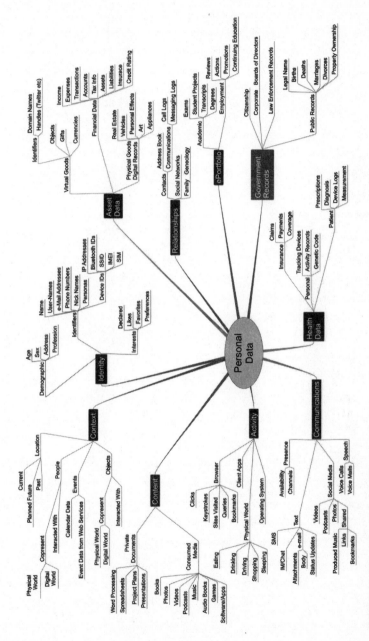

FIGURE 11.8 Personal Data Ecosystem

Copyright © 2012 Kaliya "Identity Woman" Hamlin, www.identitywoman.net, @identitywoman, while Executive Director of the Personal Data Ecosystem Consortium, www.pde.cc. Used with permission.

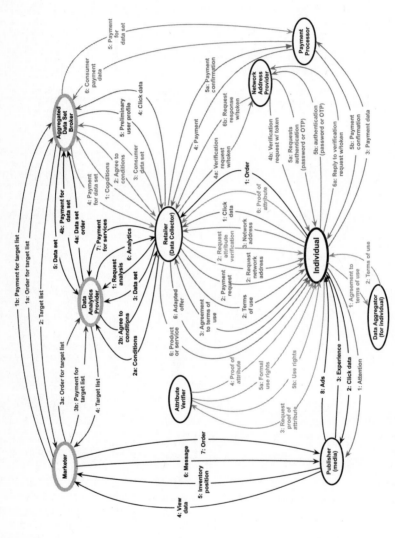

FIGURE 11.9 Personal Data Ecosystem Roles and Flows

Copyright © 2012 Kaliya "Identity Woman" Hamlin, www.identitywoman.net, @identitywoman, while Executive Director of the Personal Data Ecosystem Consortium, www.pde.cc, and Verna Allee of Value Network, LLC, and the Personal Data Ecosystem Consortium. Used with permission.

marketer has data flows between the aggregated data broker, data analytics provider, and publisher of media. The data analytics and aggregated data brokers have data flows primarily with the retailer as a data collector. The individual's data flows primarily between the retail data collector, attribute verifier, network address provider, and the individual's data aggregator.

PDE Data Sovereignty and Interoperability

Figure 11.10 illustrates flows relative to personal data sovereignty in the context of the entire data ecosystem. In order to truly understand the individual information ecosystem transformation of this future decade beyond

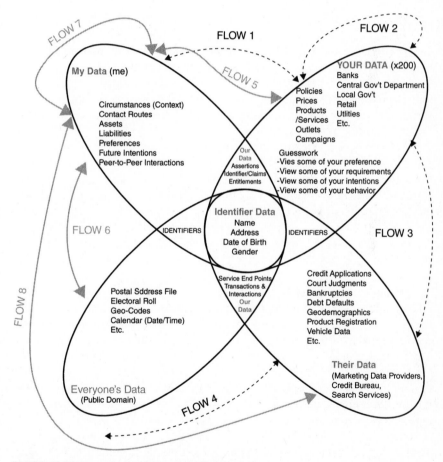

FIGURE 11.10 Data Sovereignty and Flow Graphic
Source: Iain Henderson, Information Answers, www.informationanswers.com.

the previous graphics, Figure 11.10 illustrates the macro level of the combined individual and commercial data ecosystem relative to their respective data sovereignties, and the new data flows relative to the data sovereignties.

As Figure 11.10 depicts, the personal and commercial data ecosystem can be viewed as five buckets of data intertwined with a central Identifier Data set:

1. My Data
2. Your Data
3. Our Data
4. Everyone's Data
5. Their Data

The My Data bucket is data that is undeniably and only within the domain of the individual. My Data contains all the circumstances and context of an individual's personal and commercial interactions. It also contains such things as an individual's personal contacts and interactions, location, assets and liabilities, preferences, future activities, and intentions/plans. The defining characteristics of this bucket in the future is that this data is not available to any other party or organization unless under a binding terms and conditions agreement between the individual and the other party. Historically, this bucket was under siege by organizations in order to monetize the individual's personal information ranging from subtle to overt privacy encroachment. This bucket is the epicenter of privacy for the individual. This bucket represents a constant challenge in the evolved surveillance society, whose legal issues are constantly evolving. This bucket is controlled and managed by the individuals themselves and/or outsourced to a fourth-party service that is part of the new personal data ecosystem industry. This fourth party would be akin to an accountant or attorney.

The Your Data bucket constitutes commercial entities such as banks, retailers, utilities, and central governments, and is in the domain of the organization and owned by the organization. This contains private, public, and third-sector data. Proxy views of this data exist elsewhere in the ecosystem but only proxy views (i.e., representative copies of the original data source). Your Data holds data records for entities' products and services, policies, pricing, distribution, supply chain, and campaigns. It is largely based on behavioral inferences and proxies (i.e., analytical guesses), rather than actual data that resides in the individual's My Data bucket. The Your Data bucket is where organizations hold the information proxies on their guesses of My Data's preferences, requirements, intentions, and behavior. Your Data also contains the master records of their products and services as well as pricing, costs, and their data supporting their physical distribution network.

Customer-facing views of Your Data are made available for reproduction in the Our Data intersection.

The Our Data bucket is the intersection between My Data and Your Data. It contains identifiers, claims and assertions, interactions, transactions, entitlements, and leveraged service end points. This data is jointly accessible by the individual and the organization (i.e., seller/service provider). It also includes any other parties that were involved in interactions, transactions, or relationships between the individual and the organization. Essentially, Our Data is any data that is generated when the individual and organization engage with each other (e.g., interaction or transaction). Our Data is technically owned by the organization (seller/service provider), and is in the data format that the organization determines. Organizations make an effort to present data and data formats that are interoperable with open standards.

The Their Data bucket is the data of organizations such as marketing data providers, credit bureaus, and search services. The types of data that this bucket contains are credit applications, court judgments, bankruptcies, debt defaults, geo-demographic data, product registrations, and vehicle data. The data in the Their Data bucket is built, owned, and sold by data aggregators (i.e., third parties). In this fully evolved future personal information ecosystem, this aggregated data that is created by these organizations can be resold only under a licensing agreement from the individual.

The Everyone's Data bucket is data in the public domain. The nature of this data is to be developed and made operational by large public sector entities (e.g., local governments, post offices, and mapping bureaus). Examples of this public domain data will be postal address files, electoral rules, geo-codes, and calendar (date/time). In a fully evolved personal information data store, access to this data will be under contract to the individual, with the contractual barriers being set purposefully low.

The epicenter of all these data buckets revolves around the basic Identifier Data set for the individual (name, address, date of birth, and gender). This Identifier Data set enables the personal ecosystem to exist as well as having the aspects of individual's sovereignty and privacy manageable. This includes the core personal identity data that exists in the public domain. The electoral records also are available publicly. Unlike previous decades, the individual owns and manages his or her Identifier Data set. This marks the central fundamental step change of addressing the personal data privacy issue.

Once the data buckets have been defined, now the data flows can be addressed. Historically, data flows 1 through 4 existed in the current and previous decades.

Data flow 1 represents the flow between My Data and Your Data. From a data sovereignty perspective, businesses extract data from the individual's personal data resulting from their personal and commercial activities—interactions, transactions, questionnaires. The only change from previous decades is that a business's data extraction from the individual will now be done under contract from the individual; that is, the flow does not change, just the explicit data sovereignty and contractual arrangement. Within data flow 1, My Data flows between Our Data as well; that is, individuals provide data to the organizations under the terms and conditions set by the organizations.

Data flow 2 represents the data flow inside the Our Data group of organizations, which also includes Our Data. For example, the organization that individual obtains a driver's license from sells the person's car ownership information to other organizations as in countries where volunteering drivers licenses are required when purchasing an automobile. Another example would be a telecommunication firm selling aspects of that data to marketing companies or Google AdWords selling the individual's behavior online to other organizations. Mail-order businesses also monetize their customer lists in similar fashion.

Data flow 3 illustrates the data flow between Your Data and Their Data, which again is organizations sharing and monetizing personal data between organizations. This data flow also incorporates data flows from Our Data into Their Data as well. The best example of this type of data flow is the oftentimes not explicit question: "May we share your personal data with other companies?" with a tick box that may or may not be auto-selected. This also includes whatever personal data results from the data industry monetizing the individual's activity (e.g., warranty cards, product registrations). In the future iterations, when the individual is compensated for the resale of the information, the person has an added incentive to maximize the value of the information's initial value as well as its resale value.

Data flow 4 demonstrates the flow between Everyone's Data and Their Data, which essentially is the data industry using public data (e.g., electoral rolls, court records). Data aggregators such as Axiom, Equifax, Experian, and LexisNexis extract information from public records and then package that information and offer it for resale. These data aggregators use the existing public domain information sources and apply analytics and categorization to initiate new commercial data value from the original data.

In the future personal data ecosystem, four additional individual-driven data flows will emerge (data flows 5 through 8). The sovereignty and related monetization of personal data will be tracked, managed, and enforceable by the individual as it travels through the new data flows.

Data flow 5 shows where the individual will share high-value personal information with existing and potential businesses (e.g., "I am going to buy a car next October"). In this example, this is the individual's explicit communication of a buying intent. In previous decades, the car dealership would buy secondary data from another data entity about its analytical guess about the individual's future vehicle purchase. Eliminating the uncertainty of inferring a future purchase rather than obtaining explicit future intent for the individual has far-reaching efficiency implications for businesses. Just the efficiencies in the supply chain will be significant by receiving direct personal information from individuals rather than forecasting through inference and behavioral proxy.

Data flow 6 reveals the flow between Everyone's Data and My Data, which symbolizes the individual enhancing one's own personal data store (e.g., "I will map out my favorite sushi restaurants in my area" or "Here are the top crime areas in my city"). The enhancement or extension of the individual's personal data store can range from personalizing the person's own favorite social areas to taking direct feeds off public domain sources for use with his or her own personal data mashups.

Data flow 7 is similar to data flow 6 but extends the idea by an individual enhancing another individual's personal data store. In previous decades, this type of data flow was unstructured, whereas in the future structured data flows between personal data stores of individuals will be able to be more structured and automated. For example, the individual can have a structured communication channel that allows him or her to give advice to another individual or group of individuals as to the best phone to use when traveling globally. The key to this data flow is that it is geared toward supporting the individual's needs, not the selling of products. In previous social networks, this type of peer-to-peer information sharing was common, but with this new personal data system, the enhanced version of peer-to-peer collaboration is much easier and more structured.

Data flow 8 exemplifies the new mechanics of identity in the future environment, which will function as a data flow between My Data and Their Data. In this data flow, individuals can prove their identity without revealing any other personal, identifying information to a website or a business. This new environment also shows the closer collaboration between individuals and data aggregators as individuals monetize their personal data on a broader scale.

New Customer's Voice Feeds New Business Intelligence

In this future personal data ecosystem, the new data sovereignties and flows change how business intelligence and customer intelligence are created between the two entities. More important, it changes historical processes of business. The new data flows invert many of the tried-and-true data flows:

■ **Factual updates.** Instead of businesses using various different validation data sources to manage an individual's address record, the individual maintains an accurate and up-to-date record in his or her personal data store. The business then regularly pings the personal data store for the updated and single version of the truth (e.g., "I've changed my postal address and e-mail address"). This also saves individuals time as they don't have to notify a dozen different entities that they have moved.

- **Change of circumstance.** Instead of the business using a menagerie of data sources to try to determine the individual's life situation, the individual keeps status updates on major aspects of his or her personal life (e.g., "We're getting married," "I'm buying a car," "I've just received a traffic ticket").
- **My location.** Instead of businesses using third-party companies to extract GPS and cell tower location data with the limitations to PII, individuals stream their location to their personal data store, which is available to their trusted commercial network and consequently linked to their PII.
- **Factual queries.** Individuals now have a direct link between their personal data store and businesses so they can initiate much more structured queries (e.g., "I don't understand my bill," "Where's my order?").
- **Online searches.** Instead of businesses scraping vast amounts of unstructured data for what individuals are interested in buying, the individuals explicitly communicate what they are interested in directly to the business (e.g., "I am interested in the camera right now").
- **Orders.** Instead of the business initiating commercial interactions and/ or transactions, individuals initiate interactions and/or transactions (e.g., "I would like to buy this, please").
- **Specifications.** Instead of the business passively listing features and functions, individuals request certain sets of features and functions from the business (e.g., "I would like these specific features and functions of this product/service"). This would be accomplished by a series of professional buying templates.
- **Complaints.** Instead of the business being the primary manager of complaints, individuals now have a professionalized complaint management process that is standardized and transparent (e.g., "Here's the problem I have with your product and my process to resolve it"). This is similar to eBay's Resolution Center.
- **Suggestions.** Instead of the business having the onus to solicit customer input, individuals have a professionalized suggestion process that is baked into the new interaction process (e.g., "Why don't you do X with your product and then change Y?").
- **User-generated content.** Instead of the businesses having a majority of the responsibility to create collateral on content, individuals have a standardized process to create personal and creative expressions of their commercial experiences (e.g., "Here is the video I created about your product").

- **Views, reviews, and opinions.** Instead of the business having a myriad of customer feedback types of processes, individuals' views, reviews, and opinions all are standardized with their personal data scores and then leveraged to the business (e.g., "I tried business X's product and here is what I found").
- **Shared experiences.** Instead of businesspeople managing and monitoring a myriad of unstandardized experiences and the individual having only unstructured ways to share experiences, sharing experiences is now standardized in personal data stores (e.g., "I had a similar problem so I know how you feel").
- **Peer advice.** Individuals now have a standardized process and communication between personal data stores to leverage other individual's experience and learning (e.g., "I had a similar problem and here's what I learned"). Businesses can leverage this communication if the individual opts in to the sharing.
- **If only.** Instead of businesses having the primary responsibility to create new and innovative products, businesses can crowdsource the vast personal data stores of individuals' consciousness about wishing for a product that doesn't currently exist (e.g., "What I would really like is X but nobody is offering it").
- **Future plans and intentions.** Instead of the business building predictive models on indirect data sources and third-party data, individuals would directly communicate their explicit buying intentions with the timing and location of those purchases (e.g., "I plan to buy a BMW in the next three months").
- **Expressions of interest.** A major challenge is extracting an individual's interests, both positively and negatively, from primarily unstructured data. This can be achieved by individuals listing their top likes and dislikes and storing that information in their personal data stores (e.g., "I am interested in golf but not scuba diving").
- **Preferences.** Instead of businesses extracting a limited set of preferences by inferring behavior indirectly, the individual would explicitly list preferences in a wide range of areas so the business could present products geared to those preferences (e.g., "I don't like green but I do like blue").
- **Questions.** Instead of the business managing questions through its processes, the business would have a standardized query process from all personal data stores (e.g., "I don't understand X," "What about this?," "Can you help with X?").
- **But what if ...** Instead of the businesses managing what-if scenarios in an unstructured fashion, they would manage what-if scenarios to the structure process of the individual's query (e.g., "What will happen if I do X, or if I do Y?").

- **Permissions.** Instead of the business managing data permissions from the commercial side, individuals will set up the data-sharing preferences of their personal data store and manage that process with the help of fourth parties and professionals as advocates of the individual (e.g., "I am happy for A but not B to access my data, and only for these purposes").

Notes

1. Joe Andrieu, SwitchBook.
2. ProjectVRM. http://cyber.law.harvard.edu/projectvrm/Main_Page#VRM_ Principles, VRM Principles.

About the Author

John McKean, author, researcher, and executive director of the Center for Information Based Competition, provides thought leadership to businesses to achieve a mastery level of customer information and interactions ranging from human-to-human to social network and mobile conversations. He is frequently called on by the world's leading businesses to inspire new levels of customer awareness and effectiveness through fact-based insights and a passion for customer excellence. Mr. McKean's real-world customer work is balanced with the academic rigors of guest lecturing at MIT Sloan School of Management, Kellogg School of Management, and postgraduate work at Harvard University. He also created and moderated Teradata's largest online global community for big data analytics, integrated business-to-consumer (B2C)/business-to-business (B2B) marketing, and web analytics. Members of this community include executives of many of the world's most powerful brands (e.g., Google, Amazon, Facebook, Walmart, and Disney); leading academic institutions (e.g., Harvard, Stanford, Wharton, and MIT); and respected industry analysts (e.g., Gartner, Forrester Research, and Yankee Group).

Index